THE CONSTITUTION OF THE CRIMINAL LAW

The Constitution of the Criminal Law

Edited by
R A DUFF
LINDSAY FARMER
S E MARSHALL
MASSIMO RENZO
VICTOR TADROS

OXFORD
UNIVERSITY PRESS

OXFORD

UNIVERSITY PRESS

Great Clarendon Street, Oxford, OX2 6DP,
United Kingdom

Oxford University Press is a department of the University of Oxford.
It furthers the University's objective of excellence in research, scholarship,
and education by publishing worldwide. Oxford is a registered trade mark of
Oxford University Press in the UK and in certain other countries

British Library Cataloguing in Publication Data
Data available

ISBN 978-0-19-967387-2

Printed and bound in Great Britain by
CPI Group (UK) Ltd, Croydon, CR0 4YY

Links to third party websites are provided by Oxford in good faith and
for information only. Oxford disclaims any responsibility for the materials
contained in any third party website referenced in this work.

Acknowledgements

This is the third volume to emerge from a research project on Criminalization, funded by a grant from the Arts and Humanities Research Council (Grant No 128737). We are grateful to the Arts and Humanities Research Council for the grant that made this project possible, and to our own universities for the further material and administrative support that they provided—the University of Stirling and the Stirling Department of Philosophy, the University of Glasgow and the School of Law, and the University of Warwick and the School of Law.

We are very grateful to the authors who have contributed to this volume, to those who commented on earlier drafts of the papers (Matthew Clayton, Andrew Cornford, Christine Kelly, Seth Lazar, Kasper Lippert-Rasmussen, Alan Norrie, Friedrich Toepel), and to all of the participants at the workshops and meetings from which this volume emerged. These meetings and workshops once again confirmed how productive such interdisciplinary and inter-jurisdictional discussions can be.

Antony Duff, Lindsay Farmer, Sandra Marshall,
Massimo Renzo, Victor Tadros

Contents

Contributors

C A J Coady is Vice Chancellor's Fellow and a Professorial Fellow in the Centre for Applied Philosophy and Public Ethics in the University of Melbourne.

R A Duff is a Professor in the University of Minnesota Law School, and a Professor Emeritus in the Department of Philosophy, University of Stirling.

Lindsay Farmer is Professor of Law at the University of Glasgow.

John Gardner is Professor of Jurisprudence at the University of Oxford.

Nicola Lacey is a Senior Research Fellow at All Souls College Oxford, and a Professor of Criminal Law and Legal Theory at the University of Oxford.

S E Marshall is a Professor Emeritus in the Department of Philosophy, University of Stirling.

Jeff McMahan is Professor of Philosophy at Rutgers University.

Vanessa E Munro is Professor of Socio-Legal Studies in the School of Law, University of Nottingham.

Massimo Renzo is an Associate Professor in the Department of Philosophy at the University of Warwick.

Jonathan Rogers is a Senior Lecturer in the Faculty of Laws at University College London.

Jane Scoular is Professor of Law at the University of Strathclyde.

Victor Tadros is a Professor at the School of Law, University of Warwick.

François Tanguay-Renaud is an Associate Professor at Osgoode Hall Law School, and a Member of the Graduate Faculty of the Department of Philosophy, at York University, Toronto.

Christopher Heath Wellman is Professor of Philosophy at Washington University in St Louis.

1

Introduction

The Constitution of the Criminal Law

R A Duff, Lindsay Farmer, S E Marshall,
Massimo Renzo, and Victor Tadros

This is the third volume of a series of collections arising from an Arts and Humanities Research Council (AHRC)-funded project on Criminalization. It contains revised versions of papers discussed at the project workshops in 2010–11.[1] The project's overall aims were described in our Introduction to the first volume of papers, and we will not repeat them here, save to say that our early ambition to work towards a normative theory of criminalization was soon replaced by a more realistic ambition to work towards a clearer under-standing of the complex range of normative questions that bear on the various processes of criminalization involved in a modern system of criminal law. As with the two previous volumes, this third volume illustrates some of that complexity. It is concerned with three related sets of issues about criminalization that are captured by the book's title—*The Constitution of the Criminal Law*—and addressed by the authors of these papers. In this Introduction we provide a brief sketch of those issues.

Before doing so, we should say something about the term 'constitution' and how we understand it in this context. One of the principal ways in which this term has come to be understood in contemporary writings about crim-inal law is in terms of the resources that a constitution, or some kind of constitutional court or jurisprudence, might offer as a kind of restraint or limit on state action. This is particularly evident in those whose ambitions are

---

[1] The first two volumes, also published by Oxford University Press, were *The Boundaries of the Criminal Law* (2010) and *The Structures of the Criminal Law* (2011); a fourth volume of papers, *Criminalization: The Aims and Limits of the Criminal Law*, will appear in 2013. These four volumes of papers will be followed by three monographs: Antony Duff, *The Realm of Criminal Law*; Lindsay Farmer, *The Institution of Criminal Law*; Victor Tadros, *Wrongs and Crimes*.

to correct the modern tendency towards 'overcriminalization'. Thus, Douglas Husak argues that the tendency towards overcriminalization might be limited by the identification and operation of certain internal and external constraints. These, and in particular the external constraints, can be seen as 'constitutional'.[2] Internal constraints draw on the internal structure or resources of the criminal law, and are constitutional in the weak sense that they imply that the 'constitution' of the criminal law (its form or the way that it has been constituted) imposes requirements that must be met before a rule can count as 'properly' criminal law.[3] External constraints are more traditionally constitutional, and Husak argues for changes in the political structure of law-making to require that certain conditions be met before penal laws can be enacted. These constraints are envisaged as largely procedural ways of seeking to make the law-making process more rational and evidence-based.[4]

In a similar vein, Andrew Ashworth has sought the resources to limit both the expansion of the criminal law and the development of new forms of criminal liability by drawing on what might be understood as the constitutional resources of the criminal law. For Ashworth these are once again to be found in a combination of internal and external sources, though he groups them together under the broad heading of the 'principles' of criminal law.[5] The internal principles are such things as the principle of fair labelling, or *mens rea*; these have no legislative status as such, but Ashworth argues that these, and similar principles, have come to be recognized in the jurisprudence of the criminal law, and that there are sound normative reasons for viewing them as principles which should guide the future development of the law. This is then backed up by reference to the principles contained in the European Convention on Human Rights (ECHR) and the jurisprudence of the European Court of Human Rights. In certain instances these principles,

[2] D N Husak, *Overcriminalization: The Limits of the Criminal Law* (Oxford: Oxford University Press, 2007), esp chs 2 & 3.

[3] D N Husak, n 2 above, ch 2. These constraints are that it be for a non-trivial harm, that the conduct be wrongful, that punishment be deserved, and that the burden of showing criminalization to be necessary lie on the state.

[4] D N Husak, n 2 above, ch 3. See also W. Stuntz, 'The Pathological Politics of Criminal Law' (2001) 100 *Michigan LR* 506. The external constraints that Husak proposes are that any criminal legislation must 'directly advance' some 'substantial state interest', and must be 'no more extensive than is necessary to achieve its objective'.

[5] A J Ashworth, *The Principles of Criminal Law*, 6th edn (Oxford: Oxford University Press, 2009), see esp chs 2 & 3. See also A J Ashworth, *Human Rights, Serious Crime and Criminal Procedure* (London: Sweet & Maxwell, 2002). In his project on preventive justice, with Lucia Zedner, he pursues a similar approach in seeking to identify constraints based on the internal resources of the law. See eg A J Ashworth and L Zedner, 'Preventive Orders: A Problem of Undercriminalization?', in *Boundaries of the Criminal Law* (n 1 above) 59, and 'Prevention and Criminalization: Justification and Limits' (2012) 15 *New Criminal Law Review*.

such as the principle of legality, are seen as confirming the existence of pre-existing principles of the common law; and in other instances they recognize or affirm new principles (or older principles in a different form, such as the right to a fair trial) which might act as a constraint on legislative action.

It is also worth recognizing, however, that human rights norms, as they are currently understood, provide only modest constraints on the scope of the criminal law. Rather than any general human right to a criminal law with a fair scope and content, individual rights provide some partial restrictions on the law. These restrictions have had only a modest impact on the content of the criminal law of England and Wales, and that is unlikely to change. Of course, it might then be argued that more powerful constitutional or human rights norms that are more directly and generally concerned with criminalization ought to be developed to ensure that the criminal law has a fair content.[6] It might even be argued that such rights naturally emerge from existing constitutional norms, as Dennis Baker argues in the context of the US Constitution.[7]

While we are sympathetic to these kinds of argument, we intend that the phrase 'constitution of criminal law' be understood in a wider, though not unconnected, sense (cf John Gardner's chapter). Just as we have sought to address the question of criminalization from first principles—instead of asking for reasons why we should not criminalize, or how we should respond to overcriminalization, we have begun by asking why we should criminalize—in thinking about the constitution of criminal law we are not concerned only with the question of limits (important as this is in the present context) but also with the related questions of how the criminal law is constituted and, more broadly yet, of the constitutive power of the criminal law.

In the essays in this book these questions are addressed through the consideration of three sets of issues. The first concerns the political constitution of the criminal law as part of the institutional structure of the state, or, in other words, how the criminal law is constituted through these political processes. Any adequate normative discussion about criminalization—about the ways in which and the grounds on which types of conduct can be justifiably criminalized—must attend to the character of criminal law as a particular kind of political institution (or set of institutions): to the political processes and agents through which and by whom its shape and content can properly be determined; to its relationship with other modes of law and legal

---

[6] See, further, V Tadros, 'A Human Right to a Fair Criminal Law' in J Chalmers, F Leverick and L Farmer, *Essays in Criminal Law in Honour of Sir Gerald Gordon* (Edinburgh: Edinburgh University Press, 2010).

[7] See *The Right Not to be Criminalized: Demarcating the Law's Authority* (Aldershot: Ashgate, 2011).

regulation, and to the question of how a polity can decide whether an issue of proper public concern is best addressed through the criminal law rather than (or as well as) through other legal or political routes; and to the kind of authority that a criminal law generated by such processes can claim over the polity's citizens. These issues are addressed in different ways by Nicola Lacey, by Vanessa Munro and Jane Scoular, by Jonathan Rogers, and by Kit Wellman.

Lacey sets this issue of the constitution of the criminal law in terms of two specific historical questions about the place of law-making within the British Constitution. The first asks how the changing institutional structure of the criminal law, and in particular the impact of the professionalization of legal practice, had an impact on the legitimacy of the criminal law. This is examined through a discussion of nineteenth-century debates about the legal representation of defendants in felony trials and the conceptions of crime and guilt that underlay the positions in this debate. Here she argues that as lawyers entered the criminal trial and rules of procedure and evidence became more formalized, this had the effect of undermining traditional conceptions of guilt based on lay common sense and local knowledge. This 'crisis' of legitimacy, she argues, was however ultimately resolved with the development of representative democracy, extending the franchise and securing the place of Parliament as the legitimate source of criminal law. This then points to the second question as Lacey investigates how this constitutional settlement continues to have an impact on the formation of criminal justice policy. Overall, then, her concern is with the broad constitutional landscape of the criminal law and how this should interact with normative questions about the proper scope of, and limitations on, the criminal law.

A similar set of questions is then pursued in a more contemporary context by Munro and Scoular, who examine the changes in policy and law in relation to the specific area of the criminalization of prostitution. Their concern is with what they call the constitutive relationship between law and society. In particular:

the ways in which the regulation of commercial sex markets in the UK have constituted forms of (sexual) citizenship, roles for criminal law, and bases of legitimacy for state intervention. (p. 31)

This is traced through an examination of the ways in which the justification for the criminalization of prostitution, or of associated activities, has shifted from a concern with harm and nuisance, to one of protecting the vulnerable. They demonstrate how the new concern with vulnerability is an index of a different kind of regulation and how it ties in with broader trends in government policy—in particular the regulation of trafficking and citizenship.

As Lacey notes, a central question for theorists of criminalization, whether normative or analytical or historical or sociological, concerns the distribution of the power to decide what is to count as criminal: how in fact is such power distributed among those with roles to play in the processes that lead from legislation to punishment; and how should it be distributed in a contemporary polity? The role of public prosecutors must be central to discussions of this question, and is the focus of Jonathan Rogers' chapter. It is clear that the expansions of our criminal law which have helped to generate our contemporary crises of overcriminalization have put increasing discretionary power in the hands of prosecutors who must decide which cases to pursue and to bring to trial;[8] but theorists have paid insufficient attention to questions about how extensive this power should be, how it should be structured or constrained, how it should be used, and more generally, how prosecutors should understand their role within the criminal justice system and within the polity of which that system is part.[9]

The simple story about prosecutors is that their responsibility is to apply the criminal law, rather than to make it (law-making being the job of legislators, and perhaps, to some degree, of judges); but that whereas prosecutors elsewhere in Europe are bound by a 'Legality Principle' which requires them to prosecute if there is sufficient evidence of guilt, English and Scottish prosecutors work instead under an 'Opportunity Principle' which gives them wide discretion not to prosecute, even when the evidence is sufficiently strong to ground a realistic prospect of conviction, if it would not be in the 'public interest' to prosecute.[10] That contrast is, no doubt, rather less sharp than the simple story might suggest;[11] but Rogers argues that the tests which prosecutors working under the Opportunity Principle have to apply are also more complex than the simple story suggests. In particular,

---

[8] And see also D N Husak, n 2 above, 21–30, on the significance of prosecutors' power to determine which charges to bring, and to set the terms of plea bargains.

[9] But see M M Dempsey, *Prosecuting Domestic Violence: A Philosophical Analysis* (Oxford: Oxford University Press, 2009), esp chs 3–5; J Rogers, 'Restructuring the Exercise of Prosecutorial Discretion in England' (2006) 26 *Oxford Journal of Legal Studies* 775; also C Steiker, 'Criminalization and the Criminal Process: Prudential Mercy as a Limit on Penal Sanctions in an Era of Mass Incarceration', in *The Boundaries of the Criminal Law* (n 1 above) on how prosecutors should use their discretion to help to hold back the tide of over criminalization.

[10] See *Code for Crown Prosecutors* (http://www.cps.gov.uk/publications/docs/code2010english. pdf) s 4; A J Ashworth and M Redmayne, *The Criminal Process*, 4th edn (Oxford: Oxford University Press, 2010) 199–206. See also S R Moody and J Tombs, *Prosecution in the Public Interest* (Edinburgh: Scottish Academic Press, 1982).

[11] See eg H Jung, 'Legalität oder Opportunität im Strafverfahren?' in H Prütting (ed), *Recht und Gesetz im Dialog III* (Saarbrücker Vorträge 120, 1986) 55; M Damaska, 'The Reality of Prosecutorial Discretion: Comments on a German Monograph' (1981) 29 *American Journal of Comparative Law* 119.

before they even apply the evidential test, they should employ 'the application test': do any of the legislature's reasons for enacting the offence apply to this potential defendant's alleged conduct, as a reason to condemn it, in a way that can be explained to the public? If the answer to that question is uncertain, prosecutors should then apply 'the development test': would a prosecution help to clarify the law and the reasons for enacting this offence, so as to make its application easier in future?[12] Only if either the application or the development test is passed should prosecutors go on to apply the familiar evidential and public interest tests (whose application will also differ depending on whether the prosecution is intended to apply or to develop the law).

Suppose, then, that a prosecutor has convincing evidence that two young people of fifteen have engaged in consensual sexual activity with each other. If we take the words of ss 9 and 14 of the Sexual Offences Act 2003 at face value, they cover such conduct: we might then be tempted to say that the test of evidential sufficiency is satisfied, and therefore that a decision not to prosecute would need to be based on the prosecutor's judgement that it would not be in the public interest to do so. But the decision not to prosecute should instead, Rogers would argue, be made before the evidential test is even applied, for it is clear that the legislature did not take its reasons for enacting this offence to apply to such conduct: it is absolutely clear in this case, since this was explained in Parliament during the passage of the Act.[13] For the same reason, prosecution would not pass the development test: there is no uncertainty about how the law should be applied.

This line of argument, if successful, serves to legitimate the prosecutor's official role as involving not merely the application of law that has already been determined by legislatures (or that will be more precisely determined by judges), but the interpretation, the refinement and the development of law that the legislature has passed in a, to some degree, indeterminate form. It raises, accordingly, a number of further constitutional questions about whether it is appropriate to confer this kind of power on this kind of official, if indeed we can avoid doing so;[14] but such questions must be addressed by anyone hoping to theorize the processes through which conduct is criminalized.

---

[12] Part of the background to his argument is the assumption that criminal trials have a communicative value as applying and articulating reasons for condemnation that citizens can be expected to understand.

[13] 'That is not the intention of the Bill; nor will it be its effect in practice. Strictly speaking, sexual activity between under-16s is already illegal ... There have, however, been no prosecutions simply for kissing; nor will there be in future. [I]f we find no other way to deal with this question ... we shall be able to trust the Crown Prosecution Service to ensure that that intention is followed.' (Hansard vol 409, 15 July 2003, col 248; Paul Goggins, a Home Office minister).

[14] See eg Ashworth and Redmayne, n 10 above, 218–19.

Kit Wellman's chapter takes us from the processes through which a polity's criminal law is constituted to the grounds on which it can be constituted as authoritative, and in particular to the question of whether and on what grounds it can include so-called *mala prohibita*. The traditional distinction between *mala in se* and *mala prohibita* is between crimes consisting in conduct that is (supposedly) wrongful prior to and independently of its legal regulation, and crimes consisting in conduct that is wrongful (if at all) only because it is prohibited by the law. That distinction is, of course, controversial: both its clarity and its utility have been questioned by theorists since Bentham.[15] But insofar as it can be drawn, in particular insofar as there are crimes that consist in conduct which cannot plausibly be portrayed as wrongful independently of or prior to its legal prohibition, the many theorists who take wrongdoing to be a necessary condition of criminalization face a serious problem: how can they justify the criminalization of conduct that is not already, pre-legally, wrongful? The problem is serious because it does not affect just a small area of the criminal law: in contemporary systems of criminal law the majority of offences are of this kind (and one justified complaint against many theorists of criminal law is that they focus almost exclusively on traditional *mala in se* which, though salient in public conceptions and discussions of criminal law, forms only a relatively small proportion of the offences defined by our criminal laws).[16] Wellman confronts this problem, since his account of criminal punishment (to which criminalization makes us liable) depends upon the argument that we can justly be punished only if we have forfeited our right not to be subject to penal hard treatment, and that we forfeit that right only by violating another's right:[17] for whose rights are violated by a *malum prohibitum* offence? Wellman's answer is that by committing a *malum prohibitum* offence we violate the rights of our fellow citizens, to whom we owe a duty to obey the law:[18] we can, therefore, be justly punished for such offences. He goes on to discuss two questions that such an account raises—how *mala prohibita* should be sentenced (if all

[15] See J Bentham, *A Comment on the Commentaries* (1776), in *Collected Works of Jeremy Bentham* (eds J H Burns and H L A Hart; London: Athlone Press, 1977) iii, 63, on the 'acute distinction. . . . which being so shrewd, and sounding so pretty, and being in Latin, has no sort of occasion to have any meaning to it'.

[16] See D N Husak, '*Malum Prohibitum* and Retributivism,' in R A Duff and S P Green (eds), *Defining Crimes: Essays on the Special Part of the Criminal Law* (Oxford: Oxford University Press, 2005) 65, and *Overcriminalization* (n 2 above) 103–19. In response, see R A Duff, *Answering for Crime: Responsibility and Liability in Criminal Law* (Oxford: Hart, 2007) 89–93, 166–74.

[17] See C Wellman, 'The Rights Forfeiture Theory of Punishment' (2012) 122 *Ethics* 371.

[18] He argues for such a duty in C Wellman, 'Toward a Liberal Theory of Political Obligation' (2001) 111 *Ethics* 735, and in C Wellman and J Simmons, *Is There a Duty to Obey the Law?* (New York: Cambridge University Press, 2005) ch 4.

involve the same wrong of violating our duty to obey the law), and whether we commit any rights-violating wrong in breaching an unjust *malum prohibitum* law (since it is not clear that we have a duty to obey such laws): but his chapter speaks even to those who do not share his views of punishment and of the legitimate grounds of criminalization, because it reminds us that a normative theory of criminalization must be grounded firmly in a political theory of the state and our relationship to it, and that any such theory must address the justifiability of criminalizing *mala prohibita*. That is not to suggest that a plausible normative theory must be able to justify the enormous range of *mala prohibita* that our contemporary criminal laws include, but it must have something to say on this large dimension of the criminal law, and its plausibility as a theory of a contemporary criminal law would be threatened if it could not justify at least some offences of this kind.

We have been talking so far about the ways in which the state's institutions and officials can constitute and apply the criminal law by which we are to be protected and bound as citizens. We must also ask, however, about the state and its institutions and officials not as creators, or enactors, or interpreters and enforcers of the criminal law, but as being themselves subject to the criminal law—which leads into our second set of issues. This, too, is a matter of the constitution of the criminal law: of its role as part of the polity's constitutional structure, of the authority it can claim over other parts of that structure, of how the agents of the criminal law can also be answerable to it. John Gardner and François Tanguay-Renaud address some of the questions that arise in this context.

John Gardner, in his chapter 'Criminals in Uniform', speaks directly to the relationship between the character of the state and the constitution and the justification of harm-causing action. He takes as a starting point his debate with Malcolm Thorburn about the way in which we should understand the contrasting moral positions of citizens and public officials with respect to the justifications that they may offer for their harmful actions. Gardner characterizes this debate in the following way. Thorburn treats citizens who are entitled to defences such as self-defence or lawful arrest as 'Officials in Plain Clothes'—that is, insofar as they are entitled to such defences, they are operating in the role of state officials, upholding the just law.

Gardner defends, against this view, the opposite idea that he attributes to Dicey—that when public officials are entitled to such defences, they are to be treated just like citizens—they can appeal only to the considerations that ordinary people appeal to in justifying their actions. They are merely 'Citizens in Uniform'. However, Gardner suggests, there is a moral consideration that public officials share with only some subset of ordinary citizens that may make their harming of others especially grave—that they have a duty to protect the very people that they harm. This does not render all official harming wrongful, all things considered. It does, however, raise the bar that public officials must meet in demonstrating that their conduct is justified. By considering the role of police officers in some depth, Gardner illuminates the special characteristics of official conduct and misconduct whilst endorsing a fundamental continuity in the kinds of consideration that are relevant to assessing their conduct and the conduct of ordinary citizens. Such a discussion invites us further to reflect on what it is to be a citizen and how the criminal law should be constituted in the light of such a notion.

Tanguay-Renaud's chapter is concerned with the state as a target of criminalization in a very direct sense: to what extent can the state be a criminal offender? It is very familiar that collective agents, most obviously corporations, can be criminalized for what they do. It is much less familiar, and much more unorthodox, to claim that states themselves could act in a criminally wrong way. But if objections to corporate criminal liability are not decisive, it might be argued that objections to state criminal liability are not decisive either.[19]

If states can be criminalized for what they do, what doctrines of criminal responsibility apply to them? What renders the state responsible for what it has done, and how might responsibility be undermined? What might justify the state in committing a wrong? And—the focus of Tanguay-Renaud's contribution here—what might excuse it? The idea that the state can be excused for wrongdoing seems, at first blush, difficult to swallow, but as Tanguay-Renaud demonstrates, it is in fact far more plausible than it first appears.

Finally, discussion of the constitution of criminal law cannot remain at the level of domestic criminal law and its constitution as part of the internal political structure of a nation state. In a world in which the transnational and international dimensions of both crime and criminal law are becoming so increasingly significant, we need to attend to the ways in which criminal law can be constituted as part of an international order; this gives us our third set of issues. Some of the questions that arise here are about the relations between the domestic criminal laws of different nation states; others are about the relationships between domestic criminal law and transnational or international law; others concern the authority and proper jurisdiction of international criminal law itself, and its relationship to other dimensions of the international order, including the laws of war. Jeff McMahan, Tony Coady, and Massimo Renzo address different aspects of this complex set of questions in their chapters.

---

[19] See, further, F Tanguay-Renaud, 'Criminalizing the State', *Criminal Law and Philosophy*, forthcoming.

Renzo's contribution addresses the problem of how we should understand the distinction between domestic and international crimes. In addressing this question he relies on recent developments in the literature on moral and criminal responsibility, focusing particularly on the idea that responsibility should be understood in terms of *answerability*, ie in terms of the reasons offered by the agent in order to justify her conduct.[20] Renzo provides a novel account of the distinction between wrongs for which we are answerable only to the domestic political community and wrongs for which we are answerable to the international community, and then employs this account to argue that any violations of basic human rights constitute wrongs of the second kind (whether or not they are committed as part of a wider attack against a civilian population or in the context of an armed conflict). Thus, according to Renzo's view, all crimes involving violations of basic human rights have an international dimension, and therefore trigger international criminal responsibility.

Adopting this view requires substantially revising our current way of thinking about the distinction between domestic and international crimes,[21] but doing so is not as disruptive of our current practices as we might think at first. This is because our systems of domestic and of international criminal justice should not be seen as mutually exclusive domains. As recent developments in international law confirm, domestic and international criminal law complement each other, and often overlap to a large extent. As a consequence, many crimes seem now to have both a domestic and international dimension.[22]

In his contribution, Jeff McMahan focuses on a particular type of international crime, namely war crimes. These crimes are grave violations of *jus in bello* principles, ie grave violations of the principles governing the conduct of war. After distinguishing between the legal principles of *jus in bello* and how these principles should be understood as a matter of morality, McMahan provides a revisionist account of how the latter should be interpreted. None of those who fight for an unjust cause, according to McMahan's view, are capable of respecting the moral principles of *jus in bello* (and particularly the requirements of discrimination, necessity, and proportionality), since

[20] G Watson, 'Two Faces of Responsibility' (1996) 24 *Philosophical Topics* 227; J Gardner, 'The Mark of Responsibility' (2003) 23 OJLS 157; Duff, n 16 above.

[21] Violations of fundamental human rights currently constitute international crimes only when they are committed in the context of an armed conflict, as part of a widespread or systematic attack on a civilian population, or with the intent to destroy a group (ie when they are instances of war crimes, crimes against humanity or genocide).

[22] See also M Renzo, 'Crimes Against Humanity and the Limits of International Criminal Law', (2003) 31 *Law and Philosophy* 443.

a pre-condition of being able to respect them is that combatants satisfy the requirements of *jus ad bellum*.[23]

On the other hand, the legal principles of *jus in bello* equally apply to combatants who fight with a just cause as well as to those who don't. This is because the purpose of the legal principles of *jus in bello* is to constrain the actions of the latter as well as the actions of the former. What follows is that *jus in bello* law cannot be modelled directly on *in bello* morality. Rather, *in bello* law and *in bello* morality substantially diverge. Against the background of this account McMahan considers what criteria should be employed to determine which forms of morally impermissible action in war should be treated as war crimes.

Finally, Tony Coady's contribution focuses on the questions of how terrorism should be understood for the purposes of the criminal law and of how terrorists should be dealt with by the criminal justice system. Coady defines terrorist acts as violent attacks upon non-combatants (or their property) by groups or their representatives who launch the attacks for political purposes. This tactical definition (one that takes as the distinctive feature of terrorism its specific tactic of targeting innocents) is then employed to criticize the UK Terrorism Act 2000, which relies instead on a political notion of terrorism (one that focuses exclusively on the politically motivated nature of terrorist acts).

More generally, Coady criticizes the approach to terrorism that he sees as underlying this and other similar statutes. This approach normally involves granting excessive powers to police and other state agents (power which can be too easily abused) and a resort to the use of legislation which is motivated by widespread anxiety, but lacks any justification as a way of preventing and responding to the threat of terrorism.

As with the previous two collections of this series, the aim of this volume is not to provide exhaustive answers, but rather to raise new questions and suggest possible ways of addressing them. Once again, our hope is that readers will feel compelled to engage with these questions.

---

[23] McMahan defends this view at length in his *Killing in War* (Oxford: Clarendon Press, 2009).

2

What Constitutes Criminal Law?

*Nicola Lacey**

In this chapter, I will approach two familiar questions—what defines the specific object of criminal as opposed to civil law, and what legitimizes criminalization—from the perspective of the historical constitution of English criminal law. My aim is to trace the ways in which that history echoes within, and sheds light upon, the contemporary politics of criminalization. In particular, I shall argue that a historical and institutional analysis helps to explain the much-noted difficulty in producing either a satisfactory 'definition' of criminal law[1] or a persuasive normative theory of criminalization[2]—indeed the decline, until quite recently, of scholarly attention to overall issues of criminalization as distinct from principles of responsibility.[3] My analysis sets out from an understanding of the constitution of criminal law as a process unfolding in, and shaped by, specific historical, national and institutional contexts. Among these contexts, I shall suggest that it is useful to consider two sets of salient facts which have thus

* Senior Research Fellow, All Souls College Oxford: Professor of Criminal Law and Legal Theory, University of Oxford. With many thanks to participants in the AHRC Criminalization Project workshops held at Stirling and Warwick for their comments, and in particular to Christine Kelly for her astute commentary; to Lindsay Farmer, Henry Mares, Lucia Zedner and members of the Legalism Seminar at St John's College Oxford for very helpful further comments and for discussion; and to Zelia Gallo for exemplary research assistance.

[1] See Lindsay Farmer, 'The Obsession with Definition: The Nature of Crime and Critical Legal Theory' (1996) 5 *Social and Legal Studies* 57; Celia Wells and Oliver Quick, *Lacey Wells and Quick, Reconstructing Criminal Law* (4th edn, Cambridge: Cambridge University Press, 2010) ch 1.

[2] Leo Katz, 'Villainy and Felony' (2002) 6 *Buffalo Criminal Law Review* 451.

[3] Antony Duff et al (eds), *The Boundaries of the Criminal Law* (Oxford: Oxford University Press, 2010). Classic late twentieth-century accounts of the position deriving from John Stuart Mill's harm principle include H L A Hart, *Law, Liberty and Morality* (Oxford: Oxford University Press, 1963), further refined by Joel Feinberg, *The Moral Limits of Criminal Law (4 vols)* (Oxford: Oxford University Press, 1984–8); followed by Jonathan Schonsheck, *On Criminalization: An Essay in the Philosophy of the Criminal Law* (Dordrecht: Kluwer, 1994). Douglas N Husak, *Overcriminalization* (Oxford: Oxford University Press, 2007) is exemplary of the move of criminalization to the centre of current debates in criminal law theory.

far featured little in the literature. These are facts, first, about the (relatively late and uneven) formalization of criminal law and full professionalization of the practice of criminal law; and, second, about the history of representative democracy. In each case, I assess the legacy of institutional history in terms of the constitutional and political landscape in which decisions about criminalization and decriminalization are made.[4] This contextual analysis, I argue, reveals an ambiguity about the very concept of 'crime', and about who should have the power to define the conditions for criminal liability: lawyers, politicians, medical professionals, moralists or citizens. In conclusion, I shall float some ideas about the implications of the argument for the proper design of consultative and decision-making processes in the field of criminal law reform.

I. The Decline of Theories of Criminalization

There is a substantial scholarly literature which addresses the question of why, from the mid-nineteenth century on, conceptualizing crime and criminalization became, in England, a tricky matter.[5] Why did the notion of crime as public wrong, so confidently enunciated by Blackstone in the middle of the eighteenth century, lose its resonance?[6] The expansion of summary jurisdiction, reflecting an explicit recognition of what had long been criminal law's role in the regulatory field,[7] at the hands of increasingly ambitious

[4] On the relevance of historical analysis to contemporary understandings of criminal law and the criminal process, see Lindsay Farmer, *Criminal Law, Tradition and Legal Order* (Cambridge: Cambridge University Press, 1996) ch 1; Alan Norrie, *Crime, Reason and History*, 2nd edn (Cambridge: Cambridge University Press, 2001); Lucia Zedner, 'A Political History of the Preventive State' in Andrew Ashworth and Lucia Zedner, *Preventive Justice* (Oxford: Oxford University Press, forthcoming).

[5] See Farmer, *Criminal Law, Tradition and Legal Order*, n 4 above; Katz, 'Villainy and Felony', n 1 above; Nicola Lacey, 'Contingency and Conceptualism: Reflections on an Encounter between Critique and Philosophical Analysis of Criminal Law' in R A Duff (ed), *Philosophy and the Criminal Law* (Cambridge: Cambridge University Press, 1998).

[6] See Farmer, *Criminal Law, Tradition and Legal Order*, n 4 above, ch 1; Lacey, 'Contingency and Conceptualism', n 5 above. As Farmer has recently shown ('Of Treatises and Textbooks: the literature of the criminal law in nineteenth century Britain', in Angela Fernandez and Markus D Dubber, *Law Books in Action* (Oxford: Hart Publishing, 2012), many of the great commentators of the seventeenth and eighteenth centuries confined their attention to the Pleas of the Crown, perhaps reflecting an earlier conception of the core rationale for criminalization, namely wrongs against the King: see Thomas P Gallanis, 'Making Sense of Blackstone's Puzzle: Why Forbid Defense Counsel?' (2010) 53 *Studies in Law, Politics and Society* 35–57.

[7] See Nicola Lacey, 'Historicising Criminalisation: Conceptual and Empirical Issues' (2009) 72(6) *Modern Law Review* 936–61, questioning how far this change truly expanded criminal law's regulatory role, which stretches back at least to the seventeenth century. See also Thomas

government and in the sway of Benthamite utilitarianism, provides part of the answer here. By the mid-nineteenth century, new ambiguities were emerging in the very concept of crime: a long-standing split between a moralized notion of crime as wrong or even evil (*mala in se*) and a legalized notion of crime as infraction (*mala prohibita*), already reflected in the great modern commentaries, intensified as a result of the expansion of the summary jurisdiction into new areas of regulation. Furthermore, increasing social diversity and moral pluralism put pressure on older ideas of crime as public wrong, while new theories of the aetiology of crime challenged traditional ideas of crime in terms of medicalized or otherwise scientific notions of crime as pathology or atavism. Similar dynamics were reflected in debates about and doctrines of responsibility—a closely connected issue.[8] These uncertainties brought with them an overlapping set of disagreements about the proper division of labour in defining crime as between, broadly speaking, judge, doctor, jury and (increasingly active) legislature.[9]

G Barnes, 'The Prerogative and Environmental Control of London Building in the Early Seventeenth Century: The Lost Opportunity' (1970) 58(6) *California Law Review* 1332; Bruce Smith, 'The Presumption of Guilt in the English Law of Theft 1750–1850' (2005) 23 *Law and History Review* 133. Smith shows that the number of summary offences on the statute book rose from 70 in the 1660s to over 200 by the 1770s: he argues that these summary offences were easy ways of proving what would otherwise have been charged as a felony, and that they—like their close summary cousins, vagrancy and police offences—constituted a seriously intrusive form of state power. In 1836—even before the supposed mid-nineteenth-century explosion of summary offences—Smith records 903 such charges before the Thames Police Office alone, with an 80% conviction rate. For the purposes of this chapter, the key point is that the marginalization of the regulatory offences in the treatise tradition created a tension which became more acute over time, as the conception of what was regarded as presumptively legitimating criminal law modernized around criteria of coherence, rationality and systematicity. But a balanced history of English criminal law's regulatory role remains to be written. I am grateful to Henry Mares for discussion of this point.

[8] See Nicola Lacey, 'Psychologising Jekyll, Demonising Hyde: The Strange Case of Criminal Responsibility' (2010) 4(2) *Criminal Law and Philosophy* 109–33; Nicola Lacey, 'Responsibility: law, medicine or morals?' in P Byrne (ed), *Rights and Wrongs in Medicine, King's College Studies, 1985–6* (Oxford: Oxford University Press, 1986) 139–57. For obvious reasons, the new medicalized discourses had particular implications for doctrines of defence.

[9] On the broad intellectual history of law in this period, see Gerald J Postema, *Bentham and the Common Law Tradition* (Oxford: Oxford University Press, 1986); David Lieberman, *The Province of Legislation Determined: Legal Theory in Eighteenth Century Britain* (New York: Cambridge University Press, 1989). Specifically on debates about the division of labour between law and medicine, see Roger Smith, *Trial by Medicine: Insanity and Responsibility in Victorian Trials* (Edinburgh: Edinburgh University Press, 1981); Arlie Loughnan, 'Manifest Madness: Towards a New Understanding of the Insanity Defence' (2007) 70 *Modern Law Review* 379–401 and *Manifest Madness: Mental Incapacity in the Criminal Law* (Oxford: Oxford University Press, 2012).

II. The Institutional Context and its Implications for the Constitution of English Criminal Law

The expansion and diversification of both the criminal law and ideas about what made people responsible for crime through the nineteenth century help to explain why it became increasingly difficult to come up with an integrated theory of criminalization. But they do not really pin down why this appears to have been so particularly difficult in Britain—especially in England—as distinct from the countries of the continent of Europe, which experienced successful codification of criminal law as part of a modern constitutional settlement.[10] In this section, I focus on two further features of the English landscape which may have some explanatory power: the late (and indeed still incomplete) formalization of criminal law doctrine, set in the context of the uneven development of the sort of professionalization of criminal law practice which is needed to underpin a fully formalized doctrinal system; and the specific shape taken by parliamentary democracy.

A. Criminal law: gradual professionalization yet incomplete legalization?

Notwithstanding contemporary criminal law scholars' justified respect for the great treatise writers of the seventeenth and eighteenth centuries, the fact is that criminal law formalized and professionalized in England significantly later and less completely than did much of the civil law. In particular, the structure of the felony trial and of the criminal process meant both that comprehensive criminal law doctrines were slower to develop and had less complete reach over actual practice in the courts; and that representation by legal professionals was not a regular feature of the trial process.[11] As I have argued elsewhere, other than in exceptional cases such as treason, the relatively few misdemeanour cases tried at Westminster, and very serious cases such as homicide, the criminal trial up to the early nineteenth century (and, of course, all the way up to the present day, in the forum of lay magistrates' courts) was a lay-dominated rather than a lawyer-dominated affair, and one

---

[10] See Markus Dirk Dubber, 'The Historical Analysis of Criminal Codes' (2000) *18 Law & History Review* 433; 'The Promise of German Criminal Law: A Science of Crime and Punishment' (2005) 6 *German Law Journal* 1049.

[11] Though cf the argument put forward by Cathrine O Franks in relation to the law of succession: *Law, Literature and the Transmission of Culture in England, 1837–1925* (Aldershot: Ashgate, 2010).

trained for the most part on facts rather than on law.[12] Until 1836, felony defendants had no right to be fully represented by counsel, and while no such bar affected those charged with misdemeanours, by no means all of them would have had the resources to pay a lawyer.[13] Although of distinctive social and legal importance, the misdemeanour cases initiated on the Crown side of King's Bench at Westminster seem likely to have constituted a tiny fraction of the overall number of criminal cases.[14] The vast majority of criminal trials were heard in localities, and of these the large majority were heard not by judges at the Assizes but by magistrates whose grasp of (indeed, whose access to) legal authorities was patchy. As Peter King has emphasized, this implied a highly decentralized system, featuring much local variation and an approach geared to pragmatic dispute resolution rather than formal rules.[15]

[12] See Nicola Lacey, 'In Search of the Responsible Subject: History, Philosophy and Criminal Law Theory' (2001) 64 *Modern Law Review* 350–71; 'Responsibility and Modernity in Criminal Law' (2001) 9 *Journal of Political Philosophy* 249–77; 'Character, Capacity, Outcome: Towards a framework for assessing the shifting pattern of criminal responsibility in modern English law' in Markus Dubber and Lindsay Farmer (eds), *Modern Histories of Crime and Punishment* (Stanford University Press, 2007) 14–41; *Women, Crime and Character: from Moll Flanders to Tess of the d'Urbervilles* (2008); cf Loughnan's analogous argument about the insanity defence: 'Manifest Madness' and *Manifest Madness*, n 9 above.

[13] Gallanis, 'Making Sense of Blackstone's Puzzle', n 6 above.

[14] Douglas Hay (ed), *Collections for a History of Staffordshire: 4th Series, Volume 24: Criminal Cases on the Crown Side of King's Bench: Staffordshire 1740–1780* (Staffordshire Record Society, 2010). In the Staffordshire cases from 1740 to 1800 analysed by Hay, only two per cent of all cases at Quarter Sessions, Assizes and King's Bench fell into this category (p 2). Given that misdemeanour cases have so far been the object of much less historical investigation than felony cases, my claim that they made up a 'tiny fraction' in general is a tentative one. Henry Mares' ongoing research on misdemeanours in the late sixteenth to late seventeenth centuries, for example, suggests that they may have been considerably more common than in Hay's Staffordshire sample. Mares concludes, persuasively, that 'a focus on felonies on the Crown side at assizes has served to distract us from the interest that these cases have' (Mares, 'Criminal Informations of the Attorneys General in the King's Bench from Egerton to North', in D Ibbetson and M Dyson (eds), *Law and Legal Process* (forthcoming)). Whatever their number, the distinctive importance of these cases came from the subject matter of misdemeanours, which encompassed an array of offences stretching from poaching and attempted rape to the political offences of riot and seditious libel (p 10). The more serious of these cases typically involved representation by leading barristers; significant expense; relatively high status defendants; and—hence—substantial interest in the press and in county society (pp 9, 17–18). Yet although a far higher proportion of these cases than of Assize or Quarter Sessions cases involved points of law requiring technically sophisticated professional analysis, only four of Hay's group of 129 cases featured points of law of sufficient importance to be reported in the law reports (p 21). These distinctive features of misdemeanour cases render them a fascinating object of study in their own right, but perhaps justify the primary focus in recent historiography, as in this article, on the history of felony cases, very few of which were tried at King's Bench (p 10). See also Allyson N May, *The Bar and the Old Bailey, 1750–1850* (Chapel Hill: The University of North Carolina Press, 2006) 130.

[15] Peter King, *Crime, Justice and Discretion 1740–1820* (Oxford: Oxford University Press, 2000); *Crime and Law in England 1750–1840* (New York: Past and Present Publications, Cambridge University Press, 2006) ch 1.

In this context, it would scarcely be an exaggeration to say that, even in late eighteenth-century England, criminal law was not fully legalized: in other words, findings of criminal liability turned on moral, conventional and pragmatic considerations as much as on legal standards. The institutional conditions favourable to a gradual development, refinement *and* systematic application of general doctrines—legal representation, rules of evidence, systematic reporting of criminal cases, legal education and, finally at the end of the nineteenth century, a system of appeals—were gradually constructed over a period of almost 200 years. Legal education, based in the Inns of Court, of course has a long history: but for the purposes of the argument of this chapter, it is crucial to note that its origins lay in teaching not so much legal doctrine as the application of rhetorical skills to cases and statutes.[16] A regular appellate system was not implemented until 1908, although alternative mechanisms for testing and challenging decisions did exist, notably by writ of certiorari to the King's Bench.[17] As late as 1840, there was still no authoritative written statement of the rules of the court of King's Bench—a situation which must have accorded the Court Clerks, with their 'monopoly of practical knowledge', huge power.[18] As for law reporting, the accuracy of reports was notoriously unreliable, and coverage of cases uneven, until the establishment of the Council of Law Reporting in 1865—another instance of professionalization.[19]

Of particular interest for our subject here is the defence lawyers' gradual infiltration—persuasively charted by Langbein[20] and Beattie[21]—of the criminal trial, and public reactions to this infiltration. A vigorous and long-lasting debate about legal representation, particularly in relation to felony defendants, began in the early nineteenth century and haunted not merely Parliament but also, for a further three decades after reform in 1836, the press,

---

[16] See Paul Raffield, 'The Elizabethan Rhetoric of Signs: Representations of *Res Publica* at the Early Modern Inns of Court' (2010) 7 *Law, Culture and the Humanities* 244–63 at 248. On early legal education at the Inns of Court, see also A W B Simpson, 'The circulation of yearbooks in the fifteenth century' (1957) 73 *LQR* 492–505.

[17] Hay (ed), *Collections for a History of Staffordshire*, n 14 above, p 8.

[18] Hay (ed), *Collections for a History of Staffordshire*, n 14 above, pp 28–9.

[19] C K Allen, *Law in the Making* (1964) 220 ff.

[20] John H Langbein, 'The Criminal Trial before the Lawyers' (1978) 45 *University of Chicago Law Review* 263–316; 'Shaping the Eighteenth Century Criminal Trial: A View from the Ryder Sources' (1983) *University of Chicago Law Review* 1–136; *The Origins of Adversary Criminal Trial* (Oxford: Oxford University Press, 2003).

[21] John M Beattie, *Crime and the Courts in England 1660–1800* (Princeton University Press, 1986); 'Scales of Justice' (1991) 9 *Law and History Review* 221; 'Defense Counsel and the English Criminal Trial in the Eighteenth and Nineteenth Centuries' (1991) *Law and History Review* 9, 221–67; *Policing and Punishment in London 1660–1750: Urban Crime and the Limits of Terror* (Oxford: Oxford University Press, 2001).

periodicals and the realist novel. And, as I shall argue in the remainder of this section, an analysis of this debate discloses a deep resistance to the idea of criminal law as an object of professional definition, interpretation and control.[22]

Of course, the establishment of professional autonomy and legitimacy was a huge issue across many sectors in the nineteenth century.[23] The legal profession, as compared with its counterparts, was already relatively organized—but its traditional forms of organization were inadequate in the context of the expansion of personnel and diversification of functions.[24] Hence the various branches of the legal profession were slowly reorganizing themselves so as to put their credentials on a more secure footing, through more systematic provision of training, the imposition of training requirements, and better organized professional bodies and disciplinary proceedings.

---

[22] For detailed and meticulous discussions of this history, see David J A Cairns, *Advocacy and the Making of the English Criminal Trial 1800–1865* (Oxford: Clarendon Press, 1998); Jan-Melissa Schramm, *Testimony and Advocacy in Victorian Law, Literature and Theology* (Cambridge and New York: Cambridge University Press, 2000); Allyson N May, 'Advocates and truth-seeking in the Old Bailey courtroom', (2005) 26:1 *The Journal of Legal History, The Bar and the Old Bailey, 1750–1850* (n 14 above). Thomas Gallanis has recently argued that the puzzle about why defence counsel would have been excluded for felony and treason but not misdemeanour is to be explained by the fact that prosecutions for the first two, but not the last, had been understood as an *ex officio* exercise of the King's authority since at least the time of Edward I: defence counsel would, on this view, have been committing something akin to treason. It is doubtful, however, how many defendants charged with serious misdemeanours had the resources to employ counsel. Even once the courts had begun to allow counsel to cross examine in felony cases, by the end of the eighteenth century, only about a quarter of defendants were in fact represented: 'Making Sense of Blackstone's Puzzle', n 6 above, p 36.

[23] Sir Llewellyn Woodward, *The Age of Reform 1815–1870* 2nd edn (Oxford: Clarendon Press 1962), 17–18. On the place of this debate in the contemporary novel, see Nicola Lacey, 'The Way We Lived Then: The Legal Profession and the Nineteenth Century Novel' (2011) 33 *Sydney Law Review* 599–621; Schramm, *Testimony and Advocacy* n 22 above; Jan-Melissa Schramm, 'Is Literature More Ethical than Law? Fitzjames Stephen and Literary Responses to the Advent of Full Legal Representation of Felons' in Michael Freeman and Andrew Lewis (eds), *Current Legal Issues Volume 2: Law and Literature* (Oxford: Oxford University Press, 1999) 417–35.

[24] There is a lively debate about whether this era was one of continuity or of change in the structure of the legal profession: see for example Daniel Duman, 'Pathway to Professionalism: The Legal Profession in the Nineteenth Century', 13 (1980) *Journal of Social History* 615–28; Raymond Cocks, *Foundations of the Modern Bar* (London: Sweet & Maxwell, 1983); Wesley Pue, 'Exorcising Professional Demons: Charles Rann Kennedy and the Transition to the Modern Bar' (1987) 5 (1) *Law & Hist. Rev.*, 135–74; Patrick Polden, *A History of the County Court, 1846–1971* (Cambridge: Cambridge University Press, 1999); W Prest (ed), *The Professions in Early Modern England* (London: Croom Helm, 1987). On the longer term history of the legal profession, see Paul A Brand, *The Origins of the English Legal Profession* (1992); and William Cornish, J Stuart Anderson, Ray Cocks, Michael Lobban, Patrick Polden and Keith Smith, *The Oxford History of the Laws of England* (Oxford: Oxford Scholarship Online Monographs, 2010), Part Four, 'The Legal Professions' (by Patrick Polden). On the contemporary profession, see Richard L Abel, *The Legal Profession in England and Wales* (Oxford: Basil Blackwell, 1988).

As analyses of the phenomenon of professionalization have shown, a key requirement for the effective legitimation of professional autonomy is the construction of credible markers of expertise sufficient to justify an exclusive right to perform the relevant tasks.[25] This proved especially difficult for criminal lawyers to demonstrate, for two reasons. First, there persisted a deep-rooted feeling that the definition of crime and of criminal guilt— particularly in key areas such as theft and personal violence—is a matter of common sense or morality, not to be corrupted by technicalities and professional obfuscation.[26] Secondly, criminal barristers' most evident skill was that of advocacy in their clients' interest. This made them vulnerable to the dual charge that they manipulated rhetoric to defend the guilty, for mercenary reasons; and that their rhetoric displaced the defendant's own voice, which gave better access to the truth of guilt or innocence. As Trollope's clergyman Josiah Crawley of *The Last Chronicle of Barset*, accused of theft, puts it:

I will have no one there paid by me to obstruct the course of justice or to hoodwink a jury. I have been in courts of law, and know what is the work for which these gentlemen are hired. I will have none of it . . . I say nothing as to my own innocence, or my own guilt. But I do say that if I am dragged before that tribunal, an innocent man, and am falsely declared to be guilty, because I lack money to bribe a lawyer to speak for me, then the laws of this country deserve but little of that reverence which we are accustomed to pay to them . . . . And if I be guilty . . . I will not add to my guilt by hiring anyone to prove a falsehood or to disprove a truth.[27]

In short, why would anyone need a lawyer if they were innocent: and if they were guilty, would it not be immoral to try to escape conviction through deployment of professional assistance?[28] Such scepticism about the role of

---

[25] Magali Sarfatti Larson, *The Rise of Professionalism: A Sociological Analysis* (Berkeley: University of California Press, 1977); Harold Perkin, *The Rise of Professional Society: England since 1880* (London: Routledge, 2002); Prest (ed), *The Professions in Early Modern England*, n 24 above; W J Reader, *Professional Men: the rise of the professional classes in nineteenth-century England* (London: Weidenfeld, 1966); D Duman, 'The creation and diffusion of a professional ideology in nineteenth-century England' (1979) 27 *Sociological Review* 113–38; Penelope J Corfield, *Power and the Professions in Britain, 1700–1850* (London: Routledge, 1999).

[26] See James Q Whitman, *The Origins of Reasonable Doubt: Theological Origins of the Criminal Trial* (New Haven: Yale University Press, 2008) chs 6 and 7; Loughnan, 'Manifest Madness' and *Manifest Madness*, n 9 above; Lacey, *Women, Crime and Character*, n 12 above.

[27] Anthony Trollope, *The Last Chronicle of Barset* (1867: Penguin Classics, 2002) ch 21, p 208. Mr Crawley is ultimately persuaded to accept legal assistance, and Trollope's ultimate judgement on the ethics of advocacy, reflected in the resolution of the plot, is more ambivalent than is Mr Crawley's. For further discussion, see David Luban, *Legal Ethics and Human Dignity* (New York: Cambridge University Press, 2007) ch 9; Lacey, 'The Way We Lived Then', n 23 above.

[28] As Paul Raffield has shown, this sort of scepticism about lawyers reaches back in England at least to the time of Shakespeare, though it undoubtedly had a marked intensity in relation to criminal defence lawyers in the nineteenth-century ('The Elizabethan Rhetoric of Signs', n 16

lawyers had an important bearing on the debate about reform of the criminal trial. Hence we see essayists and novelists, as well as opponents of reform in Parliament, questioning the propriety of lawyers' speaking for the defendant,[29] developing a critique of legal representation as the triumph of power, money and rhetoric exploiting specious technicalities over common sense and morality;[30] and articulating a persistent idea that true innocence needs no legal representation.

But the argument about legal representation for felony defendants also had a bearing on the legitimation of criminal law itself, and the rich literature about the ethics of criminal defence sheds light on the historical constitution of criminal law.[31] For, underlying these debates, it is clear that there are two competing conceptions of crime and of guilt in social circulation. The resistance to lawyers' developing dominance in the criminal trial represents a deep-rooted popular sentiment that the definition of criminal guilt and innocence—and hence, at some level, of crime itself—is a matter of common sense and morality, which cannot entirely be captured in law or interpreted by lawyers. In the pre-reform era, the fact that felony trials featured an 'altercation'[32] between defendant and prosecution, mediated by the judge—a figure who represents not merely the law but also both common sense and standards of fair play—provided a framework of legitimation and co-ordination which spoke to that sense of the popular ownership of crime as public wrong, itself emerging slowly from an older order in which serious crime was understood primarily as a wrong against the monarch.[33] The public nature of trials, and the location of many criminal hearings in local venues such as inns, in a world in

above; see in particular pp 246, 253 and 258–60). As Raffield puts it, from the sixteenth century, in the wake of the secularization of the legal profession, commentators saw lawyers as 'operating in an ethical vacuum' (id p 246). On the ways in which modernizing law accordingly continued to deploy images and strategies of legitimation associated with an older symbolic order, see also Lacey, 'The Way We Lived Then' (n 23 above).

[29] Key examples would include the polemical commentary on Brougham's defence of Queen Caroline and, in the 1840s, of Charles Phillips' defence of Courvoisier, in periodicals such as *Punch* and *The Examiner*. See Schramm, *Testimony and Advocacy*, n 22 above, pp 114–20; Cairns, n 22 above, pp 131–42; May, *The Bar and the Old Bailey*, n 14 above, pp 209–36; Elizabeth Gaskell's *Mary Barton* (1859: Penguin Classics, 1980); George Eliot's *Felix Holt: The Radical* (1866: Penguin Classics, 1995).

[30] Jan-Melissa Schramm, 'The Anatomy of a Barrister's Tongue: Rhetoric, Satire and the Victorian Bar in England' (2004) 32 *Victorian Law and Culture*, 285–303; and 'Is Literature More Ethical than Law?', n 23 above. For contemporary concerns expressed in fiction, see Anthony Trollope, *Orley Farm* (1861–2: Oxford World's Classics, 2000).

[31] See also Cairns, n 22 above; Schramm, n 22 above, and references at n 27 above.

[32] See Langbein, *The Origins of Adversary Criminal Trial*, n 20 above.

[33] See Gallanis, 'Making Sense of Blackstone's Puzzle', n 6 above.

which court buildings were still relatively few, constituted the interpretation of criminal law as an issue in which the community could play a role.[34] But as the lawyers gradually infiltrated the felony trial through the course of the eighteenth century—first on the prosecution side, then, by degrees, on the defence side—this fostered a further professionalization of lawyering which gave a new impetus to the refinement of distinctive criminal law doctrines, notably in the areas of evidence and procedure. As the rules of both substantive law and procedure formalized, the older equilibrium between lay and judicial conceptions of crime came under strain.[35] The most obvious sign of this strain related to the structure of the criminal trial. But the tension between technical and lay conceptions of criminal law also bore on the legitimation of law itself, with both the (ultimately unrealized) possibility of codification and the vast expansion of the criminal jurisdiction disrupting the mechanisms whereby the common law of crime celebrated by Blackstone had connected up common sense and legal judgment. And with the expansion of criminal legislation into new regulatory areas in the middle of the nineteenth century,[36] the link between common moral sense and crime was further weakened, resulting in a persistent legitimation problem for criminal law.

B. The legitimation of criminal law and the transition to representative democracy

Yet as the legitimation problem which I described in the previous section gradually presented itself, the British political system was inventing, by fits and starts between about 1820 and 1860, a new set of institutional arrangements which, potentially, solved, or at least mitigated it. If the definition of crime no longer rested in traditional values, a shared sense of public wrong, and a set of practices (notably, the non-lawyer-dominated jury trial) geared to tracking those shared sentiments, the era of reform offered a new framework for legitimation. The most vivid instance of reform—and the most urgent—was the abolition of two-thirds of the existing capital statutes in 1832, taking a decisive step towards the rationalizing modernization initiated by Romilly's reforms of 1808 by turning away from the *ancien régime* mode of threatened

---

[34] See Jonathan H Grossman, *The Art of Alibi: English Law Courts and the Novel* (Baltimore: Johns Hopkins University Press, 2002); Linda Mulcahy, *Legal architecture: justice, due process and the place of law* (London: Routledge, 2011).

[35] See Cornish et al, *The Oxford History of the Laws of England*, n 24 above, Volume XIII, Part 1 by Keith Smith.

[36] Cornish et al, *The Oxford History of the Laws of England*, n 24 above, Volume XIII, Part 2 by Raymond Cocks.

death tempered by a widespread but unaccountable discretionary prerogative of mercy. In 1820, there were well over 200 capital offences; by 1841, only murder and treason remained.[37] Also important was the comprehensive—and decades-long—reform and rationalization of criminal procedure and the foundation of a professional police force with the establishment in 1829 of the Metropolitan Police. But also key here, I would argue, was the founding of the definition of crime (as indeed of procedural arrangements and many instances of penal reform) in legislation which had the imprimatur of (albeit radically imperfect) representative democracy and—had the grand ambition of codification ever been realized—of association with self-consciously modern values such as rationality, clarity and publicity.

Though full codification never came in England and Wales, legislative domination of criminal law most certainly did;[38] and the substantial consolidating legislation steered through by Robert Peel in 1827–30 and further revised in 1861 made a significant gesture towards the rationalized common source which codification would have offered. As Lindsay Farmer has shown, notwithstanding the failure of the codification project, a gradual rationalization of criminal law during the nineteenth century is powerfully reflected in a flourishing realm of treatises, primarily written for practitioners and magistrates—itself to be supplemented and even superseded in the late nineteenth and twentieth centuries by the student-oriented textbook, a product of the development of university education in law from the late nineteenth century.[39] While not necessarily presenting criminal law as a principled, coherent body of doctrine, nor looking very deeply into the rationale for or distinctiveness of criminal law as a form of legal regulation, these treatises, as Simpson has argued, all in some sense presented criminal law as a unity—and hence as a discrete object of professional interpretation and deployment.[40] This, certainly, would have fostered co-ordination of criminal law as an integrated body of doctrine: but I would argue that it would also, in the context of modernizing sensibilities, have helped to legitimate criminal law as an object of professional interpretation. The necessity of such treatises, particularly for lower courts, was stimulated by the burgeoning of criminal legislation in new areas of regulatory concern prompted by economic and social developments

[37] See Clive Emsley, 'The History of Crime and Crime Control Institutions' in M Maguire, R Morgan and R Reiner, *The Oxford Handbook of Criminology*, 3rd edn (Oxford: Oxford University Press, 2002) 203–30.

[38] See Lieberman, Postema, n 9 above.

[39] See Farmer, 'Of Treatises and Textbooks', n 6 above: see also Michael Lobban, 'The English Legal Treatise and English Law in the Eighteenth Century' (1997) 13 *Iuris Scripta Historica* 69–88.

[40] A W B Simpson, 'The Rise and Fall of the Legal Treatise: Legal Principles and the Forms of Legal Literature' (1981) 48 *University of Chicago Law Review*, 632–79.

such as industrialization and urbanization. But that legislative origin of much criminal law itself provided an increasingly strong source of legitimation. Until at least the 1860s, the professional credentials of defence lawyers remained suspect.[41] But in the context of the increasing franchise, the parliamentary origins of a greater part of criminal law, along with the authority of a judiciary and court system itself being reorganized on more modern, systematic lines, with greater capacity for testing points of law,[42] helped to glue together the formal and the popular definition of crime—villainy and felony, as Leo Katz has put it in a thoughtful paper[43]—recreating the nexus between lay and legal constitutions of crime to a level adequate for legitimation.

Hence the history of not merely the professionalization of criminal law practice and the formalization of criminal law doctrine, but also of constitutional reform and democratization presents itself as a potentially key resource in our understanding of criminalization. Yet relatively little has been written about the impact of the transition to representative democracy in Britain or in other countries on these pressures and constraints, or about how they are filtered through political institutions and expressed in the legislative process. There is a vast literature on the parliamentary career of the effort to achieve codification and criminal law reform in the nineteenth century on which to draw in constructing such an account.[44] But it does not really engage with the larger question in which I am interested here—though a thorough analysis of that question would, of course, need to review this literature to determine who was supporting change and why, so as to be able to work out how this legal debate fits into the larger dynamics of electoral reform. Since the comparative literature on criminalization and punishment suggests that the structure of electoral democracy is an important factor in explaining country differences today,[45] the path to democracy, and the specific form of the constitutional settlement which (re)formed itself in the

---

[41] As is reflected in James Fitzjames Stephen's essay on 'The Morality of Advocacy' (1861) 3 *Cornhill Magazine* 447–59; see further Schramm, n 23 and n 30 above.

[42] See Lacey, 'In Search of the Responsible Subject', n 12 above.

[43] See Katz, n 2 above.

[44] Notably Leon Radzinowicz's monumental five volume *A History Of English Criminal Law Since 1750* (Oxford: Oxford University Press, 1948–1986). See also Coleman Phillipson, *Three Criminal Law Reformers: Beccaria, Bentham, Romilly* (London and Toronto: JK Dent and Sons, 1923); K J M Smith, *Lawyers, Legislators and Theorists* (Oxford: Oxford University Press, 1998); Richard R Follett, *Evangelicalism, Penal Theory and the Politics of Criminal Law Reform in England, 1808–30* (Basingstoke: Palgrave, 2001).

[45] See Lisa L Miller, *The Perils of Federalism: Race, Poverty, and the Politics of Crime Control* (New York: Oxford University Press, 2008); Vanessa Barker, *The Politics of Punishment: How the Democratic Process Shapes the Way America Punishes Offenders* (New York: Oxford University Press, 2009); Nicola Lacey, *The Prisoners' Dilemma: Political Economy and Punishment in Contemporary Democracies* (Cambridge: Cambridge University Press, 2008) chs 2 and 4.

nineteenth and early twentieth centuries in Britain, seem obvious objects of concern.

Unlike in the countries of continental Europe where, for all their important differences, there was a key moment of modernization and state-building which was accompanied by a formal codification of criminal law which has proved to be remarkably durable, Britain followed a more incremental path to legal modernization and (partial) rationalization, as well as an earlier path to (partial) democracy.[46] Rooted in the history of a power struggle between the monarchy and the landed aristocracy, the seventeenth-century achievement of a sovereign parliament with virtually unrestricted legislative powers survived the nineteenth-century extension of the franchise, potentially allowing a wide range of interests a say in the legislative definition of crime. Accordingly, it offered a potential solution to the legitimation problem described in the last section: the perceived gap between popular and official definitions of crime.

Of course, this solution was barely plausible in the era immediately following the Reform Act 1832; but it began to have rather more plausibility after 1867 (around the date, incidentally, at which the debate about criminal defence representation appears to have lost steam, presumably as a result of progress in both professional organization and the rationalization of legal doctrine through consolidating legislation). In short, once those who decried the power of the lawyers started to have more political power through the ballot box, the criminal law's legitimation problem reduced due to the possibility of according technical definitions of crime the imprimatur of democratic origins. At the same time, the increasing professionalization of law—reflected in both the organization of the profession itself and in phenomena like practitioner treatises—stabilized the legitimacy of judicial interpretation. Note, however, that the shape of criminal law's legitimation problem is historically specific: it presents itself in different ways at different times. The outcry in the run-up to and in the wake of the Prisoners' Counsel Act of 1836 was driven by an emerging bourgeois elite who, in the context of rapid and poorly organized urbanization, were both much concerned about crime, in particular in relation to the protection of interests in property, and rather suspicious of a *parvenu* group—the new breed of defence barristers—which they saw as lacking proper professional credentials, with patchy provision for training and a system of discipline which was both incomplete and poorly suited to the needs of a rapidly expanding profession.[47] This bourgeois elite was the very group whose electoral power was on

---

[46] James Q Whitman, *Harsh Justice* (Oxford: Oxford University Press, 2003).
[47] See Nicola Lacey, 'The Way We Lived Then', n 23 above.

the rise—a fact which enhanced the capacity of democratization to deliver greater legitimacy for criminal law, squaring the circle which combined increasing technical control over the interpretation of crime with (in principle) lay control over its legislative definition.

III. Reading Contemporary Criminalization in the Light of Institutional History

In the previous section, I have argued that the history of English criminal law has been marked by an underlying tension about who has the power and authority to define crime—the lawyer or the lay person. To conclude my analysis, I will explore the degree to which that tension, albeit in different form, continues to haunt English criminal law today. As leading comparativist Mirjan Damaska has noted, the English legal process presents an instance of what may fairly be described as a system of co-ordinate authority.[48] While the jury's role has been restricted in scope and attenuated in substance over the centuries, the role of lay decision-making in both jury trials and magistrates' courts is a striking exemplification of the implicit recognition that the definition of criminality is not purely a matter of law. Of course, magistrates are advised by a legally qualified clerk; and juries are meant to be restricted to questions of fact. But when questions of fact include findings on 'reasonableness', 'dishonesty', 'immoral purposes' and so on[49]—open-textured and incompletely specified concepts which are key to the definition of specific crimes—the line between fact and law is fine to vanishing point. Moreover, criminal courts' decision-making goes forward in a context in which lay persons outside the court will often have views about innocence and guilt, and on occasion make their voices heard on the matter, potentially producing significant social conflict about who has the better view.[50] Hence the tension

---

[48] Mirjan R Damaska, *The Faces of Justice and State Authority* (New Haven: Yale University Press, 1991).

[49] As, for example, in the case of theft as defined by the Theft Act 1968, s 1; involuntary manslaughter as defined by the common law; and soliciting for immoral purposes as defined by the Sexual Offences Act 1956, s 32.

[50] This is, of course, particularly striking in notorious cases such as the spectacular miscarriage of justice cases which haunted the English criminal process in the 1990s, and which Nobles and Schiff have analysed persuasively: Richard Nobles and David Schiff, *Understanding Miscarriages of Justice* (Oxford: Oxford University Press, 2000). Nobles and Schiff draw on systems theory to argue that there is an inherent instability in any social process in which different groups claim a right of definition, those definitions being informed by irreconcilable assumptions. In this case, the media's conception of guilt and innocence was different from that implied by the law. The self-referential nature of the legal and media subsystems hence caused a significant legitimation problem for

between lay and professional definitions of crime which underpinned the nineteenth-century argument about criminal defence continues to echo in contemporary English criminal law.

The same is true of the specific form which parliamentary democracy assumed in the course of constitutional development between the seventeenth and the nineteenth centuries. The particular structure of English parliamentary sovereignty is potentially very responsive and electorally sensitive to popular opinion, and is largely unconstrained by substantive constitutional standards. This means that, in the English system, the direct democratic legitimation of the legal definition of crime came at a price. This was not so evident during the early part of the twentieth century, in which the standard and scope of education across the populace was relatively low, and elite leadership more or less taken for granted. But it began to be a real issue from the 1970s on. As education has become better and more widespread, and as deference to established elites has diminished, a more generally populist critique of formalized definitions of crime is of increasing importance.[51] As scholars writing on criminal law in England and Wales today are only too aware, the very responsiveness of the political system to perceived swings in popular opinion means that, under certain environmental conditions, the definition of crime is liable to become highly politicized. In the absence of effective processes for a more deliberative form of popular participation, this makes for highly volatile criminal policy, and increasing incoherence in the concept of crime.

From this point of view, legitimation through a system of democratic parliamentary sovereignty which provides a direct link between electoral pressures and criminal policy is problematic. Our adversarial political system has led to law and order bidding wars and to rampant criminalization. And when criminalization is used indiscriminately and pragmatically for political ends—as, arguably, has been the case in Britain over the last fifteen years— the legal definition of crime is liable to become both ever more detached from the core popular conception, and ever harder to conceptualize or rationalize within a unitary account of its distinctive features. Hence what Husak dubs 'overcriminalization' is very much a double-edged sword as far as legitimation is concerned, as well as being a clear problem from the point of view of

---

criminal law, and one which the law had to try to resolve while being inherently incapable of doing so. This is, of course, a very particular example: but the same logic underpins the much more common complaint about defendants 'getting off on a technicality'.

[51] See Mick Ryan, *Penal Policy and Political Culture in England and Wales* (Winchester: Waterside Press, 2003).

legitimacy in a normative sense.[52] For all the obvious differences—the move to universal suffrage in 1928; the establishment of a national police force; a rationalized sentencing system—contemporary debates about the difficulty of bringing the chaotic panoply of criminal legislation within any coherent rationalizing frame are strongly reminiscent of debates in late eighteenth-century England when Parliament indulged in similarly pragmatic deployments of criminalization.[53] (Parallel problems arise for law enforcement under conditions of low legitimacy, as the police discovered at the time of the urban disorders of the early 1980s and indeed of August 2011.[54]) Note the very different situation in countries like Germany or the Nordic group, where a consensus is still prevailing around the authority of a core criminal code and around constitutional restrictions on criminalization which were part of an initial settlement of the powers of the modern state.[55]

Much of the literature on criminalization acknowledges the central part which politics plays in the process. On the one hand, the normative literature on criminalization is firmly located within political philosophy, with the role of the state and its criminal justice branch a key feature of many of the most famous political theories of the post-Enlightenment era. The vision of criminalization to be derived from Mill's (notoriously indeterminate, yet intuitively commanding) harm principle[56] is the most obvious example; but Hobbes, Hume, Locke, Kant and Hegel are equally concerned with the role of criminal punishment in the modern state.[57] On the other hand, the explanatory literature—most of it located in criminology rather than criminal law theory—is preoccupied with the role of electorally driven political pressure in widening the boundaries of criminalization;[58] while in relation

---

[52] Husak, *Overcriminalization*, n 3 above; see also Nicola Lacey, 'Principles, Policies and Politics of Criminal Law', in J Roberts and L Zedner (eds), *Principled Approaches to Criminal Law and Criminal Justice: Essays in Honour of Andrew Ashworth* (Oxford: Oxford University Press, 2012).

[53] See King, *Crime, Justice and Discretion*, n 15 above.

[54] See R Kinsey, J Lea and J Young, *Losing the Fight Against Crime* (London: Blackwell, 1986).

[55] See Lacey, *The Prisoners' Dilemma*, n 45 above, ch 3; John Pratt, 'Scandinavian Exceptionalism in an Era of Penal Excess', Parts I ('The Nature and Roots of Scandinavian Exceptionalism') and II ('Does Scandinavian Exceptionalism Have a Future?') (2008) 48 *British Journal of Criminology* 119–37 and 275–92; T Lappi-Seppälä, 'Penal Policy in Scandinavia', in Michael Tonry (ed), *Crime, Punishment and Politics in a Comparative Perspective*, Volume 36 of *Crime and Justice: A Review of Research* (Chicago: University of Chicago Press, 2007); T Lappi-Seppälä, 'Trust, Welfare and Political Culture: Explaining Differences in National Penal Policies', in Tonry (ed), *Crime and Justice: A Review of Research* (Chicago: Chicago University Press, 2008).

[56] John Stuart Mill, *On Liberty* (1859) (Penguin Classics, 1974).

[57] See Alan Norrie, *Law, Ideology and Punishment* (Dordrecht: Kluwer, 1991); Alan Brudner, *Punishment and Freedom* (Oxford: Oxford University Press, 2009); see also references at n 3 above.

[58] Katherine Beckett, *Making Crime Pay: Law and Order in Contemporary American Politics* (New York: Oxford University Press, 1997); Lacey, *The Prisoners' Dilemma*, n 45 above.

to decriminalization, the way in which changing social mores are filtered through political processes has also drawn attention.[59] In relation to Britain, electoral pressures are widely credited with (or rather blamed for) an explosion of criminalization during the last two decades[60] (there exist parallel, extensive literatures on other countries, notably the United States[61]).

In both explanatory and normative cases, the history of the institutions under scrutiny makes a real difference to the intellectual task of analysis or prescription. The nature of the state and of government has changed—and expanded—over time, encompassing functions not anticipated in the great modern political theories, and necessitating some imaginative extension of the principles which have informed liberal and communitarian thought over the last centuries. And the empirical pressures and constraints upon criminalization have also changed markedly over time. Hence large social changes such as the professionalization of criminal law and the emergence of newly democratic foundations for criminal legislation are of key relevance to the development of criminal law.

The normative task of criminalization theory can only be satisfactorily pursued if we also interest ourselves in some fundamental explanatory questions about the nature of criminalization over time and space. For the possibility of achieving valued goals or ideals can only be assessed by constructing a clear picture of the various institutional, political and social dynamics which underpin the constitution of criminal law at particular times and in particular places. The nature of the British Constitution (such as it is) affects the constitution of criminalization in both material and symbolic ways: through both the distribution of criminalizing power enshrined in the constitution and the meanings echoing through its history. We need to understand this in order to think productively about how to improve the quality of criminalization (and, if possible, to reduce its extent).

---

[59] Troy Duster, *The Legislation of Morality* (New York: Free Press, 1970).

[60] David Downes and Rod Morgan, 'No turning back: the politics of law and order into the millennium', in Maguire et al (eds), *The Oxford Handbook of Criminology* (4th edn, Oxford: Oxford University Press, 2007) 201; Tim Newburn, '"Tough on Crime": Penal Policy in England and Wales', in Michael Tonry (ed) *Crime and Justice*, Volume 36 (Chicago: University of Chicago Press, 2007) 425–70; Tim Newburn and Robert Reiner, 'Crime and penal policy', in Anthony Seldon (ed), *Blair's Britain 1997–2007* (New York: Cambridge University Press, 2007) 318–40; Robert Reiner, *Law and Order: An Honest Citizen's Guide to Crime and Control* (Oxford: Polity Press, 2007); Lacey, *The Prisoners' Dilemma*, n 45 above, chs 2 and 4.

[61] See for example Husak, n 3 above, ch 1; David Garland, *The Culture of Control* (Oxford: Oxford University Press, 2001); David Garland (ed), *Mass Imprisonment in the United States: Social causes and consequences* (London: Sage, 2001); Jonathan Simon, *Governing Through Crime: How the War on Crime Transformed American Democracy and Created a Culture of Fear* (New York: Oxford University Press, 2007).

My argument also implies, however, that we should resist the temptation to interpret 'the constitution of criminal law' too narrowly.[62] For the constitution of criminal law in the specific and narrow sense of its constitutional pedigree and structure cannot provide all the clues to escaping the dilemmas discussed in this chapter. Constitutional limits such as those to be derived from the passage of the Human Rights Act, for example, are unlikely in themselves to be effective in a system constituted as the English one is. A broader understanding of the constitutional context of criminalization— of the implications of this constitutionalization for both the content and the legitimacy of criminal law—would imply, rather, that we need to look for ways of tempering the sway of penal populism and of overcriminalization through the construction of consultative processes and/or processes of democratic deliberation at some remove from electoral pressure in the area of criminal law and penal reform. Above all, we need to reconsider a view which is one part of the historical legacy discussed in this chapter: that direct electoral accountability is the most suitable means of delivering the legitimation of power such as that of criminal law.[63]

[62] *Pace* some of the most influential scholars writing in this field at the moment: see Husak, n 3 above; see also A Ashworth and L Zedner, 'Defending the Criminal Law: Reflections on the Changing Character of Crime, Procedure and Sanctions' (2008) 2 *Criminal Law and Philosophy* 21–51; Dennis J Baker, *The Right Not to be Criminalized: Demarcating Criminal Law's Authority* (London: Ashgate Applied Legal Philosophy Series, 2011).

[63] For a development of this argument, see Nicola Lacey, 'Political Systems and Criminal Justice: The Prisoners' Dilemma After the Coalition', *Current Legal Problems* (2012) doi: 10.1093/clp/cus002 (online version).

3

Harm, Vulnerability, and Citizenship: Constitutional Concerns in the Criminalization of Contemporary Sex Work

*Vanessa E Munro and Jane Scoular**

I. Introduction

'The constitution of criminal law' engages concerns regarding the appropriate doctrinal structures, and, equally importantly, the defensible *limits*, of criminal interventions in a contemporary, liberal state.[1] More broadly, for socio-legal scholars, it also acknowledges the existence of an inevitably mutually constitutive relationship between (criminal) law and society. A number of commentators have emphasized that the ways in which law constitutes social relations reflect a complex process, which is related to the nature of the interaction between individuals and the legal system, and is refracted back in the ways in which social norms infuse both the letter and operational spirit of law.[2] Recent work in this area has also explored the ways in which criminal law is involved in a process both of creating and enforcing the boundaries of citizenship, which in turn influence the contours of criminal doctrine.[3] In this chapter, we will address these inter-related themes, focusing specifically

* The authors are indebted to the editors for their insightful and constructive feedback on a previous version of this chapter. We would also like to thank Katie Cruz for her excellent research assistance in the early stages of putting this chapter together.
[1] For recent, influential discussion, see D Husak, *Overcriminalization: The Limits of the Criminal Law* (Oxford University Press, 2008); A Duff, *Answering for Crime: Responsibility and Liability in the Criminal Law* (Hart Publishing, 2009).
[2] See, further, S E Merry, *Getting Justice and Getting Even: Legal Consciousness among Working Class Americans* (University of Chicago Press, 1990); P Ewick & S Silbey, *The Common Place of Law: Stories From Everyday Life* (University of Chicago Press, 1998); S Silbey, 'Making a Place for a Cultural Analysis of Law' (1992) *Law and Social Inquiry* 39–48.
[3] E Aharonson & P Ramsay, 'Citizenship and Criminalization in Contemporary Perspective' (2010) 13(2) *New Criminal Law Review* 181–9.

upon the ways in which the regulation of commercial sex markets in the UK have constituted forms of (sexual) citizenship, roles for criminal law, and bases of legitimacy for state intervention.[4] Our aim here is not to defend a particular normative position in relation to the contentious issue of the rights and wrongs of prostitution, nor is it to set out a detailed blueprint for any particular preferred approach to its regulation. Rather, our aim is to explore the discourses through which recent state initiatives designed to respond to prostitution have been constructed and defended. These discourses have shifted over time, and in conjunction with broader shifts towards forms of neo-liberal governance, which have in turn legitimated increased levels of criminalization and the social exclusion of sex workers. As a result, while prostitution policy is the primary terrain for our discussion, our analysis throws new, and critical, light on the processes and uses of criminalization by, and in, the modern state in a wide array of other contexts.

In the following sections, we will first outline the nature of historical and more recent responses to prostitution in England and Wales. Having done so, we will explore the ways in which the concept of 'harm', which has traditionally been seen as a cornerstone of liberal approaches to criminalization, both in and beyond the context of prostitution, has been supplemented by, and reconfigured through, an increasing contemporary reliance upon the associated, but in important ways distinct, concept of vulnerability. A number of commentators have suggested that the more expansive approach to criminalization which this shift has promoted can be attributed to a gradual colonizing of the harm principle by conservative rather than progressive liberal agendas.[5] In the specific context of prostitution, this shift has also been tied—in a not unrelated fashion—to the growing influence upon law-making institutions of a particular brand of radical or so-called 'governance' feminism.[6] Without dismissing these influences, we will suggest that the position is both more complex and more routine than these arguments imply. Indeed, recent shifts in the regulation of prostitution must be understood in the broader context of the emergence of new, neo-liberal normative frameworks for governance and citizenship, within which, we argue, the concept of vulnerability plays an enabling role.

We will move on in later sections of this chapter to explore the potential negative implications of these contemporary discourses about, and responses

---

[4] Although we do not go into the detail of reform initiatives in other UK jurisdictions, eg Scotland, the same themes can be identified here and may also be pertinent beyond.

[5] See, for example, B Harcourt, 'The Collapse of the Harm Principle' (1999) 90 *Journal of Criminal Law and Criminology* 109–94.

[6] J Halley, *Split Decisions: How and Why to Take a Break from Feminism* (Princeton University Press, 2006).

to, prostitution for the lives of sex workers. We do not seek here to trivialize the harms that those who sell sex may experience and nor do we wish to deny that the concept of vulnerability can have a legitimate role to play in constructing an appropriate response thereto. Instead, our aim is to illustrate the ways in which this concept has been deployed without sufficient critical scrutiny, becoming a mechanism through which to impose increased surveillance and coercion upon sex workers without providing the benefits of protection and security that it promises. As a result, we will suggest that recent responses to the regulation of prostitution risk creating new, or further entrenching current, axes of vulnerability.

Having highlighted these potential difficulties, in the final section, we will explore some mechanisms by which to promote a more reflexive and inclusive use of the concepts of harm and vulnerability in the context of sex work. Emphasizing the need for policy-makers, on-the-ground enforcers, and sex workers themselves, to engage legal mechanisms that exist outside of carceral and coercive confines, we will reflect on what this re-constitution might mean for the contours and possibilities of both sexual citizenship and criminal law.

II. The Regulation of Prostitution: A Brief Overview

Although the act of selling sex per se is not illegal, a long history exists in the UK of state attempts to classify and control the prostitute subject through a range of ancillary offences associated with soliciting, advertising or facilitating commercial sex. As far as the soliciting street sex worker is concerned, these responses have typically operated on the basis that punishment and incarceration provide the most appropriate mechanisms by which she could be shown the error of her ways and transformed (coercively) into a morally-upstanding citizen. From the eighteenth century, penitentiaries, lock hospitals, and Magdalene institutions were used to remove and prevent women from selling sex,[7] and in the nineteenth century, laws were created (specifically the Contagious Diseases Acts of the 1860s in England and Wales), which allowed for the arrest and compulsory medical inspection of any woman presumed to be a 'common prostitute'.[8] From the late nineteenth century, further avenues

---

[7] J Walkowitz, *Prostitution and Victorian Society* (Cambridge University Press, 1980); L Mahood, 'The Magdalene's Friend: Prostitution and Social Control in Glasgow, 1869–1890' (1990) 13(1–2) *Women's Studies International Forum* 49–61; P Bartley, *Prostitution, Prevention and Reform 1860–1914* (Routledge, 2000).

[8] This term was first used in the Vagrancy Act 1824, the Metropolitan Police Act 1839 and the Town Police Clauses Act 1847, which provided powers for the police to arrest and fine those 'common prostitutes' who caused annoyance to local inhabitants or passengers. This established an

for state intervention were also created through laws designed to penalize those deemed to have exploited the sex worker by encouraging or facilitating her prostitution, or otherwise feeding the sex markets in which she trades. In 1885, the Criminal Law Amendment Act was passed in England and Wales, which introduced new powers to penalize, through criminal sanction, brothel-keeping. This paved the way for a swathe of subsequent legislation throughout the twentieth century, which increased the state's power to raid suspected brothels and dedicate police resources to public areas frequented by street sex workers. In these more recent responses, although incarceration has continued to loom large as the ultimate sanction, it is apparent that a range of more dispersed strategies have also been operationalized by the state in order to subject those involved in sex work, both on the street and in off-street premises, to surveillance and discipline. Within these responses, while the 'rescue' and 'rehabilitation' of prostitutes has continued to be a commonly asserted objective, it has been enmeshed, but also frequently in tension, with discourses regarding public morality and nuisance.

The Wolfenden Committee Report on Prostitution and Homosexual Offences sought, in 1957, to articulate the philosophy underpinning the state's regulation of commercial sex.[9] Keen to emphasize their conventional liberal credentials, and mirroring in many regards the basic principles set out by John Stuart Mill,[10] the Committee prioritized personal privacy and autonomy (particularly in regard to sexual conduct) and insisted that this ought only to be tempered by criminal law intervention if, and to the extent that, it was necessary to ensure the avoidance of harm to others. The Report emphasized that while 'it is the function of the law to preserve public order and decency, to protect the citizen from what is offensive or injurious and to provide sufficient safeguards against exploitation and corruption of others',[11]

---

offence that could only be committed by a special category of person. A common prostitute was defined in *R v Morris Lowe* [1985] 1 WLR 29 as a woman 'who is prepared for reward to engage in acts of lewdness with all and sundry, or with anyone who may hire her for that purpose'. The term could only be applied to female, and not to male, prostitutes (*Director of Public Prosecutions v Bull* [1994] 3 WLR 1196). Despite recognition of its stigmatizing and discriminatory character, the term was retained throughout successive periods of reform (including in the Street Offences Act 1959). Some forty years later, this was gradually tackled through successive legislative interventions. The Sexual Offences Act 2003, Schedule 1, paragraph 2 amended section 1(1) of the Street Offences Act 1959 to refer to 'common prostitute (whether male or female)'. Later, section 16 of the Policing and Crime Act 2009 repealed the term 'common prostitute' in its entirety, replacing it with the term 'person'.

[9] Wolfenden Committee, 'Departmental Committee on Homosexual Offences and Prostitution 1954–57', Cmnd 247, PRO HO 345/2–16 (Home Office, 1957).

[10] J S Mill, *On Liberty* (Wordsworth Classics, 1996).

[11] Wolfenden Committee, n 9 above, paragraph 13.

'there must remain a sphere of private morality and immorality which is, in brief and crude terms, not the law's business'.[12] Thus, while it is justifiable to coercively limit (and punish in the breach) conduct which causes harm, it is not generally justifiable to do so for the sole reason that others dislike such conduct or consider it immoral. In the specific context of prostitution, this led the Wolfenden Committee to recommend the introduction of a system of fines for street soliciting, which—though representing a utilization of criminal law—was seen to be justified by the need to avoid public nuisance, which in turn would interfere with, or cause harm to, the rights of others. Beyond this, it was felt that the selling of sex in private was not an appropriate matter for criminalization, except where it was evident that harm was being caused as a result; and while the possibility of establishing a system of regulated brothels in order to deal with the displacement of street sex workers that the implementation of fines for soliciting was likely to produce was mooted, it was not pursued in earnest (mirroring the trend in recent Home Office consultations on prostitution, to be discussed below).

Thus, the Wolfenden Report developed a response to prostitution which—not without some measure of tension—depicted it both as a public offence and as a private consensual transaction. Neither abolishing nor legalizing prostitution, the Report set an agenda for subsequent legal reforms which left the commercial sexual conduct of (some) individuals unregulated, whilst strengthening the frameworks through which women publicly selling sex could be penalized. By confining state intervention to its public aspects, prostitution control was thus positioned in accordance with conventional liberal interests. The laissez-faire approach adopted 'delineated a private sphere of non-intervention, creating an unregulated market in which private forms of commercial sex are, by omission, sanctioned and as such have very much proliferated since the time of Wolfenden'.[13] At the same time, however, the punitive regime imposed upon public acts of soliciting or facilitation was also amplified. The 1956 Sexual Offence Act and 1959 Street Offences Act specifically aimed to prevent 'the serious nuisance to the public caused when prostitutes ply their trade in the street' whilst penalizing 'the pimps, brothel-keepers and others who seek to encourage, control and exploit the prostitution of others'.[14] These reforms extended the criminal

---

[12] Wolfenden Committee, n 9 above, paragraph 60.

[13] P Hubbard & J Scoular, 'Making the Vulnerable More Vulnerable? The Contradictions of Street Prostitution Policy', in D Canter, M Ioannou & D Youngs (eds), *Safer Sex in the City: The Experience and Management of Street Prostitution* (Ashgate, 2009) pp 135–53, at p 150. See also R Matthews, 'Beyond Wolfenden? Prostitution, Politics and the Law', in R Matthews & J Young (eds) *Confronting Crime* (Sage, 1986) pp 188–210.

[14] Wolfenden Committee, n 9 above, paragraph 17.

law's application to all women who solicited on the streets, irrespective of whether any complaint had been made against them by the local residents or businesses to whom it was presumed they were a nuisance, and women identified as a 'common prostitute' became liable to a loitering or soliciting charge without caution. This approach thus justified and maintained a gender-asymmetry—in many ways still evident in contemporary responses—through which it is the woman who sells sex rather than her male client who is the focus of state attention.[15]

For more than four decades, this framework for responding to prostitution remained largely unaltered in the UK, notwithstanding a number of important changes in the scale and modes of operation of the sex industry, as well as in broader socio-sexual norms, gender roles and socio-economic conditions. In 2000, a comprehensive review of sexual offence provisions in England and Wales was initiated by the Home Office.[16] While the remit of this *Setting the Boundaries* Review originally extended to prostitution, it was subsequently decided that this issue required further, and distinct, consideration. As a result, the Sexual Offences Act 2003, which emerged out of the Review, while it introduced a new anti-sex-trafficking offence, ensured a non-gender specific application of soliciting offences and modernized certain associated terminology, largely maintained the structure, tone and substance of pre-existing provisions on domestic prostitution.

Efforts to respond to the need which this process had highlighted for a comprehensive review of domestic prostitution policy, both to modernize current provisions and respond to the changing, increasingly diverse and globalized, nature of commercial sex markets were, however, subsequently undertaken. In 2004, the Home Office issued the *Paying the Price* Consultation,[17] which in turn led to the production of a *Co-ordinated Strategy on Prostitution* in 2006,[18] as well as a further narrower review on *Tackling the Demand* in 2008,[19] and to the formalization of associated proposals in

---

[15] For this reason, we focus in this chapter on the legal regulation of female sex workers. This is not to deny that men too sell sex, but it reflects the reality that women prostitutes are statistically more prevalent and more likely to be the focus of legal control, with policy-makers continuing to view prostitution as highly gendered. For further discussion of the non-regulation and non-recognition of male and trans sex workers, see M Whowell, 'Male Sex Work: Exploring Regulation in England and Wales', in J Scoular & T Sanders (eds), *Regulating Sex/Work: From Crime Control to Neo-liberalism?* (Wiley Blackwell, 2010) pp 125–44.

[16] Home Office, 'Setting the Boundaries—Reforming the Law on Sexual Offences' (Home Office, 2000).

[17] Home Office, 'Paying the Price—A Consultation Paper on Prostitution' (Home Office, 2004).

[18] Home Office, 'A Coordinated Prostitution Strategy and a Summary of Responses to Paying the Price' (Home Office, 2006).

[19] Home Office, 'Tackling the Demand for Prostitution: A Review' (Home Office, 2008).

England and Wales via the Policing and Crime Act 2009. Although the scope of these consultations and reviews extended to all forms of prostitution, the tendency exemplified in historical patterns of regulation (including the Wolfenden Committee Report) to focus attention primarily upon street-based sex work was again evident. The possibilities of creating a system of legalized brothels or permitting a small number of sex workers to work together from a private property were put forward for consideration. The former suggestion was quickly rejected, however, and while the latter did receive some support, no concrete proposals along these lines have yet emerged. Instead, the focus has remained primarily on responding to public manifestations. Prostitution continued to be characterized as street-based and castigated as 'not an activity that we can tolerate in our towns and cities'.[20] At the same time, however, the term 'commercial sexual exploitation' proliferated in policy documents and was deployed, in effect, as a synonym for prostitution. Not only did this conflate the highly diverse conditions under which such exchanges can, and do, take place, it also effaced the possibility of seeing the sale of sexual services as anything other than abusive and harmful. Thus, while the criminal law continued to formally abstain from intervening in private transactions, the doctrinal insistence on stepping in to prevent exploitation interacted with this pervasive finding of the harmfulness of prostitution to legitimate far greater encroachment, as well as the emergence of more explicitly protectionist rationales for state intervention in relation to public acts of soliciting.

The overall aim of this emergent framework is declared by officials to be one of the eradication of prostitution. This is to be achieved through the increased criminalization of clients and the continued intolerance of prostitution-related 'nuisance', combined with the co-ordination of welfarist policing that is designed to divert, deter and rehabilitate (coercively if necessary) individual women from sex work. The conclusion that the law can legitimately play a more significant role in 'encouraging' women to leave prostitution underlines the belief that it is an inherently exploitative industry which no one would freely choose to work in, and paves the way for policing designed to disrupt sex markets through anti-social behaviour orders, raids and closures of brothels, and greater punishment of purchasers. Though wholesale client criminalization has not been realized, the Policing and Crime Act 2009 now renders it a strict liability offence for anyone to purchase or promise to purchase sexual services from a prostitute who is 'subjected to force, etc'. This extends to transactions with any person subject to exploitative conduct (defined in the statute as involving the use of force,

---

[20] Home Office, n 18 above, p 1.

threats, coercion or deception) by a third party, where that conduct is of a sort likely to induce or encourage her engagement in prostitution and is undertaken in expectation of gain for the third party, or someone other than the prostitute or client. While this move has been welcomed by some of those commentators who objected to the traditionally asymmetric focus of the law on the women who sell sex rather than their male clients,[21] the tendency to depict such clients uniquely as 'exploiters and transmitters of disease' has been challenged.[22] In addition, as we will explore in detail below, the significant risk that enforcement of such coercive interventions will merely exacerbate existing gender inequalities and will increase surveillance and control without securing attendant protection has been highlighted.[23]

III. From Harm to Vulnerability?

While the Millian 'harm principle' which, as noted above, found applied expression in the context of the Wolfenden Committee Report, continues to be regularly deployed in debates regarding the appropriate remit for criminalization, we suggest in this section that it has been supplemented and, to some extent at least, reconfigured in the context of contemporary prostitution regulation by the increased reliance upon a related but distinct concept of vulnerability. While the exact meaning of this concept is contested and its boundaries are amorphous, abuse of another person's vulnerability typically attracts strong normative condemnation. Vulnerability relies on recognition and accreditation by others, which leaves scope for manipulation in line with divergent socio-political or socio-economic agendas. But in contrast to harm, the concept of vulnerability implies a predictive, forward-looking character. It attaches to identities, circumstances or conditions more than to incidents, and it connotes a state of precariousness that is perpetually threatened rather than a concrete instance of violation that can be identified. These characteristics, we would argue, help to explain why the concept has been so enthusiastically invoked as part of the recent turn towards more actuarial forms of criminal justice policy. When conjoined with the fact that we are all—as embodied and connected beings—vulnerable to some degree, it also provides support to those

[21] S Jeffreys, *The Industrial Vagina: The Political Economy of the Sex Trade* (Routledge, 2009).

[22] T Sanders, 'Blinded by Morality? Prostitution Policy in the UK' (2005) 86 *Capital and Class* 9–17.

[23] J Scoular & M E O'Neill, 'Legal Incursions into Supply/Demand: Criminalising & Responsibilising the Buyers and Sellers of Sex', in V Munro & M Della Giusta (eds), *Demanding Sex: Critical Reflections on the Regulation of Prostitution* (Ashgate, 2008) pp 13–34.

who—for various paternalistic or punitive reasons—lobby for greater levels of state intervention.

Despite paying lip-service to the concept of harm, the extent to which recent prostitution policy initiatives in the UK have been framed by conventional liberal readings of the harm principle has been contested.[24] Critics have argued that the *Setting the Boundaries* Review, though purporting—in accordance with values of freedom and privacy—to reject state intervention other than where it was necessary to prevent harm to others, was informed by a blend of other rationales for criminalization, including a 'quasi-moral' justification which reflected 'the idea that sexual offences embody social standards of right and wrong'.[25] Thus, Lacey concluded that 'though the shade of John Stuart Mill stands behind the Review's references to harm and its appeal to the value of autonomy, an equally important concern is that of protection'.[26] Similarly, Munro has argued that on the underside of the Review lay an ideology that was 'more in keeping with Devlin than Mill—an approach within which a shared moral fabric not only exists, but needs to be protected, through criminal law, from the deleterious effects of deviance'.[27] In the context of prostitution, where the nature, extent and origins of any harm associated with commercial sex are highly contested, it has been observed that the Review's focus on the *harmfulness* of such conduct provided little determinative guidance, creating space for a reliance on more moralistic or conservative forms of reasoning that were rarely formally acknowledged. In the service of her 'protection', the prostitute subject was cast unequivocally as both victim and vulnerable; and set apart from the norms of inclusive citizenship in the process. Indeed, despite debate over the inevitability of harm, key policy-makers introduced the *Protecting the Public* White Paper,[28] which followed the *Setting the Boundaries* Review, by insisting that the sex industry is a 'sub-world of degradation and exploitation' to be purged and a 'terrible trade' that 'bedevils' communities.[29] This characterization has

---

[24] For a recent engagement with, and defence of, the use of paternalistic (as distinct from moralistic) arguments grounded in concerns about 'harm' within a liberal response to prostitution, see P Marneffe, *Liberalism and Prostitution* (Arizona State University Press, 2009).

[25] N Lacey, 'Beset by Boundaries: The Home Office Review of Sex Offences' (2001) *Criminal Law Review* 3–14, at 5.

[26] Lacey, n 25 above, p 5.

[27] V Munro, 'Dev'l-in Disguise? Harm, Privacy and the Sexual Offences Act 2003', in V Munro & C Stychin (eds), *Sexuality and the Law: Feminist Engagements* (Routledge-Cavendish Publishing, 2007) pp 1–18, at p 4.

[28] Home Office, 'Protecting the Public: Strengthening Protection against Sex Offenders and Reforming the Law on Sexual Offences', Cmnd 5668 (Home Office, 2002).

[29] Hansard, House of Commons Debate, 19 November 2002, Column 507, per Mr David Blunkett.

subsequently been seized upon by critics who have argued that this reflects, paradoxically, the extent to which prostitution was conceived of as an exception to, rather than exemplar of, the liberal mantra of non-intervention in the absence of identifiable harm.[30]

Similar patterns of a shifting discourse, operating in preference to (or at least in conjunction with) a more conventional focus upon the harm principle can also be identified in subsequent reviews and recent legislation. At the heart of this new discourse is a concern to trace, problematize and respond to the position of 'vulnerability' that is presumed to be the condition of the life of the sex worker. In the debates that preceded the Policing and Crime Act 2009, for example, Jacqui Smith, the then Home Secretary, insisted that 'the mark of any civilized society is how it protects the most vulnerable'.[31] Within this frame, *what* it was that the individual was deemed to be vulnerable to was often left imprecisely stated and the risk of its actualization was left without quantification. While harm continued to lurk in the background of this discourse, its role in justifying criminalization became increasingly obscure, with a designation of vulnerability in itself being used as a marker that demanded and legitimated a coercive state response. The concept was relied upon repeatedly by policy-makers and campaigners in the discussion that surrounded the 2009 Act. It was deployed to describe (with or without empirical evidence) the difficult position of those involved in prostitution (who were presumed to be vulnerable by virtue of their engagement in commercial sex), to defend the criminalization of those (clients, 'pimps' and traffickers) who supported their prostitution (who were presumed to *abuse* vulnerabilities), to support rehabilitative measures to remove the immediate personal circumstances (ie engagement in prostitution) that were deemed—often via a restricted notion of causality—to give rise to vulnerability, and to bolster the image of the state as a benevolent force in this process.

At one level, of course, there is little new in this narrative of saving 'vulnerable' women involved in prostitution. Recent initiatives have been predicated precisely upon a goal of rescuing and protecting those 'trapped' in prostitution, and so seeking to do 'what Josephine Butler attempted over 100 years ago, in a very different era and in a very different way'.[32] Yet this is more than just the same old story. As we will argue in the next section, this

---

[30] Lacey, n 25 above; A Bainham & B Brooks-Gordon, 'Reforming the Law on Sexual Offences' in B Brooks-Gordon et al (eds), *Sexuality Reposition: Diversity and the Law* (Hart Publishing, 2007) pp 261–96.

[31] Hansard, House of Commons Debate, 19 January 2009, Column 524, per Ms Jacqui Smith.

[32] Mr David Blunkett (Home Secretary), quoted in Mark Oliver and Alan Travis, 'Victorian Reformer Inspired Blunkett', *The Guardian*, 30 December 2003, p 2.

new narrative has evolved to fit a changing socio-political context, and more specifically, the constructions of the 'vulnerable community' and the 'vulnerable female victim of commercial sexual exploitation' that have emerged have been framed, at least in part, to legitimate increased criminal law regulation. The imagery that was chosen to preface the Home Office's *Paying the Price* Consultation provides a vivid illustration of this. The juxtaposition of broken windows and a 'broken child' is utilized to represent the subject of prostitution. This tokens vulnerability, signals the need for protection and connotes a risk of contagion if left unaddressed. Crucially, it also sidesteps the contradictions and complexities that are more aptly at issue in cases involving those adult women engaged in prostitution, who become the consultation's primary focus for surveillance, control, intervention, and rehabilitation.

IV. Conservativism, Feminism and Neo-Liberalism

It was suggested in the previous section that, in the context of prostitution regulation in the UK, there has been an increasing deployment of the concept of vulnerability in conjunction with, but also often in preference to, the associated concept of harm, which has conventionally been posited as pivotal to assessing the legitimacy of criminalization. It was argued that the indeterminacy of competing claims to harm in the context of prostitution may have undermined its usefulness and permitted scope for reliance on a range of other, more protectionist—and often more morally conservative—agendas. While the context of prostitution may provide an acute illustration of these claims, we do not believe that these developments are peculiarly tied to it. On the contrary, we suggest here that not only is the indeterminacy of the harm principle and the rise of the significance of 'vulnerability' as a trigger for action evidenced in other contexts, but so, too, is the use of more protectionist narratives that justify expansive state intervention.

In a diverse modern society in which our frequently individualistic rights consciousness greets legal restrictions upon personal freedom with marked scepticism, concerns have increasingly been raised regarding whether the harm principle does, or indeed can, provide the kind of boundaries for legitimate state intervention that it purports to offer. Harcourt, for example, has argued that with the passage of time 'the harm principle is effectively collapsing under the weight of its own success'.[33] As the concept has gained argumentative and rhetorical currency, claims which may previously have

---

[33] Harcourt, n 5 above, at p 113.

been framed through alternative discourses (for example, of morality or equality) have increasingly turned instead to notions of harm. An ever-wider variety of harms have thus been identified (environmental, psychological, etc) and this has led to a deluge of potential claims of harm in any given context in which the criminal law needs to determine the scope and terms of its involvement. In addition, the harms that are claimed by one individual or group are increasingly being met with counter-claims of different types of harm from others. This has had significant ramifications for those who rely upon the harm principle to determine the proper boundaries of state intervention and criminalization. Indeed, as Harcourt has observed, 'the issue is no longer whether a moral offence causes harm, but rather what type and what amount of harms the challenged conduct causes, and how the harms compare'; but on those issues, 'the harm principle is silent'.[34] Resolution can thus only be secured by selecting one interpretation, or one hierarchy, of harm over another, and this selection is based necessarily on ideological or pragmatic considerations that are external to the formula of the harm principle itself.

Of course, the extent to which it was ever purported that the harm principle could operate as a sole and sealed limiting principle with regard to the legal enforcement of morality can be contested. While many commentators have raised concerns regarding the lack of clarity in Mill's account of what constitutes harm and of how competing experiences of harm are to be responded to,[35] Mill and subsequent advocates of this basic liberal principle were not oblivious to these concerns.[36] Its contextualization within the broader framework of political liberalism, which—amongst other things—prioritizes human self-development, deplores human suffering, and seeks to ensure equal concern and respect, provides at least some assistance in resolving these difficulties.[37] It may be appropriate, then, for us to direct greater attention to the *realpolitik* that frames the operation of the harm principle in any given context. Equally, however, the difficulties that it labours under in modern times may emerge less as a result of its inherent indeterminacy per se, and more as a result of its contemporary replacement with, or the co-existence of, a new normative paradigm that speaks to alternative forms of citizenship and legitimation.

Drawing on the contemporary US context, Harcourt argues that while there has been a steady uptake in the language of harm, it has been deployed

[34] Harcourt, n 5 above, at p 113.

[35] See, for example, J Fitzjames Stephen, *Liberty, Equality, Fraternity* (originally published 1873), R J White (ed) (Cambridge University Press, 1967).

[36] H L Hart, *Law, Liberty and Morality* (Stanford University Press, 1963); J Feinberg, *The Moral Limits of the Criminal Law: Harm to Others* (Oxford University Press, 1984).

[37] For one recent exploration of how this might operate and be applied in the context of prostitution regulation, see Marneffe, n 24 above.

increasingly in the service of a conservative, rather than conventionally pro-gressive, liberal agenda. It has been conjoined with a 'broken windows' theory of crime prevention,[38] which charts a trajectory from minor crimes, like prostitution and loitering, to serious criminality and neighbourhood decline, in order to lobby for the increased regulation and prohibition of a range of human activities.[39] Thus, as conservatives have increasingly made use of the harm principle, 'liberal theory has colonized moral conservatism and, it would appear, is being colonized by conservatives in return'.[40] While there may indeed be some merit in this analysis, we suggest that the processes involved are more complex than merely an undermining of the progressive liberal harm principle by a conservative moral agenda. In the specific context of prostitution regulation, a surprising level of affinity and alliance has emerged between this conservative outlook and radical feminist arguments which insist upon the inevitably exploitative, harmful and non-consensual nature of commercial sex work. Though the extent of its influence amongst policy-makers has been overestimated in some quarters (at the same time as the risks of its co-option have been underestimated),[41] it is apparent that the binary stories of unagentic, victimized women and exploitative clients, pimps or traffickers, which often inform this genre of feminist theory, have been deployed strategically by the state to support increased intervention.

While, at one level, these conservative and radical feminist discourses are undoubtedly playing an important role in framing contemporary responses to prostitution, at another level, these developments must also be understood in the broader context of 'structural shifts both in discourses of citizenship and in practices of criminalization'.[42] Recent years have seen a significant expansion of criminalization, both in the UK and US.[43] Such interventions have, however, often taken a peculiarly modern form, imposing an obligation on citizens to self-govern and to manage crime risks throughout their daily activities. A vision

[38] J Wilson & G Kelling, 'Broken Windows: The Police and Neighbourhood Safety', *The Atlantic Monthly* (March 1982). Available for on line access at http://www.theatlantic.com/magazine/archive/1982/03/broken-windows/4465/.

[39] Harcourt, n 5 above, at pp 149–50; see, further, B E Harcourt, 'Reflecting on the Subject: A Critique of the Social Influence Conception of Deterrence, the Broken Windows Theory and Order-Maintenance Policing New York Style' (1998) 97 *Michigan Law Review* 291–389.

[40] Harcourt, n 5 above, at p 116.

[41] Halley, n 6 above; K Bumiller, *In an Abusive State: How Neoliberalism Appropriated the Feminism Movement against Sexual Violence* (Duke University Press, 2008).

[42] Ahoronson & Ramsay, n 3 above, at p 182.

[43] D Garland, 'Governmentality and the Problem of Crime: Foucault, Criminology, Sociology' (1997) 2 *Theoretical Criminology* 173–214; J Simon, *Governing Through Crime: How the War on Crime Transformed American Democracy and Created a Culture of Fear* (Oxford University Press, 2007); A Ashworth & L Zedner, 'Defending the Criminal Law' (2008) 2 *Criminal Law and Philosophy* 21–51; and Husak, n 1 above.

of criminal justice has emerged which posits 'the citizen-as-potential-victim as its consumer, on the one hand, and its "responsibilized" crime preventing active participant on the other'.[44] This, in turn, has produced and sustained a paradox within which 'a political commitment to rolling back the state' is increasingly combined with 'unprecedented reliance on criminalization as a policy means'.[45] But, as Ramsay has observed, this encroachment may be best understood not as some illiberal aberration but rather as flowing from a new— or at least a newly reconfigured—normative basis for criminalization, which is grounded in the protection of 'vulnerable autonomy'.[46]

The selective focus in recent sex work regulation in the UK on public places, risky practices and dangerous people, coupled with an increasing rhetorical reliance on claims of vulnerability certainly chime with this analysis. As discussion in the following section highlights, we find in this context evidence of what Sullivan refers to as 'schizophrenic' criminal justice policy, which is marked by a coexistence of socially inclusive neo-liberal techniques of regulation with more overt forms of control and repression.[47] Within this frame, amongst other things, inclusion has no intrinsic value but becomes utilized as a feature of risk management and responsibilization. It is contingent on offender change and compliance, and when it fails it can quickly be substituted for more effective means, such as custody and incapacitation.[48] To this extent, contemporary prostitution regulation provides, we suggest, a particularly vivid illustration of the ways in which new normative frameworks are being forged, which both work with, and against, more conventional understandings of harm, morality, citizenship and the state.

V. Re-visiting Vulnerability in Neo-Liberal Frame

We have suggested above that contemporary policy responses to, and discourses around, prostitution in the UK (and, indeed, elsewhere) have become

---

[44] Ahoronson & Ramsay, n 3 above, at p 182.

[45] Ahoronson & Ramsay, n 3 above, at p 182.

[46] P Ramsay, 'Overcriminalization as Vulnerable Citizenship' (2010) 13(2) *New Criminal Law Review* 262–85; P Ramsay, 'The Theory of Vulnerable Autonomy and the Legitimacy of the Civil Preventative Order', LSE Law, Society & Economy Working Paper Series 1/2008, available at www.lse.ac.uk/collections/law/wps/wps.htm; P Ramsay, 'Vulnerability, Sovereignty and Police Power in the ASBO', in M Dubber & M Valverde (eds), *Police in the Liberal State* (Stanford University Press, 2008) pp 157–76.

[47] R Sullivan, 'The Schizophrenic State: Neo-Liberal Criminal Justice', in K Stenson & R Sullivan (eds), *Crime, Risk and Justice: The Politics of Crime Control in Liberal Democracies* (Willan, 2001) pp 29–47.

[48] Garland, n 43 above, at p 6.

increasingly animated by the concept of vulnerability. Depictions of the community as vulnerable to the harms associated with sex work have been conjoined with accounts of the vulnerability of individual women engaged in prostitution, which have been deployed by a number of feminist commentators with varying degrees of reductiveness. There is, no doubt, a legitimate role to be played by the concept of vulnerability in this context, for example in problematizing the dynamics of power that may be in play between a sex worker and her 'pimp'/brothel-owner/trafficker. At the same time, however, we have concerns about the loose and pervasive ways in which the concept has increasingly been invoked. It has come to label a condition presumed to be shared by all those engaged in commercial sex, irrespective of the complexity of individual experiences and narratives. Its predictive nature has mitigated the requirement to clearly correlate concerns about risk to the feasibility of their coming to fruition. What is more, as we will argue in this section, its conjunction with neo-liberal forms of governance has facilitated an individualized focus upon the conditions that give rise to vulnerability, distracting attention from the state's role in their creation and privileging coercive intervention as the means of their redress.

While it is too soon to fully assess the impact of the Policing and Crime Act 2009, concerns have been expressed over the extent to which—through its wider range of controls and increased scope for professional intervention—it may prove to be more coercive than the previous fine and caution system, with increased 'protection' being mirrored in the increased policing of women's lives.[49] Critics have argued that any symbolic value secured by acknowledging the perceived culpability of those who create a demand for commercial sex may be undermined by the legislation's selective targeting of sections of the sex trade where control is presumed to be most prevalent. This in turn may encourage an over-policing of transactions involving foreign women as an anti-trafficking strategy, which overlooks the forms of control practised on domestic prostitutes and those who migrate freely from overseas.[50] Prosecution rates for the offence in England and Wales (and for similar offences in other jurisdictions) have been low and police forces have reported both that they do not find the

[49] J Phoenix, 'Youth Prostitution Policy Reform: New Discourses, Same Old Story', in P Carlen (ed), *Women and Punishment: The Struggle for Justice* (Willan Publishing, 2002) pp 67–93, at p 82.
[50]]See, for example, V Munro, 'An Unholy Trinity? Non-Consent, Coercion and Exploitation in Contemporary Responses to Sexual Violence in England and Wales', in G Lestas & C O'Cinneide (eds), *Current Legal Problems* (Oxford University Press, 2010) pp 45–71; Scoular & O'Neill, n 23 above; A Carline, 'Perspectives on Trafficking and the Policing and Crime Act 2009: Challenging Notions of Vulnerability through a Bulterian Lens', in S FitzGerald (ed), *Regulating the International Movement of Women: From Protection to Control* (Routledge-Cavendish, 2010) pp 135–53.

provisions particularly helpful and do not have the resources necessary for their enforcement in any event. At the same time, the fact that the possibility of prosecution for this offence lurks in the background may have a significant and detrimental impact on the way in which commercial sex transactions are structured and negotiated. Fear of prosecution may lead clients to insist on hastily made agreements, or require sex workers to seek out clients in less visible (and hence less safe) environments, transact with a riskier client base or engage in less safe sexual practices. In these regards, critics argue that an initiative implemented under the auspices of helping sex workers (by quashing the demand that is seen to 'entrap' them in prostitution) may ultimately render them more 'vulnerable'.[51]

Moreover, while the new regime for the disposal of persons convicted of soliciting, which requires them to attend a series of rehabilitation meetings with a supervisor, designed to secure their exit from prostitution in lieu of conventional punishment, offers some progressive potential, the fact that it only offers inclusion to those sex workers who responsibly exit and adopt 'normal' lifestyles continues the hegemonic moral and political regulation of prostitution.[52] This approach relies on a rationale of 'rescue' and 'reintegration', irrespective of the conditions under which the sexual exchanges in question took place or the personal history and expressed motivations of the individual woman involved. Moreover, it promotes a close and mutually reinforcing engagement between criminal justice and welfare systems which also increases the scrutiny and discipline to which the sex worker is subject. In line with the neo-liberal models of governance that Ramsay identifies in other contexts,[53] this is a strategy that seeks to 'responsibilize' the individual seller of sex—it is no longer the job of the state to rehabilitate, but the job of the prostitute to become compliant. Thus, the 'problem' of prostitution's perpetuation is reduced to 'one of recalcitrant individuals unwilling to accept offers of help and support'.[54] But this underestimates the difficulties of imposing 'order' onto the frequently chaotic lives of sex workers and distracts attention from the state's obligations both to tackle the conditions that give

---

[51] See, for example, V Munro & J Scoular, 'Abusing Vulnerability? Contemporary Law and Policy Responses to Sex Work and Sex Trafficking in the UK' *Feminist Legal Studies* (2012, Volume 20, Issue 3, forthcoming); A. Carline, 'Of Frames, Cons and Affects: Constructing and Responding to Prostitution and Trafficking for Sexual Exploitation' *Feminist Legal Studies* (2012, Volume 20, Issue 3, forthcoming); Hubbard & Scoular, n 13 above.

[52] J Scoular & M O'Neill, 'Regulating Prostitution: Social Inclusion, Responsibilisation and the Politics of Prostitution Reform' (2007) 47(5) *British Journal of Criminology* 764–78.

[53] Ramsay, n 46 above.

[54] M Melrose, 'Trying to Make a Silk Purse from a Sow's Ear? A Comment on the Government's Prostitution Strategy' (2006) 5(2) *Community Safety Journal* 4–13, at 12.

rise to prostitution in the first place and to provide the material resources necessary as a prerequisite to sex workers' 'exit' and personal change.[55] At the same time, it also presumes and preserves the criminal law's role as enforcer of sex workers' desistance and rehabilitation, by offering them the 'opportunity' to 'be helped or else'.[56] The perpetual prospect of imposing further censure (including incarceration) on women who fail to comply with rehabilitative meetings 'renders the notion of voluntarism highly questionable' in this context.[57] Despite its welfarist overtones, it promotes a preoccupation with punitive and carceral responses, legitimated on the basis of community protection and security.[58]

At the heart of these recent initiatives, then, remains a somewhat schizoid approach to the prostitute subject. On the one hand, she is a vulnerable individual, marginalized and victimized, and in need of assistance from the state both to quash the client demand that drives her prostitution and to help her 'choose' a less risky, more conventional, lifestyle. At the same time, since she is always in need of containment and control, she must not be too comfortable in this position. Her presence, particularly on the street, can (re)position her as an aggressor, a threat to orderly society and respectable communities, which in turn increases the vulnerability of others. Moreover, her refusal—or inability—to engage with rehabilitation 'effectively' can see her (re)positioned as anti-social, corrupting, wilful and liable to punishment. While this precarious construction has been increasingly built upon, and justified through, a discourse of 'vulnerability', it cannot be dislocated from claims about the 'harm' of prostitution as a trigger for criminalization. Equally, nor can the framework for regulation which it promotes be divorced from the legacy of the Wolfenden Committee Report. Linked in important ways to these previous paradigms, it cannot thus be understood as a wholly novel phenomenon; but at the same time, it is far from being simply a modern manifestation of old agendas and responses. In being framed through the lens of neo-liberal forms of governance, and influenced by 'conservative liberal' and/or radical feminist rationales, it has a distinctive and pioneering

---

[55] Melrose, n 54 above; Scoular & O'Neill, n 52 above; J Phoenix, 'Be Helped or Else! Economic Exploitation, Male Violence and Prostitution Policy in the UK', in V Munro & M Della Giusta (eds), *Demanding Sex: Critical Reflections on the Regulation of Prostitution* (Ashgate Publishing, 2008) pp 35–50; Munro, n 50 above.

[56] Phoenix, n 49 above.

[57] J Scoular, J Pitcher, R Campbell, P Hubbard & M O'Neill, 'What's Anti-Social about Sex Work? Governance through the Changing Representation of Prostitution's Incivility', in J Phoenix (ed), *Regulating Sex for Sale* (Policy Press, 2009) pp 29–46, at p 43.

[58] L Zedner, 'Security, the State, and the Citizen: The Changing Architecture of Crime Control' (2010) 13 *New Criminal Law Review* 379–403.

feel, and the ways in which this feeds through into policy poses disconcerting implications both for our understanding of the concept of vulnerability and our responses to commercial sex.

By prioritizing 'exit' from sex work as the primary means of facilitating social inclusion, the current response risks moving us further away from the pursuit of justice, becoming instead a tool of individualized risk assessment and facilitating 'rehabilitation' only according to unchanged, dominant norms.[59] In addition, and crucially, it fails to address the vulnerability that arises from the continued criminalization of soliciting, and, more broadly, distracts from the 'the larger context, the situations, the chains of influence, within which [sex workers'] vulnerability is *created*, we might even say produced, may be perpetuated'.[60] As Edstrom has observed, then, perhaps the key difficulty with using vulnerability as a conceptual tool is not that it suggests a position of passivity or powerlessness (although, as we have seen in recent prostitution discourses, it very often does), but that it pushes the analysis 'back to individuals and their bodies... at the expense of power relations, accountability, structures, and dynamics'.[61] Moreover, by justifying interventions on the basis of predictions of future events, it relies on risk assessments that are inevitably negative and pessimistic, typically premised on the presence of a 'villain' and often 'built upon stereotyped or discriminatory attitudes towards certain decisions, or the different socio-cultural contexts within which these decisions are made'.[62] In the current context, this can— and has been—tied to the pivotal place that prostitution occupies in the radical feminist imagery—inherently degrading, selling sex is an activity that is paradigmatic of a wider, all-encompassing system of male power,[63] and instances of violence, abuse, and exploitation which take place within and outside the context of prostitution, become *the* context of prostitution, assuming a transnational, acultural and ahistoric meaning. By collapsing a multiplicity of issues into an accessible and linear story of good and bad sex, of victimized, unagentic women and bad men, this imaginary thus appeals to a particular binary social and cultural mindset.

---

[59] Scoular & O'Neill, n 23 above; B Cruikshank, *The Will to Empower: Democratic Citizens and Other Subjects* (Cornell University Press, 2004).

[60] C Philo, 'The Geographies that Wound' (2005) 11 *Population, Place and Space* 441–54, at 443.

[61] J Edstrom, 'Time to Call the Bluff: (De)-Constructing "Women's Vulnerability", HIV and Sexual Health' (2010) 53(2) *Development* 215–21, at 217.

[62] M Dunn, I Clare & A Holland, 'To Empower or to Protect? Constructing the "Vulnerable Adult" in English Law and Policy' (2008) 28(2) *Legal Studies* 234–53, at 244.

[63] C MacKinnon, *Toward a Feminist Theory of State* (Harvard University Press, 1989); K Barry, *The Prostitution of Sexuality* (New York University Press, 1995); Jeffreys, n 21 above.

This binary also suits a neo-liberal approach that encourages the grafting of relatively crude criminal justice solutions onto complex issues, in a way that bolsters state security and protects economic freedom.[64] Both feminism and criminal law lose much of their transformative power when they are reduced to binaries within which subject positions are presumed to be 'settled' and the realities of contradiction, constraint and struggle in the lives of those selling and buying sex, or the ways in which the activity can both challenge and reinforce norms of heterosexuality, femininity, and community, are not acknowledged. Thus, while vulnerability as a concept may have a useful role to play in increasing our understanding of, and improving our responses to, commercial sex, it is unlikely to be of assistance, and may be of concern, where it fails to engage with these complexities, and where those who invoke it do not articulate clearly the parameters of its meaning, the thresholds for intervention and the significance of what is left beyond.

VI. Sex Work, Citizenship and Criminal Law: Towards a New Engagement

While several commentators have welcomed the turn to vulnerability in general,[65] we have explored in previous sections its more problematic potential when applied within the frame of dominant neo-liberal forms of governance to the issue of contemporary prostitution. As noted above, our aim here is not to call for the abandonment of the concept per se but rather to call for closer and more critical engagement regarding what it means to be vulnerable in this context, and to insist that policy-makers engage more consciously with the complex realities of sex workers' lives in charting this vulnerability and determining how best to respond to it. We will argue in this section that, amongst other things, this requires critical re-engagement with the indexical relationship between criminal law's regulation of sex work and wider citizenship norms. While the constructions of the 'vulnerable public' and the 'vulnerable sex worker' that have emerged in recent reforms promote regulatory norms which are reframed to fit with modern times, we will suggest that they preserve a problematic legacy by continuing to relegate the sex worker—as both irresponsible and anti-social—to outside the polity.

---

[64] Scoular & O'Neill, n 23 & n 52 above; Zedner, n 58 above.

[65] M Fineman, 'The Vulnerable Subject: Anchoring Equality in the Human Condition' (2008) 20(1) *Yale Journal of Law and Feminism* 1–23; P Kirby, *Vulnerability and Violence: The Impact of Globalization* (Pluto Press, 2006). For further discussion of these approaches, and of our alternative appraisal of the concept of vulnerability, see Munro & Scoular, n 51 above.

There are, we believe, reasons to be concerned about the current uses to which the criminal law is being put in the context of prostitution, particularly where vulnerability is invoked without contextualization in order to legitimate intervention. But simply reasserting a conventional liberal version of the harm principle is unlikely to have much currency as a means of pushing back/resisting state interference. The principle itself is replete with tension and indeterminacy, and in any event, countering problematic instances of criminalization on the basis that they are 'illiberal' may miss the point that, in a larger sense, they reflect new liberal frames in which the role of criminal law and the parameters of responsible citizenship are conceived and deployed differently, in the name of protecting our 'vulnerable autonomy'.[66] To engage effectively with the issue of sex work regulation and the role of criminal law therein, then, we require—amongst other things—a more situated discussion of the citizenship issues raised by these new normative processes of inclusion and exclusion. This will highlight the extent to which 'citizenship is a set of contingent and unco-ordinated interactive politico-legal processes' rather than a static legal status or philosophical concept.[67] It will require us to consider the conditions of neo-liberalism, including the inequalities experienced by those, like sex workers, who fall outwith, or are relegated beyond, its purview. The limits of law in this context reflect the limits of our current understandings of community. Yet this is being challenged by sex workers themselves and by writers who draw on more expansive notions of citizenship. Scoular and O'Neill, for example, invoke theories of radical democracy and sex workers' demands regarding rights, recognition and redistribution, to counter the exclusionary aspects of neo-liberal citizenship.[68] Meanwhile, Pitcher et al explore the complexity of the experience of sharing spaces where sex work takes place to move beyond pre-existing binaries and reveal the potential for more supportive relationships between sex workers and local communities, as well as between sex workers and law enforcement.[69] Such approaches demand that we do not silence 'vulnerable' stakeholders in the name of protection or demarcate their activities as so harmful as to militate against their inclusion, but deal head on with the complexity of their vulnerability, and their rights, in situ. This may not be easily achieved in the context of prostitution, where competing normative positions are often fiercely defended and personal narratives are typically

[66] Ramsay, n 46 above.
[67] M Valverde, 'Practices of Citizenship and Scales of Governance' (2010) 13(2) *New Criminal Law Review* 216–40, at 218.
[68] Scoular & O'Neill, n 23 & n 52 above.
[69] J Pitcher, R Campbell, P Hubbard, M O'Neill & J Scoular, *From Conflict to Coexistence: Living and Working in areas of Street Sex Work* (Policy Press, 2006).

complex, fluid, and frequently contradictory. Yet, it is crucial to achieving a more 'holistic' account of human vulnerability which, as Dunn et al observe, requires that 'the (law) engage with the question of how "vulnerable adults" incorporate the issue at hand into the ways that they interpret, and ascribe meaning to, their lives'.[70]

Moving beyond circular, abstract and typically indeterminate debates about harm, morality and community in the context of sex work regulation will be a challenge. However, the seeds of an enlivened engagement between stakeholders in relation to the criminal law and its role in the construction and recognition of citizenship may be identifiable in the recent case of *Bedford v Canada*.[71] Here, current and former female sex workers argued before the Ontario Superior Court of Justice that three Criminal Code provisions criminalizing activities related to prostitution (specifically running or working in a bawdy house, communicating for the purposes of prostitution or living off the avails of prostitution) breached section 7 of the *Charter of Rights and Freedoms* because they endangered the lives of sex workers. It was argued that, although prostitution was officially legal, the virtual criminalization of the activity through such measures contributed to a growing incidence of physical and psychological violence. The laws prevented sex workers from protecting themselves by hiring security, working in groups, working inside or screening their clients through initial questioning. In a sense, then, their claim suggested that the law prevented them from acting *responsibly*, as individuals who could protect themselves from risk—or, in other words, as appropriate neo-liberal subjects. As such, it arguably tapped into a claim with particular currency. Giving the Superior Court of Justice's judgment, Justice Susan Himel upheld the applicants' claim. She rejected arguments from the Government of Ontario, who claimed that permitting bawdy houses commodified women and so violated sex workers' dignity and equality; and that the criminal law therefore had a legitimate role to play in preventing sex work from becoming normalized. Moreover, the Court rejected arguments presented by REAL Women Canada, the Christian Legal Fellowship and the Catholic Civil Rights League as interveners in the case, which asserted that sex work was not a 'Canadian value', that it was harmful to the women involved, and that the state was permitted to protect against 'moral corruption' through its criminal laws. This approach, which was largely upheld in appeal in *Canada (Attorney-General) v Bedford*,[72] provides a valuable illustration of the way in which, by enforcing the inclusion of sex workers within the polity and securing them access to the public discourse of

[70] Dunn et al, n 62 above, at p 252.   [71] *Bedford v Canada* (2010) ONSC 4264.
[72] *Canada (Attorney-General) v Bedford* (2012) ONCA 186.

law, the Charter allowed the contested terms of 'harm', 'dignity' and 'Canadian values' to be openly debated and tested. The judgment recognized that citizenship required that the sex workers' safety and rights be evaluated in situ and in all their complexity. Moreover, without displacing the important role of the criminal law in dealing with the violence that is experienced by sex workers, it acknowledged the ways in which the criminal law itself structures patterns of violence and designates certain groups as the instigators of offence and nuisance, as well as the subjects of vulnerability.

VII. Concluding Remarks

It has been argued that the 'risk of harm test', which has been relied upon in relation to the regulation of pornography, although it invokes neo-liberal connotations through its reliance on the language of risk and has the potential to merely perpetuate existing 'patriarchal and heterosexist moral regulation', also has the innate potential for more progressive outcomes, since it 'allows a multivocality of views' from different communities, as they speak to law about their divergent perceptions of harm.[73] It can thus emerge as 'a site upon which to reflect on the ways in which courts continuously open up new avenues for political challenges even as they attempt to reinstitute sovereignty and limit epistemological 'pluralism'.[74] To the extent that this is what Harcourt suggests may bring about the collapse of the harm principle, it seems, then, that it should not necessarily be feared. Such a collapse may 'increase our appreciation that there is harm in most human activities' and 'help us make more informed arguments and reach more informed decisions'.[75] The rise of vulnerability as an allied, but distinctive, discourse in the context of prostitution policy does not preclude these more progressive opportunities; indeed, as noted above, there are several commentators who suggest that it may increase the likelihood of their fruition, and Kirby has suggested that 'vulnerability points decisively and unambiguously to the need to strengthen our networks of solidarity and mutual obligation'.[76] At the same time, however, this can only be achieved when this multivocal engagement around the meaning and parameters of both harm and vulnerability co-exists alongside a critical reflection upon the role of criminal law as a

---

[73] M Valverde, 'The Harms of Sex and the Risks of Breasts: Obscenity and Indecency in Canadian Law' (1999) 8 *Social & Legal Studies* 181–97, at 181.

[74] Valverde, n 73 above, at p 181.

[75] Harcourt, n 5 above, at p 120.

[76] Kirby, n 65 above, at p 220.

creator of exclusions, risks, and precariousness, as well as a source of protection and redress. A frame that allows considerations of dignity and equality to engage reflexively with considerations of vulnerability is essential in order to explain and justify criminalization. In this way, while harm may still have an important place, it is less likely to act as, or be able to be depicted by policy-makers as, a bright line that determines the legitimate limits of criminal law. Instead, it emerges as a vehicle through which multiple voices can demand inclusion within a more pluralistic community and, through doing so, can secure a platform from which to contest and ultimately reconfigure associated norms.

4

The Role of the Public Prosecutor in Applying and Developing the Substantive Criminal Law

*Jonathan Rogers**

In this chapter, we are concerned with the effects of criminalization decisions on the decision-making process in the public[1] prosecutor's office when it comes to making charging and prosecution decisions in individual cases. Those who write on criminalization are aware that views on which activities should and should not be criminalized cannot be translated into legal rules without further ado. Those rules will need to be comprehensible to the lay community, if they are to guide them; they will have to be interpreted by lawyers who advise citizens, and they will have to be given effect in individual cases by judges. There is considerable scope for the underlying reasons behind the law to become lost in the process, and for the offence to become employed more (or, depending on the text, less) widely than was originally envisaged. But this need not be a ground for pessimism. If we can agree how the prosecutor should go about applying and developing the law, then our criminalization decisions might be made in better anticipation of how the law is likely to be applied and developed. We focus here on the prosecutor's understanding of the substantive law (and not, say, that of the police, important though that is too) on the assumption that the prosecutor has the 'final word' on the application of the substantive law and decides which cases come to trial. Indeed a study of his[2] application of the criminal law is of extra

* I am very grateful to the editors and to all the participants at the workshops who commented on my earlier draft. Special thanks are due to Friederich Toepel, who provided an insightful commentary which has influenced this final version. The responsibility for any remaining short-comings is my own.
[1] This means that we will not be discussing private prosecutors.
[2] References to the male pronoun should be taken to include the female pronoun.

theoretical interest because it combines an acknowledgement of the various reasons for criminalization with a study of the value and purposes of the criminal trial; in light of this, it is surprising that not more has been written on this subject.

In this chapter, I shall assume that (1) every criminal trial is to have some communicative value regarding the norms of the criminal law (though many trials will have other objectives too) (2) citizens are not merely subjects of the criminal law; it is their law too, and it must be capable of their comprehension. On those bases, it will be argued that the public prosecutor should have a role in identifying the reasons why an alleged activity seems to have been criminalized and considering whether these reasons are comprehensible to the rest of the community. If he cannot both identify *and* explain any possible reason for condemning D for what he is alleged to have done, then discontinuance for the alleged offence is justified and even required. Otherwise he would not be applying the law as recognized by the community, and so the trial will have no communicative value (nor indeed could the prosecutor effectively communicate to the defendant his decision to prosecute him, if called upon to do so). But where he is unsure whether the alleged conduct is intended by the lawmaker to be criminal and has too little relevant legal material to make an informed opinion, then he may only prosecute in order to develop the law. This means that we will draw a distinction between *applying* the law (which requires him to be able to understand it and to explain its reasons, whether or not he personally agrees with them) and *developing* the law (which he may only do if he is unable to apply it). The importance of the distinction will be clearer when we suggest that the standard tests in prosecutorial decision-making (the evidential test, the public interest test and the fairness test[3]) should apply differently depending on whether the prosecutor is trying to apply the existing the law, or to develop the law (so that he may be in a position to understand and to apply it in future).

The likely objections to this will be that it is only for the lawmaker to consider the reasons for the law, and their likely comprehensibility, and similarly, that the prosecutor acts in an executive role in sending cases to court, and should leave the problems in communication of the criminal law to the courts themselves. But neither objection convinces.

To start with the first objection, the presupposition of an objective view of what the law may be as applied to any situation, *without thinking of its*

---

[3] By the 'fairness' test, I refer to the decision whether the defendant can fairly be expected to cope with being prosecuted. For an argument that this is properly regarded as separate from the public interest test, see J Rogers, 'Restructuring the Exercise of Prosecutorial Discretion in England' (2006) 26 *OJLS* 775, but it is not necessary to resolve this debate for the purposes of this chapter.

underlying reasons, is unrealistic. Many prohibitions are cast in evaluative terms (failing to take reasonable care in some matter, or acting in a way likely to cause distress, and so on). In deciding whether a court would be likely to convict on a certain set of facts, the prosecutor is likely to be substituting his own view on the sort of activity that *should* merit condemnation—at least, when he first enforces the law and has no precedents to guide him. It may be that he thus discontinues some cases which would in fact be declared criminal if only they were to reach court.[4] Secondly, nothing is said of the situation where the law is under-developed, eg, where some exculpatory defence might be widely assumed to be available but no clear source of law exists. Here it is too difficult to speak of the prosecutor 'applying' the law. Moreover, even if he openly brings a prosecution to test or to develop the law, then that too is a choice which needs to be made on the basis of some criterion, which is nowhere spelt out. So there are value-laden decisions to be made regarding the substantive law under any model. To be sure, we would agree that 'any official or public organization that substitutes its own judgement for one reached through the appropriate democratic channels is behaving uncon-stitutionally'.[5] But while the prosecutor cannot 'substitute' his own pre-ferred norms of the substantive law to those which clearly apply, he may and should adopt his own views as to whether the reasons behind the law *do* apply as reasons also to condemn the alleged conduct, if he is meaningfully to enforce it.

The second objection, that the prosecutor should leave the courts to deal with cases where liability seems to arise on a literal application but no good reason for the application of the law can be communicated, is also too much. Prosecutorial discretion should not be wholly an executive operation. Coun-tries that explicitly recognize a 'public interest' test accept that prosecutors may have regard to their resources in making individual decisions; and even countries that don't wish to grant 'discretion' in this matter for serious offences tend to have different arrangements for less serious offences.[6] This already suggests that it is natural to consider the likely gains in communi-cation in selecting a case for trial. Moreover, the prosecutor may be required to assume legal and quasi-judicial duties too—and this is so even in jurisdic-tions which try to limit the ambit of the prosecutor's discretion in gauging the public interest. The prosecutor will act as a lawyer when he interprets the law, reviews the evidence and considers potential procedural issues, and as such

[4] M Damaska, 'The Reality of Prosecutorial Discretion: Comments on a German Monograph' (1981) 29 *Am J Comp L* 119, at 121–2.
[5] A Ashworth, *The Criminal Process*, 2nd edn (Oxford University Press, 1995) at p 79.
[6] Damaska, n 4 above, at 120.

professional ethical standards may apply to him.[7] He may act in a quasi-judicial capacity when considering whether the defendant can fairly be expected to cope with the burden of being prosecuted for the offence in question, as opposed to being subject to a less formal disposal.[8] Often his ethical lawyerly duties may seem to overlap with his duties of fairness to the defendant, eg when we might say that he should select only the appropriate charges rather than to over-charge in order to extract a favourable plea bargain. We often say that he acts as a 'minister of justice' when exercising such functions.[9] If we treat him as answerable to the defendant in some respects,[10] then it should not be surprising if he were also expected to explain to a prosecuted person (if called upon to do so) *why* his alleged activity is criminalized. This is not to deny that there is a substantial executive role in what he does, and the rule that he may not promise not to prosecute in advance of an offence[11] may be regarded as a valuable safeguard which disables him from 'licensing' criminal offences. But his role is not *purely* executive, and from this standpoint the argument that applying the substantive law requires him to think about why D's alleged conduct is condemnable, and whether the reasons are at least comprehensible to the lay community, need not be radical at all.

I. Alternative Criminalization Questions

I shall argue in this chapter that where the prosecutor believes that D's alleged conduct was intended or assumed to be criminal, then his first step is to ask himself whether any of the lawmaker's reasons for enacting the offence can apply as a reason for condemning D's alleged conduct; and then whether he could explain this link to the lay community. We will call this the *application* test. Where he is sure that an explicable reason does apply, then he *may* prosecute, subject to the evidential, public interest and fairness tests. If he is

---

[7] On which, see A Sanders and R Young, 'The Ethics of Prosecution Lawyers' (2004) *Legal Ethics* 7(2) 190.

[8] See Rogers, n 3 above, at pp 800–1.

[9] See A Ashworth and M Blake, 'Some Ethical Issues in Prosecuting and Defending Criminal Cases' [1998] *Crim LR* 16, at 17. Sanders and Young suggest that '(I)f we are to test the "Minister of Justice" claim, the place to start is pre-trial prosecutorial discretion', n 7 above, at 196.

[10] In England, this arises in some abuse of process cases where the courts stop a prosecution because the prosecutor has reneged on an undertaking not to prosecute. See generally J Rogers, 'The Boundaries of Abuse of Process in Criminal Trials' (2008) 61 *Current Legal Problems* 289.

[11] In England, see *Yip-Chiu-Cheung v R* [1994] 3 WLR 415 (PC); *R v DPP, ex p Pretty* [2002] 1 AC 800 (HL).

sure that no reason can apply (or at least, none that can be explained), then he *must* discontinue. But he may not be able to answer the question in either way, because he may not even be sure that liability is today intended or assumed by the lawmaker, and in that event he should apply the *development* test, which is concerned with whether the prosecution of an offence would help him better to understand the scope and reasons for the offence, or other areas of the law (including the general part of the criminal law). Again, subject to the evidential, public interest and fairness tests, he may prosecute if he thinks that to do so will assist him in understanding the law so that he may be able to deploy the application test in future cases. Together, these may be thought of as alternate 'criminalization questions' and they should be regarded as mutually exclusive: the prosecutor should only apply the development test if he *cannot* apply the application test. Further, whichever criminalization test applies should be the first test to be applied, once a possible charge has been identified; because the operation of the subsequent evidential, public interest and fairness tests will differ depending on which of the two criminalization questions originally applies.

The *application* test relies on a premise that the public prosecutor should be equipped with an ability to think about the criminal law not merely as a set of texts which fall to be interpreted, but also as a set of normative messages; to understand, as academics do, that criminal prohibitions must be based on some reason why the defined conduct ought to be condemned by the community. However, the prosecutor need not be a philosopher in his own right. He need not believe in any particular theory of criminalization. Indeed it might be preferable if he did not. For his task is not to design or to redesign the criminal law, nor even to justify the laws that have been passed, but only to be able to perceive and then to explain the reasons why they were passed. Thus, he may personally find it difficult to justify an offence of blasphemy but he could probably find reasons, albeit unpersuasive ones (relating to variant theories of morality or offence), which might explain its criminalization. He should next consider whether he would be able to explain any such reason, so that ordinary members of the lay community might understand him (and again it would not matter whether they *agree* with any of the reasons offered). Thus, the prosecutor's true role in using the application test is that of a (hypothetical) philosophical educator—he should only want to enforce laws the reasons for which he believes that he could explain, and which the lay community could understand, even though neither he, nor his audience, might find them convincing.

Provided that the prosecutor believes that he could explain the reasons behind the law, and how they relate to D's conduct, then the law is comprehensible even if bad, and so falls to be applied. For it is still possible for proceedings to have proper communicative value. The defendant and others (maybe even the prosecutor) might become persuaded that the reasons behind the law are in fact good. Alternatively, the court proceedings might assist in confirming suspicions that the law is bad (something that would be most effectively communicated by a decision by the jury to nullify the law and to return an acquittal, or by the judge granting a discharge from penalty upon conviction[12]). But the public evaluation of laws through the process of trial and punishment is only possible insofar as there are comprehensible norms to be communicated. In contrast to bad laws, there is no purpose in prosecuting offences the reasons for which either no longer sensibly apply or at any rate cannot be explained to a comprehending lay public. The House of Lords in England, in declaring that it would be absurd to think that nine-teenth-century treason laws could possibly apply today so as to prohibit incitement of a peaceful abolition of the monarchy (eg, in newspapers or school debating societies) said that any prosecutor who insisted upon charging the offence would become a 'laughing stock'.[13] This seems to be a suitable way of articulating the difference made here between an interpret-ation of a law which is not so much harsh or controversial but rather nonsensical to modern eyes.

It should be clarified that the prosecutor should embark on the application test only when he thinks that the lawmaker *intended* or *assumed* criminal liability to arise. The lawmaker's intention may be garnered not only from the legislation as clarified by case law, but also from perusal of external sources (such as debates in Parliament and previous government papers) and, if necessary, through consultation with experts. But the lawgiver's intention or assumption of criminality is what matters; where it is present, the application test applies even if it is possible that there may be a legal obstacle to conviction (this is a matter that rather falls to be considered when applying the evidential test). Thus, it was doubtful whether the old English offence of obtaining property by deception covered frauds committed by electronic means, because the form of the property which the victim trans-ferred was not technically the same form of property which the defendant obtained. But there could be no doubt that liability *was intended* in such situations. So the prosecutor should next have considered the *reasons* for the offence of obtaining property by deception, and he would have found (explicable) reasons which would also suffice to condemn D's conduct. The

---

[12] On the significance of discharges, see M Wasik, 'The Grant of an Absolute Discharge' (1985) 5 *OJLS* 211.

[13] *R (on the application of Rusbridger) v Attorney-General* [2003] UKHL 38.

technical legal hurdle would arise only at the next (evidential) stage; but that need not rule out the prosecution either, as we shall see.[14] Thinking in this way may also require the prosecutor *not* to prosecute by applying the letter of the law, if criminal liability is clearly not what the lawmaker intended or assumed, as may be the case with an obvious legislative drafting blunder. The prosecutor should too consider whether the lawgiver intended or assumed the availability of *defences* which may arise in any case; if not, then the prosecutor should be ready to prosecute even though for legal reasons the courts might have to accept the defence. If a defence seems to have been intended or assumed, again the prosecutor should ask whether the lay community could understand a reason for it, and he should again be prepared to prosecute if he imagines a negative answer.

But the application test cannot always apply from the outset. The prosecutor will not always be so confident whether the lawmaker intended liability (or a defence) to apply. It may, for example, not be so clear whether a legislative omission was a blunder or whether it was deliberate. New cases may have thrown into confusion the legal community's understanding of the law. Or, old legislation may seem to apply so awkwardly to new situations that he may wonder whether the lawmaker, if he wanted criminal sanctions, would since have addressed the problem separately; or by contrast, some new legislation may be so vaguely drafted that only case law may clarify its scope into confusion, etc. In these situations, thinking about the reasons behind the law can make no sense, since the prosecutor should only embark on this exercise when determining the *lawmaker's* reasons for criminalization— which he cannot do if it is not clear what he intended or assumed the law to be. Indeed, the lawmaker may have intended the scope of the offence to develop incrementally through prosecution and trial; or he may have neglected a problem, perhaps for political reasons, and have left the common law to find interim legal solutions. Here, if he should decline to prosecute, the prosecutor may be depriving himself of his only possible opportunity to understand and apply it in the future. This is where the *development* test must apply instead.

It follows from this that the justifications for bringing prosecutions, according to either of the criminalization questions, are in some way independent from the outcomes at trial. If it were proper to prosecute to develop the law, then that need not be undercut by an acquittal; and if it were improper to apply the law where the reasons for criminalization are incomprehensible, then the decision to prosecute cannot become justified by a

---

[14] See n 35 below and accompanying text.

conviction. But this should not be surprising. The prosecutor does assume the responsibility for causing the harms occasioned to prosecuted persons pending trial, which will occur regardless of whether D is convicted or even if the charges are later dropped,[15] and that should alert us to the point that the justifications for *prosecuting* and for *punishing* are related but separate. The argument here is that the prosecutor's role requires him to send cases to trial where either the comprehensibility of the law is of a minimum level such that the trial may have communicative value, *or* at least where the law can be developed to the minimum extent that he can *apply* it in future cases. The perspective of the court may be different, of course—the court may feel that a provision is so clear that it cannot be interpreted so as to give effect to the lawmaker's undoubted intention[16]—but that will not of itself undermine the decision to have prosecuted.

In the vast majority of cases, there will be no doubt that the lawmaker intended to criminalize the alleged activity and there will be one or more likely several explicable reasons why so. But some aspects of the proposed application and development tests merit further consideration.

II. The Application Test

In deciding what the lawmaker's reasons for criminalization were, the prosecutor may attribute to the lawmaker reasons for criminalization which he did not express but which, it is believed, would make sense and would not have been rejected if they had been mooted. This may include paternalistic or moralistic reasons which today would seem unfashionable. Moreover, such reasons may be inferred from the text of the law, as may be necessary where there is no contemporary indication of the various different reasons for criminalization. Thus, it may well be that the offence of assisted suicide was prompted by a religious stance on the sanctity of life, and that criminalization reflected the views of the moral majority of the time. But it is also possible to argue that the offence of assisted suicide is premised on a variation of the harm principle, perhaps on the 'slippery slope' basis that some vulnerable and uncertain people may wish to be assisted in order not to be

---

[15] A person prosecuted may find that the stress, inconvenience, and cost in finding legal advice and temporary difficulties whilst the case is pending (eg, if a prospective new employer, or money-lender, asks whether he or she is currently facing any charges) are the greatest impositions of all—and the prosecutor himself is responsible for imposing these harms. See M Feeley, *The Process is the Punishment* (Russell Sage Foundation, 1979).

[16] As happened in the electronic fraud case of *R v Preddy* [1996] AC 815.

a burden to others, and it may be too difficult for family members to understand their vulnerability and motivations, meaning that only a blanket ban will be effective in protecting the vulnerable.[17] To the extent that this is plausible (whether or not it is convincing), and is consistent with the text of the offence and not inconsistent with anything said when the Suicide Act was passed in 1961, then prosecutors are right to have been prepared to prosecute under the Act on that basis, This is so even if they should consider that society has become so secular that the original moral reasons for criminalization are no longer comprehensible.

Further, some 'drift' may have occurred such that by incremental development the law is accepted to be more (or less) expansively interpreted today than originally intended. Thus, the scope of the law of murder today is surely different from the medieval concept of 'killing under the Queen's peace with malice aforethought', and the law of self-defence has developed from being an excuse in murder cases where the defendant had retreated until literally facing a wall, to a potential justification to various charges, where the reasonableness of his actions falls to be judged by all the circumstances. Here, the prosecutor should identify possible reasons for the modernized law, and apply them—thus, he may now speak too of justificatory reasons for self-defence which may apply to certain forms of alleged conduct.

Once he has identified a reason for what the law is assumed or is intended to be, the prosecutor must decide that the lay community could understand the reason and its applicability for condemning D's conduct. It may be unusual for the lay community not to perceive any reason for the law at all. This is perhaps most likely to happen with obsolete offences or with certain laws which are arguably so remote from the concerns of the community that they do not recognize them as 'their' laws but rather as edicts which they are mandated to obey, or as the impositions of an intellectual elite.[18] One likely situation where the community representative will not recognize a law as being in any way 'theirs' will be one where democracy has broken down and the lawmaker has been free to make oppressive laws. Where East German law apparently allowed officials to shoot citizens who tried to climb the Berlin Wall, it was quite right that prosecutions should have taken place after reunification; because presumably the lay members of the community in

---

[17] See the approach of Lord Bingham in *R v Secretary of State for the Home Department, ex p Pretty* [2002] 1 AC 800 at [26]–[28].

[18] No separate test need apply should the prosecutor be called upon by the defendant to explain the reasons of the law for which he is charged; he need only supply the same reasons which he would have explained to the hypothetical member of the community.

East Germany could not understand why it might be justified to shoot them for wanting to escape to another country.[19] More commonly, one suspects, the reason behind a prohibition will be comprehensible but it may not be understood why it should apply to what D is alleged to have done. Suppose that D possessed arguably indecent photographs of children in books which he was found to have bought from reputable high street shops. The lay person would understand why the offence has been enacted but perhaps not why that reason should apply to condemn D in this case: the circumstances might elicit the response that one could fairly expect reputable shops not to sell anything that might be thought to violate obscenity laws.[20]

There is perhaps not the necessity to define as closely what is meant by the 'lay community' here as may be the case, say, with juries. Certainly it is not suggested that the prosecutor should necessarily imagine talking to a group of people, much less a cross-section of the community in terms of political or social categories.[21] He may even imagine the outcome of a conversation with *one* lay person. In imagining the likely outcome, the prosecutor might assume only that the lay citizen is of average intelligence, adult age, resident in the community during adulthood, unprejudiced against any class or category of persons and reasonably well informed about current events. The citizen would be prepared to revise his intuitive views on any subject when confronted by facts and reasoned argument and would be able to understand views with which he nonetheless still disagrees. At the same time he is not a Herculean figure. He may be so familiar with certain practices which he knows are widely tolerated in the community that it will be too hard for him to understand why they should have been criminalized. This lay community test does mean that the application test will vary from community to community in terms of philosophical sophistication. Some communities may be very quick to understand offences based on common morality, whilst others might find them so bizarre as to be incomprehensible.

---

[19] For further discussion of this case, see G Fletcher, 'The Nature of Justification' in J Gardner, J Horder and S Shute (eds), *Action and Value in Criminal Law* (Oxford University Press, 1993), arguing that the statutory justification should not bind the court either.

[20] In *R v Neal* [2011] EWCA Crim 461, the Court of Appeal effectively suggested that prosecutions should not take place on such facts, when giving its reasons for denying the prosecution a retrial 'in the interests of justice'—though they did not deny that the possession might, legally, have been criminal.

[21] This brings us back to our earlier point that the community need not *agree* with the reasons for any criminalization decision; only to understand them. Different conceptions will apply to communities which allow jury nullification; here cross-representation is likely to be vital.

Decisions *not* to prosecute on the basis of the application test should be discussed within the public prosecution service, and the decision should be publicized and communicated, together with the relevant facts of the case, both within the legal community and in the lay community. They would be open to review, and the decision not to proceed could be relied on by other prosecutors and by subsequent defendants.[22] Ideally, such publications would trigger fast-track procedure by which the legislature could consider amending or abolishing an incomprehensible offence, in much the same way that laws which are held incompatible with human rights obligations may have fast-track systems in some states.

A. The lawmaker's explicit reliance on prosecutorial discretion

Perhaps the most challenging questions for the prosecutor arise where the lawmaker openly concedes that the law is very broad, and offers a view that certain activity which he may have criminalized would properly not be prosecuted in practice. Here, depending on the authority and precision of such statements and the extent to which they seem to have been instrumental in allowing the apparent over-criminalization to occur, the prosecutor may seem to be on particularly strong ground in some cases to think that, although the lawmaker intended to criminalize the activity, he had no reason to condemn the activity as may apply to the instant case.

Here, it seems that we may need to distinguish between different reasons for knowing over-criminalization. If the reason is openly one of political compromise *and* it seems that there is no criminalization-based reason for the width of the law, then the application test should fail. It would not even be necessary to consider the perspective of the lay community, for there would be no reason to explain to it. But there may be some reasons for over-criminalization which may be put in the language of criminalization discourse. For example, the lawmaker may wish to send an unequivocal message to the community that the safety of certain activities cannot readily be gauged in advance, such as assistance to dying relatives who commit suicide. Here, routine discontinuance in minor cases (albeit combined with

---

[22] But there does remain the danger that some defendants will not perceive important distinctions between the publicized case and their own, against which the prosecutor should try to warn. It is beyond this chapter to discuss the appropriate level of review of decisions to prosecute in similar but distinguishable cases, and indeed the appropriate forum. But if the ground for distinction in a later case is important, and means that D's own conduct *was* intended to be criminal *and* that an explicable reason can be found to explain why it should be criminal, then in principle it may serve the public interest to prosecute the case in order to communicate that conclusion.

prosecution of those who only did act in risky situations, ie, those where the deceased was not fully ready to die) would send out the contrary message—that people *can* judge the safety of their own conduct in such situations, or at least that one cannot be condemned for so thinking if one appears to be right. This may be a case where the reason for criminalization is unconvincing but nonetheless it is one which can probably be understood by the lay community. In these cases, relief (if any) must be sought in the public interest test.

By contrast, other reasons for knowing over-criminalization may be premised on a policing or prosecutorial system which consists of engaging with the defendant about his conduct over a period of time, when he is at risk of non-compliance with some obligations. Thus some strict liability offences may be passed on the basis that any decision to prosecute will only arise from that ongoing experience. This may happen with so-called regulatory offences, where factory inspectors issue warning notices before contemplating prosecutions for health and safety violations.[23] The point is that 'fault' as it is usually understood in the substantive criminal law may not be evident on the instant occasion, but this may have nonetheless been the latest in a series of incidents during which the factory owner clearly had been at fault and it may be supposed, though not proven that he was at fault in the instant case too. Imposing strict liability might then be the most effective way to enable such a system to work. In some contexts the lawmaker might take the view that other state agents, such as social workers, could be responsible for advising and warning prospective defendants. This explains Horder's suggestion that strict liability may be legitimate when imposed on parents who fail to ensure that their children attend school, provided that Parliament's intention is that prosecutions will only follow after social services have monitored a pattern of non-attendance.[24]

In cases where there is *no* belief from the relevant state agent in any fault over the incident in question *and* no belief in any ongoing fault on the part of the defendant, the prosecutor does apply the law properly by discontinuing, notwithstanding that the cases could be proven on the basis of strict liability. That is, he would be applying the *application* test, and not merely the public interest test, because the lawmaker had no intention (and no reason) to criminalize such activity. The problems arise where the state agent does perceive there to have been present or ongoing fault. Now strict liability *is* intended, but could the prosecutor expect to explain to the public the reason for condemnation of D (namely that the state agent is trusted to assess his fault)? Here the reputation of the state agent for fairness and good organization is important.

[23] See further K Hawkins, *Law as Last Resort: Prosecution Decision-Making in a Regulatory Agency* (Oxford University Press, 2002).

[24] J Horder, 'Whose Values should determine when Liability is Strict?' in A Simester (ed), *Appraising Strict Liability* (Oxford University Press, 2005) at pp 114–20.

For example, social workers in a country might be widely distrusted, so that the lay community could not understand why this power has been afforded to them. It may, for example, be thought that they would enjoy the exercise of power or would discriminate against certain members of the community in assessing fault for non-co-operation. The public distrust may, in some cases (they will be forced to conclude), even apply to some extra-judicial decisions about fault that fall to be made by the prosecutors themselves.[25] Where this distrust is perceived, the prosecutor should cease to proceed with *all* such cases insofar as they are prosecuted in reliance in court on a strict liability basis, though prosecutions might be proper in cases where the prosecutor could prove to the requisite standard a level of fault which the lawmaker would have intended to penalise (and the reason for which could be explained).

III. The Development Test

We now consider those cases where the application test *cannot* be applied. These are the cases where it is unclear to the prosecutor what the law was actually intended (or assumed) to be, as it applies to the alleged facts. Many such cases will involve issues relating to the general part of the criminal law, or general defences, which may be pivotal to applying the law to the facts of the case, but were quite neglected by the lawmaker; and it may not even be possible to make inferences from legislative silence, or to guess what the lawmaker assumed the law to be. One example may be found in the law on causation (whether a man who beats his wife can be liable for manslaughter upon her suicide).[26] Another is the law relating to decisions to withdraw life-preserving medical treatment from comatose patients. The prosecutor, were he called upon to try to apply the law of murder at the first time of asking, would have had the difficulty that the norms of murder arose from a time when it was barely possible to preserve life by artificial feeding in the first place; and there were no directly helpful precedents to guide him. Nor was it clear whether a defence of necessity might apply, or even exist. The special

---

[25] It may alternatively become thought in the community that special prosecution agencies which only rarely prosecute have become the subjects of 'corporate capture': cf Sanders and Young, n 7 above, at p 197.

[26] *R v D* [2006] EWCA Crim 1139. See the prosecutor's account where it was said

Through our appeal we wanted to establish the principle, which the Appeal Court accepted, that if you harm your partner and cause them physical and mental harm and subsequently drive them to suicide, then you can be guilty of manslaughter.

No jurisdiction in the world, to our knowledge, has case law or legislation to guide us and we believe that this was a ground breaking prosecution.

http://www.cps.gov.uk/news/press_releases/129_06/index.html (last accessed 15 November 2011).

part of the criminal law may also be unclear, likely because of inconsistent decisions (eg, whether a person may 'appropriate' property belonging to another by receiving a gift).[27]

It will be evident that the development test is of a much more technical nature than the application test. It is a matter of legal judgment whether the law is so unclear that the application test cannot be used. The prosecutor will consult textbooks (including practitioner works) and legal experts in the area, and if he remains unsure of the law, he does not *apply* it. But he may wish to develop it. It is true that he *himself* will not develop the law by prosecuting, but he may legitimately prosecute (subject to the evidential and public interest tests) on the basis that he facilitates the possibility of judicial clarification. In the same way that he owes duties to courts and to defendants to *apply* the law only where it is comprehensible to the lay community (and necessarily, it must be assumed, to the defendant too), the prosecutor may also be said to owe duties to the rest of the legal community to facilitate development of the law so that they can advise clients and argue points of law more appropriately. Here, communication of the criminal law by trial drops from the forefront in favour of the benefits of legal clarity; and even quite complicated cases which would not be understood by the lay community may yet be brought if the legal community would gain in understanding of the law from the process. Accordingly, as we shall see, when the development test applies, the prospects of obtaining further clarity from the courts will be the driving factor between the subsequent evidential and public interest tests.

An ancillary point is that the prosecutor may and perhaps should be neutral about the *outcome* of any case brought in order to develop the law; for he is seeking clarity rather than a 'better' law. That is not to say that he should not *have* views about the substance of various legal changes, but he should pursue any such views through democratic channels and not through individual case decisions. Thus, the decision to prosecute a man for raping his wife in 1990[28] on the basis that the scope of the marital rape immunity had been continually shrinking, and that it was no longer certain whether it necessarily still existed at common law at all, was one that fell to be made by applying the development test. The prosecutor should have taken it on account of the benefits in legal clarity (which would obtain however the case may be decided). Had there instead been merely a growing perception of the injustice of the immunity and of the serious wrongs that were inflicted by marital rape, then that could only have justified making representations to the legislature. If the prosecutor were able to consider the *merits* of legal *change* (as opposed to the

27 *R v Hinks* [2000] 4 All ER 833.
28 *R v R* [1991] 4 All ER 481.

potential *legal* effects of *clarification*) then there would be the prospect of his (even inadvertently) either becoming an oppressive figure or of manipulating the natural development of the law. He would be oppressive if he sought legal development through prosecuting unpopular or excluded defendants (eg, if he tried to clarify public nuisance laws by prosecuting prostitutes instead of other potential defendants).[29] Alternatively, he might manipulate legal development by choosing a particularly strong or weak case from a list of candidate cases. Thus, selecting a case where an undercover policeman instigated a minor crime in order to thwart a terrorist atrocity could be thought of as a way of securing a beneficial precedent for the police on the scope of the defence available for undercover officers.

Here we can see two further benefits of concentrating on legal clarity rather than legal content. First, the cases will be self-selecting simply by virtue of being perceived as legally difficult (something which other, independent, lawyers may confirm). So the first candidate case should be prosecuted, and then no issue need arise from his choosing one case above others. Second, the prosecutor does not need to consider whether the judiciary will be able to deliver the desired outcome in terms of substance—because he will have no such outcome in mind. Thus, he need not concern himself with the limits of judicial law-making; that is a matter which the courts must resolve for themselves (as indeed they did in deciding to abolish the marital rape immunity without legislative fiat). For the prosecutor at least, it should not matter if the legislator has preferred not to act on certain matters. Provided that the lack of action has created genuine legal uncertainty, he should be prepared to prosecute.

One may think that when the prosecutor seeks only legal clarity, then the state should allow *all* important points of substantive law to be dealt with by other avenues (eg, declaratory proceedings on a set of hypothetical facts) and that the necessity to bring a prosecution is a mark of failure in the law-making machinery in that state. It almost certainly is the case that declaratory jurisdictions have a lot to offer.[30] But in *some* cases prosecution will still be the best method of clarification, because there may be a subsidiary aim to

---

[29] In the context of applying the public interest (ie, determining which low level offences, if any, should be vigorously prosecuted), Ulliver suggests that community outrage against certain behaviour may be legitimate: H R Ulliver, 'The Virtuous Prosecutor in Quest of an Ethical Standard: Guidance from the ABA' (1973) 71 *Michigan LR* 1145, at 1152. This is disputed by Sanders and Young who fear the spectre of the lynch-mob; and similar concerns should apply to the choice of which areas might be considered ripe for legal development.

[30] That is, if criminal courts are granted the jurisdiction to make declarations and if prosecutors can seek declarations as well as potential defendants. Neither is the case in England, and Lord Mustill said in *Airedale NHS Trust v Bland* [1993] 1 AC 789 at 889 that 'it will be necessary to be sure . . . just how it is that the civil courts can do in a criminal matter what the criminal courts themselves cannot do'.

secure punishment of the accused if he *is* found to have offended. It may be that, when the law is clarified, it nonetheless becomes so clear that it can at once be communicated to the community through that punishment. Marital rape is a clear example here. More generally, there may be cases where the defendant has unscrupulously taken advantage of what he hoped would be a lacuna in the law. If it were thought that unclear law would not be developed by prosecution, but only by hypothetical resolution, then this may be an invitation for some persons to pursue selfish ends without taking any risk of answering for their consequences.[31] That is to say nothing of practical problems which would otherwise arise in cases where it is clear that *some* law can be applied against the defendant. If it is uncertain whether a domestic abuser can be guilty of manslaughter on the suicide of his wife, then it would seem incongruous to prosecute him for battery (by virtue of the application test) and to refer the causation problem for a hypothetical resolution for future reference.

One final point is that the lawmaker can directly pre-empt the application of the development test by granting *immunities from prosecutions that are designed to develop the law* in relation to certain defendants and in relation to certain (typically valuable) activities. It may be that there are some situations where there is perceived to be a low risk that persons will take advantage of the fact that they cannot be prosecuted in order to develop the law. Typically, this will apply where values held dear by the criminal law (such as the right to life or the right to liberty) are at stake even though the working environment is far from criminal. In return for the immunity, the potential offenders will also be subject to other methods of review (including disciplinary and ethical committees) and there will be other ways in which legally unclear points which relate to their activities may be clarified.[32] Good examples of such immunities might apply to those who perform certain forms of abortions, euthanasia or treatment of compulsorily detained patients. It should be emphasized that the prosecutor should still *apply* the law where he believes that he *can* ascertain what it is intended or assumed to be. It is hard to think of such immunities in English law, but that is partly because we do not think of punishment and prosecution as being separate harms, and so immunities from prosecution which

---

[31] The facts of *Hinks*, n 27 above, where the defendant befriended a vulnerable and mentally subnormal man with the probable aim that he would offer to give her as much money as she might say she needed, and over time accepted some £60,000 from him, is one good example.

[32] Eg, they may be issued with guidelines from a governing body which could be subject to review or arbitration of some kind.

are brought primarily to clarify the law, rather than to seek punishment, have not arisen for consideration.

IV. Consequential Effects of the Two Criminalization Questions

It will be recalled that every prosecutorial decision is traditionally said to comprise of an evidential test, a public interest test and a test of fairness (to the defendant).[33] But prosecutorial codes typically consider these tests only on the assumption that the prosecutor is *applying* the law; and so even states which openly recognize a public interest test say nothing of the relevant interests in seeking legal clarity through prosecution.[34] In this section, we shall assume that the prosecutor has decided whether he is seeking to apply *or* to develop the law; and our concern is to see how differently the subsequent tests may apply as a result of that initial decision. Perhaps the most important conclusion will be that fairness to the defendant is more likely to weigh heavily as a factor towards discontinuance where the motivation of the prosecutor is to develop the criminal law.

A. The evidential test

Where the alleged facts would satisfy the *application* test, then it is possible to have a presumptively demanding evidential test, such as a rule that the prosecutor should think that he is more likely than not to prove his case in court. Whether this should be quite so inflexible as to apply to all cases is perhaps dubious. For, having considered the reasons behind the law and their comprehensibility, it may occur to the prosecutor that the lay community would both understand *and* strongly support the reasons for criminalization as they would apply to the alleged conduct. It is possible that at the stage of the evidential test, some such cases should attract a lower threshold regarding points of substantive law; and indeed public confidence in the prosecutor may be undermined if he indulged his doubts about the law to such an extent that he does not even attempt to bring a prosecution. Thus, as already indicated,[35] it was surely right to bring

---

[33] Albeit that many writers simplify this by including the fairness test within the public interest test; but this need not concern us for present purposes (see n 3 above).

[34] See generally section 4 of the Sixth Code for Crown Prosecutors (2010) at http://www.cps.gov.uk/publications/docs/code2010english.pdf.

[35] See n 14 above and accompanying text.

prosecutions over frauds which were perpetrated by electronic means, even if it may have been thought relatively likely that they would be legally flawed.

However, the prospects of conviction are not relevant when the prosecutor acts in order to *develop* the law. As already mentioned, the outcome is not important now; and the equivalent evidential test is whether the prosecution would likely be an effective way of clarifying the scope of the law. The efficacy of prosecution for this purpose is likely to vary between different jurisdictions. Some may have fast-track procedures for legislative consideration of problematic points or, as already discussed, for judicial resolution of important academic points on hypothetical facts which do not require an individual to be prosecuted. Where such alternative effective methods exist and are appropriate, they might be preferred. But some cases should yet need to be prosecuted.[36] In deciding whether there is a reasonable prospect of clarification of the law, much will depend upon the facts and the prospects of creating a precedent. Perhaps the most efficacious prosecution that was brought to test the law in England was that of *Dudley and Stephens*,[37] where the court maximized the opportunity to create a meaningful precedent by recording a special verdict on the facts so that the final verdict would be reasoned and delivered by a panel of judges.

B. The public interest test

When deciding whether it is in the public interest to prosecute, the governing question when *applying* the law ought to be whether there is a worthwhile aim in seeking punishment. Different theories of punishment are conceivable; undoubtedly the pursuit of simple general deterrence through punishment explains many prosecutions. Whether it is worthwhile to pursue the punishment will depend upon the perceived gains and the costs of bringing the case. But the prosecutor must bear in mind that in criminalizing an activity, the lawmaker implicitly decides that the costs may justify at least occasional enforcement; and so any policies to discontinue prosecuting certain conduct altogether should not be absolute, and should be made by reference to the criteria that apply to discontinuing individual prosecutions in general.[38] The prosecutor (after suitable consultation with his peers) may put certain low priority cases 'on the back burner' for a while, but, if so, he should reconsider

---

[36] See the earlier discussion of *Hinks*.

[37] (1884) 14 QBD 273. See the magisterial account of the background and of the judicial proceedings in A W Simpson, *Cannibalism and the Common Law* (Chicago University Press, 1984).

[38] See the decision of Laws LJ in the High Court in *R v DPP, ex p Kebeline and ors* [2000] 2 AC 326 at 351.

such decisions regularly in the light of subsequent putative patterns of behaviour, and the perceived needs of deterrence and to communicate the criminality of the conduct. The temporary nature of the system is of importance, and ideally any policy of discontinuance ought to be stated to be subject to regular revision.

This leads us to one important difference between the prosecutor deciding that conduct is not criminal because none of the reasons for its criminality could be understood by the lay community (such a decision should have permanent effect) and a decision that a certain type of offending is rather trivial, or controversial, and/or too costly to enforce. In the latter case discontinuance should be temporary and citizens should know that they take some risk by committing the offence. This should not mean that the application of the law has become arbitrary or unduly unpredictable, but the prosecutor should have a system to ensure broad consistency between cases which are and are not prosecuted while there is a temporary decision to put certain types of cases 'on the back burner', and which enables him to explain his decisions to affected defendants. Provided that the prosecutor's system is accessible to the public, then temporary 'public interest discontinuance' should not be regarded as unconstitutional. It is possible that it may even be required in some sensitive cases, such as the prosecution of assisted suicide.[39] Similarly, the prosecutor may accept plea bargains, and may devise codes whereby his policies for accepting lesser pleas are set out for the sake of consistency and transparency. The main safeguard here is that any policy of discontinuance or downgrading should be applied on a case-by-case basis, so that the policy does not effectively substitute for the substantive law, and the charge still reflects the wrong done by the defendant. The prosecutor should again be prepared both to deviate from his own policies in exceptional cases and to explain deviations when they occur.[40]

In jurisdictions where jury verdicts are final and need not be reasoned, one may ponder the public interest element in controversial cases where the jury might acquit in defiance of the law. Such cases may pass the application test, provided only that the prosecutor considers that the lay community would *understand* the reason behind the law, and also the evidential test (applying the law objectively to the evidence). But, arguably, if punishment is nonetheless thought to be unlikely, then the costs may yet be harder to justify. It may

[39] For example, where human rights of the defendant are engaged or where the lawmaker explicitly relies on prosecutorial discretion in difficult cases, both of which apply in assisted suicide cases. For details of how such systems might operate, see J Rogers, 'Prosecutorial Policies, Prosecutorial Systems, and the *Purdy* Litigation' [2010] *Crim LR* 543–64.

[40] See eg J Rogers, 'The Ian Tomlinson Affair—An Examination of the Case' (2010) 174 *Criminal Law and Justice Weekly* 517–19.

be that much depends on the interests of victims in such cases. Where a victim's right to vindication for a wrong done to him may be in issue, that extra factor may yet justify the prosecution in the public interest (as perhaps may arise when police officers are charged with using excessive force against a known offender).[41] But cases where no such rights are at stake (for example, the possession of cannabis for medical purposes) may be different. Where a number of jury nullifications of the law have already occurred in such cases, the prosecutor may wonder whether any conviction would rather tend to communicate the arbitrary way in which some trials by jury may be resolved.

By contrast, where the prosecutor aims to *develop* the law, then the public interest test should focus on the potential gains to be made in terms of legal clarity and subsequently better informed prosecution practice, against the financial costs of the proceedings. A case will be especially valuable if it involves a version of a commonly recurring set of facts or may require the court to rule upon a general legal principle which may apply in a variety of factual settings. Thus, we can see that to prosecute Dudley and Stephens for murder may have been of great legal interest at the time, because cannibalism at sea was sufficiently common in the nineteenth century, not to mention the greater benefits from a better understanding of a general necessity defence. By contrast, it may have been right that a naval officer should not have been prosecuted for shooting dead a colleague who was burning to death after an incident in combat and who asked to be killed immediately.[42] The outcome of such a case would be of great interest to legal academics and philosophers, but the facts are unusual and in terms of precedent the case would be so fact specific that it may not greatly improve the prosecutor's (nor the legal community's) understanding of the wider defence of necessity or any defence of consent. Such a case then might not be cost-effective.

As well as against the costs of proceedings, the prosecutor should consider the gains in legal development against any short-term alarm among the law-abiding community that may be caused by the institution of the prosecution. The very institution of a prosecution may already deter many persons from repeating like activity, and the prosecutor should have to consider the 'chilling effect' that prosecution might then have. So, valuable as it would be to determine whether there is a defence (and if so, then also its scope) for

---

[41] In *R (on the application of B) v DPP* [2009] EWHC 106 (Admin) a victim's right to be free from degrading treatment was said to be violated by a decision to discontinue the prosecution by a careless application of the evidential test. Possibly the same would be said of a decision to discontinue on the supposed 'public interest' ground that a perverse jury acquittal would render the case as non-cost-effective.

[42] This apparently real life example is offered by the Law Commission, *A New Homicide Act for England and Wales* (2005) Consultation Paper No 177, at para 8.43.

crimes committed by undercover officers whilst trying to gather evidence of serious crimes,[43] such a prosecution may disrupt several other ongoing operations which may themselves turn out to be perfectly proper, leading to serial offenders managing to evade detection. Here, a combination of the interests of individual victims in securing vindication for the (arguable) wrongs done to them and the value of the type of activity that may be deterred by prosecution may prove to be decisive in weighing the public interest. In cases of undercover police officers who incite crimes there may be distinctions to be made between prosecuting officers who were trying to uncover conspiracies to exploit or harm individuals (eg, paedophile rings, gangs who offer contract killings) and those who are trying to uncover drug dealing. Protection of victims may point against prosecuting the former category of cases as a means for testing the law. Admittedly this is a difficult area, which will depend somewhat on one's conception of a 'victim' (eg, in cases where the limits of voluntary euthanasia are in issue), but the questions themselves seem to be the right ones.

C. Fairness to the defendant

Finally, fairness to the defendant involves taking into account the effect of prosecution upon him. When prosecuting under the *application* test, the prosecutor assesses the effect of prosecution upon the defendant and decides whether he can fairly be expected to bear them as a prelude to his own possible punishment, taking into account the weight of the perceived public interest in seeking his punishment. In doing so, he should consider that in criminalizing the activity, the lawmaker has already anticipated that suspects can, in the normal run of events, be expected to cope with the pains of prosecution in being tried for the offence. So the perceived harms to the defendant would have to be somewhat over and above the ordinary effects in order to justify discontinuance on the grounds of fairness.

When prosecuting under the *development* test, the prosecutor must similarly weigh any unusual pains of prosecution against the relative assessment of the public interest in seeking legal clarification. But there are further factors to consider. The prosecutor here is calling the defendant to participate in a trial for conduct that is not necessarily already thought to be criminal, and it may be that D's *willingness* to engage is of greater importance for that reason. Any suspect of a recognized crime may be expected to care about his guilt

---

[43] See A Ashworth, 'Testing Fidelity to Legal Values: Official Involvement and Criminal Justice' (2000) 63 *MLR* 633–59.

and to want to participate in his trial; but not everyone can be expected to care as much about the legal niceties which the prosecutor wishes to clarify. It is D's willingness to argue for the non-criminality of his conduct which should matter; and not merely the fact that he was willing actually to perform the conduct. It is of course acknowledged that the legal arguments will likely be made by defendant's counsel, but that is not decisive. It is D's own inherent *belief* that the law is, or should be, on his side which may help to justify the decision to prosecute him to clarify the law relating to his conduct, and not his own level of legal articulation. Where there is no such inherent belief which he has been prepared to communicate, and his only reasons for forming views on his own actions would be to defeat a prosecution, then his unwillingness to participate in any quest for legal clarity is a factor that points against prosecution (though this unfairness needs yet to be balanced against the perceived gains in legal clarification).

A willingness to account can be manifested directly, perhaps by informing the prosecutor of what one has done,[44] though a willingness to argue the propriety of one's actions to *anyone* is of value. But prosecutors might infer a willingness to argue from the type of activity and perhaps from the status of the defendant. Thus, we can see that doctors who regularly performed abortions in the early twentieth century, before the Abortion Act 1967 clarified the grounds for doing so, may have been thought to be willing to defend their actions; for they were in positions of responsibility and presumably thought strongly that their acts were justified. In turn, it may be that immunities for prosecutions to develop the law may be thought by the lawmaker to be needed for some such persons.[45] But those who act through the perceived call of duty only (perhaps acting under superior orders) or who assume that their acts are lawful and do not see any occasion for holding strong views about its legality are possibly in a different position. It may be too much to infer from their actions alone that they are prepared to argue for their propriety, and so their presumptive unwillingness to engage with the purposes of the prosecution should be weighed against the public interest in seeking legal clarity.

---

[44] In *R v Bourne* [1939] 1 KB 687, the leading common law case on justifications for abortions, the defendant (an eminent surgeon) had notified the Attorney-General of his conduct and of the circumstances.

[45] See n 32 above and accompanying text. In some jurisdictions, the doctors may also have the opportunity of seeking clarity on their own part.

V. Conclusions

We have noted in this piece that the act of prosecution is itself one that needs to be justified; it imposes restraints and harms on the person who faces the process and as such it needs to be justified independently from any subsequent punishment. The primary justificatory purpose of a prosecution is to facilitate the function of the criminal courts in communicating the reasons for the criminal law, and the evidential, public interest, and fairness tests are the means by which individual decisions are justified. On these occasions, the prosecutor employs what we call the application test. But if he cannot even determine what the applicable law is intended or assumed to be, then he may be justified in prosecuting if—but only if—to do so would facilitate the *development* of the law in order that he may apply it in future; and here again, the evidential, public interest, and fairness tests will guide individual decisions (in different ways).

The distinction between the application and the development tests has been made at the level of principle, but it would not be difficult to suggest potential practical applications. Insofar as a prospective prosecution might not be expected to be successful, then it matters whether the prosecutor is understood to be trying to apply the law or to develop it—for in the latter case the apparent lack of prospects of conviction need not be fatal.[46] Where a prosecution is justified to develop the law, it will be for the criminal courts to have regard to such matters as their own proper role in developing the law, and whether mistakes of law should be more freely granted in some such cases.[47] In these cases, prosecutors should only think about the worthwhileness of trying to obtain the legal ruling.

From the constitutional perspective of the prosecutor's relationship with the substantive law, the important point is that, whatever his motivation for bringing a case, the prosecutor should be neutral. He must apply bad or unpopular laws (provided that they are comprehensible), and he cannot choose which areas of the law to develop on the basis of his own philosophical

---

[46] In *R (on the application of Da Silva) v Director of Public Prosecutions* [2006] EWHC 3204 (Admin), it was said that the prosecutor was right not to prosecute a firearms officer for shooting an unarmed man several times at close range because at law self-defence would likely have succeeded. But arguably the prosecutor should have been trying to develop the law, since the rule on which the decision was based may have been open to challenge under the Human Rights Act 1998; and here the low prospects of securing a conviction should not matter so much. See J Rogers, 'Stockwell Revisited' (2007) 157 *NLJ* 286.

[47] A Ashworth, 'Ignorance of the Criminal Law, and Duties to Avoid it' (2011) 74 *MLR* 1, argues that defendants who claim a defence should have tried to ascertain the law.

convictions of what the law should be. Lawmakers should be particularly careful to bear in mind his perceived neutrality when making certain criminalization decisions. Two examples have been noted here. Regarding the matter of defences for undercover police officers who incite crimes, the public interest test might suggest that the consequences of developing the law by prosecution would be unjustifiable on account of the possible abandonment of valuable operations—and yet the public perception of a failure to prosecute a close working ally might be negative. Here, Parliament should state the relevant law or perhaps allow some limited immunities against prosecutions which would otherwise be properly brought to develop the law. Similarly, strict liability offences which are premised on the assumption that prosecutors will only prosecute in cases of ongoing fault are problematic because (I have argued) the prosecutor could only properly enforce them if he considers that he could explain to the lay community why the lawmaker has trusted him with this responsibility. But we are saying here *only* that the prosecutor must be *neutral* in applying the law and in deciding when to develop it. Undoubtedly the proper exercise of his duties still requires him to think about, and to be prepared to explain, *why* the law prohibits what it does; and about which issues he would welcome judicial clarification in order to apply the law more often.

5

Rights Forfeiture and *Mala Prohibita*

*Christopher Heath Wellman**

I am inclined toward the rights forfeiture theory of punishment, which contends that a criminal may permissibly be punished only when he or she has forfeited his or her right not to be subjected to the hard treatment constitutive of punishment. This approach strikes me as particularly well-suited to explain the permissibility of punishing those who commit *mala in se* crimes.[1] It is much less clear, however, whether this account leaves sufficient normative space for *mala prohibita* crimes. In particular, if we begin with the intuitively attractive assumption that one cannot forfeit any of his or her rights without violating someone else's right, advocates of the rights forfeiture theory of punishment who want to defend a state's right to punish those who commit *mala prohibita* crimes must explain whose rights are violated by the commission of *mala prohibita* crimes. I attempt to provide such an explanation in this chapter.

This chapter is divided into four sections. First, I briefly outline the rights forfeiture theory of punishment and its difficulties with the category of *mala prohibita*.[2] Next, I explain how I think a rights forfeiture theorist might best

* This chapter was vastly improved thanks to the critical feedback from audiences at the University of Stirling and the University of Warwick. I am also grateful to Lindsay Farmer, Zachary Hoskins, Sandra Marshall and Carl Wellman for written comments on earlier drafts.

[1] I understand *mala in se* crimes to be actions (like murder) which are wrong in and of themselves and *mala prohibita* crimes to be actions (like driving on a public road without displaying a valid vehicle registration sticker on one's front windshield) which are wrong only because they have been legally prohibited. As Lindsay Farmer has pointed out to me, even if this construal of the distinction has recently become the orthodox view, *mala in se* originally referred to an idea of crimes as sins, or crimes against nature, in the sense of breaking God's law. According to this earlier understanding, the wrongness of *mala in se* crimes was often thought to be self-evident. For the purposes of this chapter, I do not presume the wrongness of *mala in se* crimes is necessarily self-evident.

[2] I do not mean to suggest that *mala prohibita* crimes pose a problem for only rights forfeiture theorists. Notice, for instance, that my interest in this question was sparked by Douglas Husak's treatment of the subject in *Overcriminalization* (Oxford: Oxford University Press, 2008), which in turn engages with Stuart Green's article, 'Why It's a Crime to Tear the Tag Off a Mattress: Overcriminalization and the Moral Content of Regulatory Offenses' (1997) *Emory Law Journal*

solve this problem. In the third section, I grapple with difficult questions about how severely one may be punished for committing a *mala prohibitum* crime. And finally, I comment briefly on what rights and duties stem from unjust *mala prohibita* laws.

I. The Rights Forfeiture Theory of Punishment

Given that punishment, by definition, involves visiting hard treatment upon those who are punished, and persons typically have a right not to be subjected to this hard treatment, it would seem natural to conclude that the permissibility of punishment is centrally a question of rights.[3] This insight is lost on the vast majority of theorists working on punishment who focus instead on the *aims* of punishment. According to retributivism, the general justifying aim of punishment is to serve justice by giving criminals the hard treatment they deserve; utilitarianism suggests that the aim is to produce better consequences (chiefly by deterring everyone from committing crimes); moral education theory insists that the aim is to help morally educate the criminal and society at large; expressivist theory claims that the chief aim is for society to express its emphatic denunciation of the criminal; restitutive theory alleges that the aim is to restore the victims; and societal safety-valve theory claims that the aim is to provide an effective, peaceful outlet for socially-disruptive emotions. I think that all of these aims help explain why we should *want* a properly constructed system of punishment, but none shows why it would be permissible to institute one. Only a rights-based analysis will suffice here, because the type of justification we seek for punishment must demonstrate that punishment is permissible, and it would be permissible only if it violated no one's rights.[4]

To appreciate this basic point about the relationship between aims, rights and adequate justification, imagine that I want some of your money, so that

46 1533) and R A Duff's paper, 'Crime, Prohibition, and Punishment' (2002) *Journal of Applied Philosophy* 19 97–108, and all three of these theorists struggle with *mala prohibita* crimes even though none is a rights forfeiture theorist.

[3] On the definition of punishment, see Joel Feinberg's landmark paper, 'The Expressive Function of Punishment', reprinted in Joel Feinberg, *Doing and Deserving* (Princeton: Princeton University Press, 1970) 95–118. I am largely sympathetic to Feinberg's analysis, but for the purposes of this chapter I take no stand on what conditions in addition to hard treatment must be satisfied for punishment to occur.

[4] Although moral theorists sometimes distinguish between an action's being merely permissible and its being fully justified, I use permissibility and justification interchangeably here. For the purpose of this chapter, then, I assume that one supplies an adequate justification for punishment if one can show why it is permissible.

I might take a year off from teaching to write a book defending the rights forfeiture theory of punishment. This admirable aim may well explain why I *want* some of your money, but it does not by itself explain why I would be *justified* in taking your money, because it says nothing about the various *rights* involved. In particular, absent some sort of explanation to the contrary, you stand in a privileged position of ownership over your money, a position which entails that I may not unilaterally help myself to it, no matter how laudable my aims are. Now, if you had promised to financially support my research, then this might well explain why I may permissibly help myself to the funds in question, but in this case, your promise rather than my aim is the crucial variable. Indeed, even in a scenario in which you agree to fund my leave from teaching precisely because I have such an important project, my aims are not by themselves a sufficient justification. Without your consent, I may not permissibly take your money. In light of this, the centrality of rights (and the inadequacy of aims) is apparent.

Because being killed, or locked in a cell, or forced to give up some of one's money appears in normal circumstances to violate one's life, liberty and/or property rights, the permissibility of punishment seems to hinge on whether such actions, as criminal punishment, are compatible with these rights in a way that they normally are not. After all, just as the fact that you own your money entails that others may not permissibly commandeer it, each individual's privileged position of moral dominion over his or her own affairs entails that others may not permissibly incarcerate or otherwise punish him or her. However, just as you can waive your right to your money (if you give it to me, for instance), one can forfeit one's right against being punished. When one wrongly harms another, for instance, one forfeits the privileged position of dominion over one's self-regarding affairs. Moreover, one loses this moral shield in direct proportion with how badly one mistreats others. This is why the innocent may not permissibly be punished, those who misbehave only a little may be punished only a correspondingly small amount, and those who behave worse may be punished more severely. As W D Ross puts it:

the offender, by violating the life or liberty or property of another, has lost his own right to have his life, liberty, or property respected, so that the state has no *prima facie* duty to spare him, as it has a *prima facie* duty to spare the innocent. It is morally at liberty to injure him as he has injured others, or to inflict any lesser injury on him, or to spare him, exactly as consideration both of the good of the community and of his own good requires. If, on the other hand, a man has respected the rights of others, there is a strong and distinctive objection to the state's inflicting any penalty on him with a view to the good of the community or even to his own good.[5]

---

[5] W D Ross, *The Right and the Good* (Oxford: Oxford University Press, 1930) 60–1.

Thus, contrary to the traditional strategy of citing the valuable aims that punishment can realize, I believe the best approach for those who seek to demonstrate the permissibility of punishment would be to focus on explaining how criminals have forfeited their rights against hard treatment. Because of a variety of powerful criticisms of rights forfeiture theory, however, very few have pursued this lead. Elsewhere I have attempted to respond to each of these standard objections, but I will not rehearse those arguments here.[6] For the purposes of this chapter, I shall assume *arguendo* that a suitably refined theory of rights forfeiture is not vulnerable in any of the ways critics typically allege, so that I can focus on a new potential problem: the justifiability of punishing those who commit *mala prohibita* crimes.

To see why *mala prohibita* crimes pose special difficulties for rights forfeiture theorists, notice Ross's suggestion that one retains one's right not to be punished unless one violates the rights of some other party. If Ross is right about this, then *mala prohibita* crimes raise special questions because, unlike in the case of *mala in se* crimes, it is not obvious whose right the criminal violates. To appreciate this problem, compare the *mala in se* crime of driving recklessly to the *mala prohibita* crime of driving on a public road without a valid vehicle registration sticker displayed in the legally required spot on one's front windshield.[7] It seems clear that reckless drivers violate the rights of others by exposing them to unacceptable risks, but whose right is violated by one's failure to display a vehicle registration sticker on one's car? In the same vein, compare the more complicated cases of rape and statutory rape. In rape, a thirty-year-old man forces a thirty-year-old woman to have sex at gunpoint. In statutory rape, a thirty-year-old man has 'consensual' sex with a seventeen-year-old girl in a jurisdiction that criminally prohibits men older than twenty from having sex with girls under the age of eighteen.[8] The case of rape poses no special problems for the rights forfeiture account; given that the rapist clearly violated the rights of his victim, it follows straightforwardly that he has forfeited his right not to be punished. But the case of the statutory rapist is more difficult. To see why, it would be helpful to step back and consider the rationale behind statutory rape laws.

I presume that statutory rape legislation is typically motivated by the recognition that one's consent is morally valid only if one is sufficiently mature. If one is not mature enough to intellectually understand and/or

---

[6] See C H Wellman, 'The Rights Forfeiture Theory of Punishment' (2012) *Ethics* 122(2) 371–93.

[7] I am grateful to Antony Duff for this paradigmatic example of a *mala prohibita* crime.

[8] For the purposes of this chapter, I shall refer to females who are at least eighteen years old as women and those who are younger than eighteen as girls, whether or not they are mature enough to give their morally valid consent.

emotionally appreciate all of the stakes involved in a given situation, then we do not think that one's consent is morally valid in this arena. If a five-year-old girl agrees to have sexual intercourse with me if I buy her some candy, for instance, the fact that she 'consents' to the sex is of no moral consequence whatsoever.[9] Although we may have to provide a slightly different explanation of why it is wrong for me to have sex with this young girl, it clearly seems just as wrong as the rapist who forces himself on his victim at gunpoint. In light of this, it is altogether understandable that states would criminally prohibit even what might appear to be consensual sex with those who are not mature enough for their 'consent' to be morally valid. Given how difficult it would be to conclusively determine whether any given person is (or was) in fact sufficiently mature, states understandably seek to avoid these foreseeable administrative nightmares by using age as a proxy for maturity. Thus, a statute prohibiting sex with someone under a certain age is typically utilized as a workable solution to the problem in question. When a jurisdiction insists that a man over the age of twenty may not have sex with a girl under the age of eighteen, for instance, it is thought that this formulation will enable the law to come acceptably close to ensuring that no girls who are insufficiently mature will have their rights violated by what might appear to be consensual sex. In addition, setting a clear age limit enables us to avoid worries about punishing people for violating excessively vague laws the boundaries of which are difficult for even a conscientious citizen to discern. If the law clearly states that statutory rape involves a man over the age of twenty having sex with a girl under the age of eighteen, for instance, then men can ensure that they will not be liable to punishment merely by refraining from having sex with anyone under the age of eighteen.[10]

In any event, the crucial point is that the age components of statutory rape laws are administrative tools designed to *approximate* rather than *perfectly track* maturity levels. Thus, when legislators pass a law prohibiting sex with girls under the age of eighteen, everyone recognizes that there is no magical psychological transformation that occurs on one's eighteenth birthday; many girls will be sufficiently mature before that date and some remain insufficiently mature long after they turn eighteen. Interesting questions can be

---

[9] As Sandra Marshall has suggested to me, if one adopts a normative conception of consent (as the law appears to do), then an immature person's agreeing to something may not count as consent, since there would be no such thing as *immature* consent.

[10] Another controversial aspect of statutory rape legislation is the strict liability with which it is often imposed. Thus, even if a man takes every reasonable precaution to ensure that he is not sleeping with a girl under the age of eighteen, he may become liable to punishment if (through no fault of his own) he has sex with a seventeen-year-old girl. Although this is obviously an interesting issue, it is distinct from those on which I seek to focus in this chapter.

raised about both of these types of cases, but for our purposes here, problems emerge for those girls who are sufficiently mature before they turn eighteen. In particular, notice that the statutory rapist may have consensual sex with a seventeen-year-old girl who is in fact sufficiently mature to give her morally valid consent to this sexual intercourse. But if so, then it seems as though the statutory rapist did not violate any of his sexual partner's rights. And if Ross is right that we cannot forfeit any rights without violating someone else's rights, the statutory rapist does not appear to have forfeited any of his rights. The rights forfeiture theorist thus appears unable to explain why the statutory rapist may permissibly be punished.

There seem to be three salient options here: one could (1) deny that states may permissibly impose *mala prohibita* crimes, (2) deny that one forfeits rights only when one violates a right, or (3) provide an explanation as to why one violates rights when one breaks *mala prohibita* laws. I regard (3) as the most promising alternative, and I shall pursue this option at length below. Still, it is worth pausing to say a little bit about the first two options, because, while I suspect that most would be considerably more receptive to the second option, I actually think (1) is more defensible than (2).

To appreciate why one may plausibly deny that the state may permissibly punish *mala prohibita* criminals, notice that not all rights forfeiture theorists are statists. In the quote cited above, Ross takes it for granted that the state is the party who will be doling out punishment, but not all rights forfeiture theorists presume that this must be so. Consider the positions of John Locke and John Simmons, for instance. Locke is a rights forfeiture theorist who believes that everyone in the state of nature has a competitive right to punish and the state acquires its monopolistic right only when each of us voluntarily agrees for the state to have sole authority over this domain. Simmons agrees entirely with this normative picture, but, unlike Locke, he denies that existing states have in fact garnered the requisite consent from all of their constituents. Thus, without abandoning his rights forfeiture theory of punishment, Simmons denies that any existing state has an exclusive right to preside over the criminal legal system. In other words, Simmons believes that when it comes to punishing wrongdoers, existing states merely have the same competitive right as the rest of us.

Against this backdrop, consider the theorist who denies that states may permissibly punish *mala prohibita* criminals. In particular, notice that, while this position leaves considerably less room for state discretion over the criminal law than many presume is warranted, it does not amount to anarchism. A critic of *mala prohibita* crimes might well believe that existing states enjoy exclusive moral dominion over the punitive process; he or she will merely insist that criminal law contain itself to *mala in se* crimes. Put in terms of our earlier example, for instance, this theorist does not object to the state's having exclusive authority to punish those men who have sex with insufficiently mature girls; he or she alleges only that the state may not punish all men who have sex with girls under a certain age specified by the state. A theorist of this stripe can therefore remain a statist because he or she need not object to the state's claiming a monopoly on punishment; he or she questions only the permissibility of a state's enacting laws with age limits that can result in men who have not in fact had sex with an insufficiently mature girl being punished as if they had done so.

Let me stress that I am not suggesting that this position is correct. On the contrary, my own view is that this stance leaves too little room for a legitimate state's discretion over the criminal law. The two points I seek to emphasize here are merely the following: first, it is neither incoherent nor incompatible with statism to deny that states may permissibly punish *mala prohibita* criminals; and second, even if rights forfeiture theorists were forced to adopt this position, it would not necessarily show that rights forfeiture theory should be rejected. It may instead be that rights forfeiture theory helps reveal why and in what ways *mala prohibita* legislation is objectionable.

Turning to (2), many theorists are likely to be attracted to the idea that one can forfeit a right without violating the rights of another. After all, there is more to morality than rights and their corresponding duties, so it seems obvious that one can behave culpably without violating anyone's rights. If the person in line behind me at the market is purchasing only one item (some medicine for the sick twin infants she is struggling to keep quiet, perhaps), this may not entitle her to go ahead of me, but it nonetheless seems plausible to say that I ought to offer to let her go first. In other words, while I may be well within my rights to stay in front of her, I would clearly be displaying a vice if I either failed to notice this struggling mother's plight or, even worse, recognized her situation and remained unmoved by it.

I agree with much of this, but I still think that we should follow Ross in supposing that one retains one's right not to be punished unless one violates someone else's right. In my view, one can behave culpably, even deplorably, without acting impermissibly. The example of my insisting on my right to remain in front of the weary mother at the market is a good example of this. Perhaps the best way to characterize this behaviour is in terms of the suberogatory, a category of behaviour which, though not forbidden by duty, nonetheless reflects badly on an agent. The important point for our purposes here, though, is that it seems natural to think that one may not permissibly be punished unless one acts *impermissibly*; we may criticize but not punish those who act in a suberogatory fashion. I believe this stance is confirmed by reflecting on cases like that of my acting culpably at the market.

That is, while I certainly believe that others are right to deplore and even criticize my behaviour, it seems wrong to say that anyone might permissibly punish me. And the best explanation for this judgement, I think, is that one remains morally immune to punishment as long as one acts permissibly, where the bounds of permissibility are set by the rights of others.

Insofar as I have merely described how I think we should analyse what I take to be a paradigmatic case of the suberogatory, I must confess that I have no conclusive argument against someone with opposing intuitions. In other words, I have no way of rebutting someone who thinks that I may permissibly be punished for failing to let the weary mother go ahead of me even though she had no right to do so. Because my own stance on this issue makes it more rather than less difficult for the rights forfeiture theorist to contend with *mala prohibita* laws, however, I shall just assume for the sake of argument that one forfeits one's right not to be punished only if one violates a second party's rights. And, given this assumption, a rights forfeiture theorist who seeks to defend the category of *mala prohibita* crimes must explain how those who commit these crimes violate someone else's rights. In the next section, I shall explore the possibility that those who commit *mala prohibita* crimes violate the rights of their compatriots when they break a just law of a legitimate state.

II. Why *Mala Prohibita* Criminals Violate Rights

Framing the issue of a state's right to enact *mala prohibita* legislation in terms of the anarchism/statism debate as we did above is illustrative, because it suggests the promise of explaining the permissibility of punishing *mala prohibita* criminals as connected to a citizen's obligation to obey the law. In particular, if one's compatriots have a right that one obey the law, then perhaps the best way for a rights forfeiture theorist to explain why a *mala prohibita* criminal may be punished is because, in disobeying the law, the criminal has violated the rights of his or her compatriots. With this in mind, let me quickly explain why there is a moral duty to obey the law.

The first question is, why be a statist? After all, given that states coerce everyone within their territorial boundaries, we must begin with a strong presumption in favour of anarchism. Despite this presumption, I am a statist because I believe that states are permitted (indeed, obligated) to impose themselves upon their constituents because this imposition is necessary to provide crucial benefits that would be unavailable in their absence, and I believe that states can supply these benefits without imposing unreasonable costs upon their constituents. As political theorists have long emphasized, it would be virtually impossible to pursue rewarding projects and nurture meaningful relationships unless everyone within a territorial district adheres to a common, clearly promulgated and impartially adjudicated set of rules. And since states seem necessary to secure an environment in which everyone can count on each other to defer to a common set of rules, states perform an incredibly important function that justifies their coercive presence.

Given that states perform their valuable functions by co-ordinating all of their constituents, it is tempting to conclude that each citizen has a duty to obey the law because his or her legal obedience is necessary for the production of the important benefits of political stability. But this inference is too quick. While it may be true that a state could not perform its justifying political functions unless *a sufficient number* of its constituents complied with this state's legal commands, a typical individual's obedience to the law is clearly not essential to the state's capacity to secure the goods of political stability. My country's capacity to perform its functions will not be discernibly affected by whether or not I pay my taxes this year, for example. And if it is descriptively inaccurate to say that my legal obedience is necessary for the provision of the benefits of political stability, then we cannot explain an individual's duty to obey the law with the same straightforward consequential line that justifies the state as a whole. This does not mean that citizens have no duty to obey the law, of course, but it does highlight the need to invoke an additional, extra-consequential consideration. I believe this supplemental element is fairness. In my view, each citizen has a duty to obey the law as his or her fair share of the collective political task. Thus, if states are justified because they perform the incredibly important task of rescuing all of us from the perils of the state of nature, then each of us has a duty to obey the law as his or her fair share of this larger communal project. And most importantly for our purposes here, someone who wrongly disobeyed the law would be treating his or her compatriots unfairly. In other words, even if there were no discrete harms that followed from the legal disobedience, he or she would be taking unfair advantage of his or her fellow citizens.

I have developed and defended this account of the duty to obey the law at some length elsewhere, but I shall not say anymore about the details of this approach here, so that we can return to the question of *mala prohibita*.[11] In particular, let us see whether this account of the duty to obey the law can help illuminate why *mala prohibita* criminals necessarily violate rights. We shall return to the example of statutory rape laws below, but let us start with a couple of easier cases: the requirements that drivers neither (1) exceed the

---

[11] See C H Wellman, 'Toward a Liberal Theory of Political Obligation' (2001) *Ethics* 111 735–59.

posted speed limit nor (2) drive a vehicle that lacks a valid vehicle registration sticker on its front windshield.

Let us begin by analysing the requirement that I not drive faster than 65 miles an hour on a given stretch of highway. Before doing so, it is important to highlight that one can violate another person's rights without actually injuring him or her. If my reckless driving causes me to run into another person, then obviously I have violated this second party's rights. But I can also violate another's rights without actually colliding into anyone else, because others have a right against being exposed to unreasonable risk of harm. And because the risk one poses to others is a function of the speed at which one drives, there is nothing necessarily problematic about saying that one can violate the rights of others by driving too fast. Even if I am lucky enough to hit no one as I speed through a crowded intersection at 100 miles an hour, for instance, I have still violated the rights of those people in the vicinity. But while this reasoning might seem to justify the state's enforcing designated speed limits, this inference does not automatically follow. In particular, note that there is a huge difference between a state's criminally prohibiting reckless driving in general and its criminally prohibiting driving over the speed of 65 miles an hour on a given stretch of road. The problem, of course, is that there will presumably be many cases in which one can safely exceed this speed limit (perhaps by a considerable margin) without exposing others to unreasonable risks. And if the state punished a professional race car driver like Danica Patrick for driving ten miles over the posted speed limit when, given the quality of her car and her driving skills, she could in fact have driven considerably faster without posing unacceptable risks to others, then it appears as though the state is punishing her when she has not violated the rights of others. And since we are assuming both that (1) one cannot forfeit one's rights without violating anyone else's rights, and (2) one may not permissibly be punished unless one forfeits one's right not to be exposed to the hard treatment of punishment, this routine case of *mala prohibitum* punishment appears unjust.

But if the state has a right to impose the more specific legal requirement that no one exceed 65 miles an hour on this particular stretch of road, and all of the state's citizens owe it to each other to obey laws such as this, then perhaps the punishment would be justified after all because, by violating her compatriots' rights that she obey the law, Danica forfeited her right against being punished. With this in mind, the crucial question is why a state might permissibly require that no one drive faster than 65 miles an hour when, before this legal pronouncement, everyone had only the more general duty not to expose each other to excessive risks. And the answer here presumably features the great benefits that come with having a publicly known and uniformly enforced specification of what speed everyone must treat as excessively risky.

Among the basic ideas here is the well-known worry about the harms that would predictably ensue if each of us was left to interpret for himself or herself what speed is required by the more general injunction against exposing others to unacceptable risks. Given the room for reasonable disagreement about the specifics here, our roads would be much less safe, there would be more accidents, and the arguments over who was responsible for these accidents would be considerably more frequent and intractable. If this is right, then it seems plausible to conclude not only that the state may permissibly impose speed limits, but also that each citizen owes it to his or her compatriots to obey these limits. If a citizen exceeds the designated speed limit, then he or she is not doing his or her fair share to contribute to the benefits that these laws provide, and thus is violating the rights of his or her compatriots. In other words, each of us is morally prohibited from exposing others to unreasonable risks, but being part of a political community can also require one to refrain from relying solely on one's personal judgement as to which risks are in fact excessive. The duty not to expose others to unreasonable risks is owed to all other *humans*, and the duty to defer to the state's uniformly imposed assessment of which particular risks are unacceptable is owed to one's *compatriots*.[12]

The legal requirement that one not drive a vehicle without a registration sticker on its front windshield is in some ways distinct from speeding laws because, whereas the prohibition against exceeding 65 miles an hour corresponds to the general right others have not to be exposed to unreasonable risk, others would seem to have no rights related to your duty to put stickers anywhere. Nonetheless, I think a similar justification can be given. Notice, for instance, that the quality of one's car is among the factors that affect the level of risk one's driving poses to others. If the brakes on one's car did not work well, for example, then your driving at the legally posted speeds might well pose unreasonable risks to others. Given this, there seems nothing illegitimate about a state's prohibiting people from driving unsafe cars on public roads. And if the state is going to enforce this legal requirement, it does not seem unobjectionably demanding for it to require that drivers periodically confirm that their vehicles are in fact roadworthy. Finally, in order for the state to actually oversee this issue without prohibitive administrative costs, the state might require drivers to publicly display evidence that their cars have passed the requisite tests by placing a sticker in

---

[12] Putting this point in terms of what we owe our compatriots is a little misleading, because I think one would be equally bound to obey the traffic laws in the countries one visits as a tourist, for example.

the designated spot on the car. Thus, while others initially have nothing like a right that one display stickers on one's windshield, once a state requires that drivers demonstrate the safety of their vehicles in this fashion, it seems plausible that citizens acquire a duty to do so.

If the foregoing arguments are on target, then perhaps the fact that we have a duty to obey the law—a duty that is owed to our compatriots—enables a rights forfeiture theorist to explain why someone may permissibly be punished for driving faster than 65 miles per hour or in a car that does not have the requisite registration sticker affixed to its front windshield. One might worry, however, that this explanation proves too much. In particular, if someone may permissibly be punished merely for breaking the law, then does this not give the government a blank cheque to punish any behaviour whatsoever, as long as it criminally prohibits it first? This is an important objection. As much as we might hope to justify punishing *mala prohibita* crimes, it certainly does not seem permissible for a state to punish people for putative 'crimes' such as failing to wear last week's dirty underwear on their heads, even if the state enacted clear prospective laws requiring everyone to do so. To avoid this criticism, then, we need some principled way of distinguishing those *mala prohibita* laws whose violators we can legitimately punish from those whose violators we cannot. The most natural place to draw this distinction, I would presume, is between just and unjust *mala prohibita* laws. And if this is right, then we may permissibly punish someone for driving in excess of the posted speed limit while we may not punish those who fail to wear last week's dirty underwear on their head because the former law is just while the latter is unjust.

Although this solution appears promising, critics may object that it saddles us with an unacceptable position regarding the duty to obey the law. In particular, if we suggest that one may be permissibly punished only for violating just *mala prohibita* laws, this must be because we have a moral duty to obey only just laws. But one's theory of political obligation cannot discriminate among laws based upon whether or not they are just, because doing so is inconsistent with this duty being content-independent. Let me explain.

Not everyone believes that there is a duty to obey the law, but those who do typically distinguish between legitimate and illegitimate regimes and allege that we have duties to obey only the commands of the former. I agree that there is no general duty to obey the laws of an illegitimate state, but, as I have argued elsewhere, neither do we necessarily have an obligation to obey all of the commands of a legitimate state.[13] In my view, we have a general duty to obey only the just laws of a legitimate regime.

[13] See C H Wellman and John Simmons, *Is There a Duty to Obey the Law?* (New York: Cambridge University Press, 2005) ch 4.

Now, some reject the conclusion that we have a duty to obey only the just laws of a legitimate regime, because they worry that it amounts to denying that we have content-independent reasons to obey the law. After all, critics opine, if the obligation to obey the law is to do any work, then presumably it must be able to obligate us to do things we would not otherwise be required to do. But if we are obligated to obey only the just laws of a legitimate state, then it is the justice of the commands, rather than the fact that they are required by the state, which generates the duty. This objection misses the mark, however, because it presumes that all acts are either required by justice or prohibited by justice. This is a false dichotomy, though, because some acts are neither required nor prohibited; they are simply permissible acts which we are at liberty to do. Thus, those acts that are *required* by justice are a subset of just (ie, permissible) acts. Given this, insisting that there is no obligation to obey an unjust law is perfectly compatible with there being content-independent reasons to obey the law. A traffic law requiring all drivers to drive on a particular side of the street, for instance, is but one example of a just law which might obligate citizens to do something that they would not otherwise be morally required to do.

It is worth noting that this analysis is confirmed by our intuitions regarding promising. In particular, promising is typically regarded as a paradigmatic source of content-independent duties, since we routinely become obligated to do things that we would not otherwise be required to do (like meeting a friend for lunch) once we promise to do so. And notice: it is standardly supposed that promises to perform an injustice are null and void. That is, even if one promises to do X, one cannot have a duty to fulfil this promise if doing X is prohibited. But if our recognition that there is no duty to fulfil unjust promises is perfectly consistent with there being content-independent reasons to keep one's promises, then why think that my contention that there is no obligation to obey unjust laws is incompatible with the existence of content-independent reasons to obey the just laws of a legitimate regime?

If this is right, then it would be permissible to punish *mala prohibita* criminals only if the particular laws they violated were just, and the reason that it seems perfectly reasonable to punish someone for driving faster than 65 miles per hour or for driving a car that has no registration sticker on its front windshield is because the state is justified in enacting each of these particular laws. With this in mind, let us return to the case of a statutory rape law that prohibits a man over the age of twenty from having sex with a girl under the age of eighteen. At first blush, the state's setting these age requirements looks no different than its setting speed limits. Just as the state sets a uniform speed of 65 miles per hour even though different drivers in various cars in distinct weather conditions can drive safely at dramatically different speeds, the state sets a uniform age of eighteen even though some girls will be sufficiently mature well before their eighteenth birthday and others will not be mature enough until later. Despite these clear parallels, for two reasons we cannot infer the justice of a statutory rape law from the justice of a speeding limit. First of all, the punishment for statutory rape is typically dramatically more severe than the penalty for speeding, and so we should not be so quick to assume that we are not violating the rights of those punished for statutory rape. Second and less obviously, it may demand much more of a person to ask him to refrain from having sex with a given person than it does to ask him to avoid speeding. This claim may seem curious, but one must remember that not every man who wants to have sex with a girl under the age of eighteen is a deplorable sexual predator. There is no reason that a man over the age of twenty cannot be deeply in love with a girl under the age of eighteen, and in these cases criminally prohibiting this couple from having sex is morally tantamount to prohibiting two gay men who are in love from having sex together.

Thus, even if a state violates no rights when it punishes all those who exceed a designated speed on any given stretch of road, it does not automatically follow that it similarly acts justly when it punishes all men over a given age who have sex with girls under a certain age. I will say more below about what I think a just statutory rape law would look like. For now, I will conclude more modestly by emphasizing only that the justifiability of any given *mala prohibita* law will depend upon a number of factors, including (1) the importance of the rights of the potential victims protected, (2) the severity of the punishment imposed, (3) the number and proportion of people punished who in fact committed no corresponding *mala in se* crime, and (4) the availability of alternative means of achieving the aims the particular law is designed to achieve.

III. The Problem of Sentencing

If all of the foregoing arguments are sound, then a rights forfeiture theorist can explain why a legitimate state may punish someone guilty of committing a *mala prohibita* crime when the particular criminal statute is not unjust. Potential problems remain, however, because it is not clear that the rights forfeiture theorist can recommend appropriate sentences for all such crimes.

To see why the question of sentencing raises such difficult issues, let us return to the case of statutory rape. Because rape is such a horrific violation of the victim's rights, presumably it would be permissible to impose a correspondingly onerous punishment.[14] But remember, in the cases of statutory rape, there is no guarantee that the presumptive rapee's rights were in fact violated. If the legally underage girl was actually sufficiently mature, then her consent was morally valid, and the sex did not violate her rights. It does not follow that no one's rights were violated, however, since, as I argued above, the statutory rapist may have violated the rights of his compatriots by breaking a just law. And if the statutory rapist violated the rights of his compatriots, then presumably he has forfeited his right not to be punished. But how much may he be punished?

I know of no algorithm that reliably generates specific answers to questions like this, but presumably one's compatriots' rights that one obey the law are not terribly weighty—certainly they are not as weighty as one's right not to be raped—and thus the statutory rapist may not permissibly be punished anywhere nearly as severely as may the rapist. Because of this, justice apparently requires the state to punish a statutory rapist much less severely than it may punish a rapist. Putting this point in terms of admittedly arbitrary numbers that will be helpful simply for purposes of illustration, let us suppose that, while a rapist forfeits his right not to be imprisoned for as many as ten years, a statutory rapist forfeits his right not to be imprisoned for no more than ten weeks. If so, it would be unjust for a state to punish statutory rapists for more than ten weeks.[15] This is problematic, however, because, while not all statutory rapists will have had sex with a girl who is not mature enough to have given her morally valid consent, many will have. And since these particular statutory rapists will have violated an extremely important right of those girls with whom they had sex, they will be woefully underpunished by any sentence which does not exceed ten weeks. Indeed, for those statutory rapists who had sex with an immature girl, an appropriate punishment would presumably be more like ten years.

Thus, even if the arguments outlined in the previous section enable the rights forfeiture theorist to explain why *mala prohibita* criminals may be punished for committing crimes like statutory rape, they do not seem capable of providing the types of answers we would like to secondary questions that might be asked about sentencing. Interestingly, our analysis began with a worry about statutory rapists who had not violated the rights of their sexual

---

[14] I take it for granted that a rights forfeiture theorist, like a retributivist, can endorse some type of rough proportionality between crime and punishment without embracing a corollary of *lex talionis*.

[15] On page 112 of *Overcriminalization*, Husak raises these types of questions about Duff's views on *mala prohibita*. I am grateful to Andrew Cornford for pointing out that, because my view is similar to Duff's, I must also address these issues.

partners being over-punished, but we now see that there is a more sophisticated worry about statutory rapists who have violated the rights of their sexual
victims being under-punished. Combining these two observations, we can
put the objection to rights forfeiture theorists in the form of a dilemma:
statutory rapists might be sentenced to punishments of either ten weeks or ten
years in prison. If they are imprisoned for ten years, then the state will be
violating the rights of those statutory rapists whose sexual partners were
mature enough to give their morally valid consent, but if they are imprisoned
for only ten weeks, those statutory rapists whose victims were not old enough
to give their morally valid consent will be dramatically under-punished.

Those familiar with the literature on the morality of punishment will likely
notice that we have now stumbled onto a more localized version of an
objection that is commonly invoked against what are often called 'fairness'
theories of punishment. Fairness theorists allege that punishment is justified
because, by enjoying the benefits of everyone else's legal obedience and then
breaking the laws themselves, criminals have unfairly taken advantage of the
benefits of legal co-operation without contributing their fair share. This
approach clearly has intuitive appeal, but most theorists reject it for two
related reasons. First, in the case of many standard crimes, it offers a patently
misguided account of the criminal's culpability. If Harry rapes Sally, for
instance, Harry's moral liability to punishment presumably stems straightforwardly from his horrible mistreatment of Sally, rather than from some
elaborate story about how he took unfair advantage of all of his compatriots
who did their fair share by obeying the law against raping Sally. Put more
succinctly, the punishment is warranted principally because Harry wronged
Sally, not because he wronged his compatriots. And second, if a criminal's
culpability is explained in terms of his taking unfair advantage of his compatriots, then we should punish Harry similarly regardless of whether he stole
a pencil from Sally or raped her, because in both cases the wrong was the
same: he took unfair advantage of his compatriots. But this seems crazy.
Clearly Harry should be punished more for raping Sally than for stealing one
of her pencils.

In general, the rights forfeiture theory of punishment is strong where
fairness theory is weak. Regarding *mala in se* crimes, the rights forfeiture
account focuses on the victim's violated right, and, as a consequence, it
supplies straightforward and compelling explanations as to why and how
severely the criminal may be punished. The particular account of *mala
prohibita* crimes I have developed in this chapter, however, is echoic of the
fairness theory of punishment. It should therefore come as no surprise that
I now face the same problem with sentencing of *mala prohibita* crimes that
fairness theory faces more generally. Highlighting the ways in which my

account of *mala prohibita* resembles the fairness theory of punishment also calls our attention to the prospect that the account defended here may sometimes misdiagnose why punishment is warranted. In particular, the punishable wrong committed by the statutory rapist who has sex with an insufficiently mature girl is presumably his violation of his victim's rights, not that he has somehow treated his compatriots unfairly. In sum, even if my account allows rights forfeiture theorists to explain why *mala prohibita* criminals may permissibly be punished, in some cases it offers a clearly misguided explanation that generates inappropriate recommendations for sentencing.

There may be no fully satisfactory solution to the dilemma of over or under-punishing the distinct types of statutory rapists, but two salient options would be to (1) set the default punishment either at ten weeks and then allow the state to raise it as high as ten years in those cases where it can prove that the girl in question was in fact immature, or to (2) set the default punishment at ten years but provide conditions for the defendant to prove his innocence by establishing that the girl was mature enough to give her morally valid consent.[16] Of these two options, the second strikes me as more promising.

Setting the default punishment at the lower level of ten weeks and then evaluating the maturity of each girl in question seems problematic for two reasons. First, if the state determines that the apparent victim of a statutory rape was actually sufficiently mature, it is not clear that the statutory rapist should be punished at all. Secondly, states are motivated to utilize criminal legislation like statutory rape laws in order to avoid the administrative costs and complications of making these difficult psychological assessments in each and every case. Thus, requiring states to make these difficult judgements on the back end, after conviction but before sentencing, defeats the purpose for which the laws were initially designed.

Given these problems, it seems better to set the default punishment at ten years and then build in institutional mechanisms that provide an opportunity for the defendant to prove his innocence if he can convince the court that the girl in question was sufficiently mature. Importantly, the statutory rapist should not be sentenced to the lesser charge of ten weeks if he can establish his innocence. Instead, I recommend that this mechanism should function similarly to self-defence. Just as a defendant who killed someone is not guilty and should not be sent to prison at all if he or she acted in self-defence, a man who had sex with a girl who was sufficiently mature to give her morally valid

---

[16] A third option would be to split the difference, so to speak, and sentence all statutory rapists to, say, five years in prison. This option appears to be a non-starter, though, since it would over-punish some, under-punish others, and give no one the punishment he deserves.

consent is not guilty and may not permissibly be sent to prison, even for ten weeks. One additional wrinkle that I would propose for statutory rape laws, though, would be that there should be some avenue available for girls to legally establish their maturity in advance of any potentially criminal action. I recognize that it may sound crazy to speak of girls under the designated age going to some state bureaucrat to apply for what essentially amount to licences to have sex, but it seems to me that this would be an important improvement over the status quo. Imagine that a twenty-one-year-old Jack is in love with a seventeen-year-old Jill in a jurisdiction that criminally prohibits men over the age of twenty from having sex with girls under the age of eighteen. If Jill and Jack want to have sex, and if Jill is in fact mature enough to give her morally valid consent, then one can imagine that they would be thrilled to have the opportunity to take the necessary steps to ensure that Jack would not be legally vulnerable to being imprisoned for ten years if they were discovered to have had sex. What is more, if a state provided such an opportunity, then it could without injustice set a weightier presumption that all girls under the age of eighteen are in fact insufficiently immature. In other words, if states provide ample opportunity for girls under the age of eighteen to antecedently establish their maturity, statutory rapist defendants have less grounds for complaint if they are subsequently saddled with a greater burden of proof to establish their innocence.

Finally, I recognize that requiring states to amend their laws in this fashion burdens them with additional costs, but it strikes me that these costs must be borne if states are to avoid egregious injustice. Having a criminal legal system in which killers can establish their innocence by demonstrating that they acted in self-defence also requires the legal system to be more costly and complicated, but no one doubts that these protections are required to ensure that innocent people are not wrongly punished. The only difference between our existing arrangements for self-defence and the amendments I am proposing for statutory rape laws, I would suggest, is that the issues surrounding *mala prohibita* legislation are less obvious than those attached to self-defence.

Of course, even if states sought to institute each of the changes I have recommended, such a system would inevitably make some mistakes, so we should expect that some men who had sex with insufficiently mature girls would wrongly escape prison and others who had sex with girls who were mature enough would wrongly be sent to prison for ten years. But no legal system can be expected to work perfectly. The important point for our purposes here is that there appears to be no reason that a rights forfeiture theorist cannot plausibly defend *mala prohibita* criminal laws, even statutory rape legislation that attaches severe penalties to those duly convicted. As long as these laws provide adequate institutional mechanisms which enable those who have not in fact violated anyone's rights to establish their innocence, states are at liberty to construct their criminal laws with sharp, salient boundaries that admittedly only approximate actual guilt and innocence, even for crimes that carry substantial penalties.

IV. The Injustice of the Status Quo

I have suggested that rights forfeiture theory is compatible with *mala prohibita* criminal laws, but I have also argued that justice requires that many existing *mala prohibita* laws must be amended to provide greater assurances that innocent people are not wrongly punished. But the fact that my characterization of a just statutory rape law differs in important ways from many that are currently in existence raises additional questions. Specifically, given that I believe both that (1) one has a moral obligation to obey only the just laws of a legitimate state and that (2) many existing statutory rape laws are unjust, are those who are convicted under existing laws justly punished? And do they have a moral obligation to accept their punishment? My answer is: 'it depends'. More specifically, it depends upon whether the girl with whom the convicted criminal had sex was in fact insufficiently mature to give her morally valid consent. If the girl was not in fact mature enough, then the man did violate her rights, he forfeited his own right not to be punished, and there is no injustice in the state sending him to jail for ten years. In this case, I believe that the injustice of statutory rape law is not germane, and the man is obligated to accept his punishment. If the girl was sufficiently mature, however, then the man did not violate her rights, and he did not forfeit his right not to be punished. And because the statutory rape law does not provide the requisite mechanism for the defendant to establish his innocence, it is a seriously unjust law. And just as it would be wrong for a state to punish someone who killed in self-defence if this state gave defendants no opportunity to establish that they had acted in self-defence, it would be wrong for this state to punish a statutory rapist for ten years. And finally, since there is no obligation to obey an unjust law, the statutory rapist whose sexual partner was in fact sufficiently mature has no moral obligation to accept his punishment.

V. Conclusion

Even those readers who agree with all of my arguments and conclusions may worry about the extents to which I have had to go in order to show why rights forfeiture theory is compatible with punishing those guilty of committing *mala prohibita* crimes. Should the twin facts that I have had to work so hard and *even then I have not been able to justify the status quo* lead us to be suspicious of rights forfeiture theory? I do not think so. Even though most who work on the morality of punishment take *mala prohibita* for granted and are anything but receptive to the rights forfeiture theory of punishment, I regard the difficulty we have had squaring this approach to punishment with existing *mala prohibita* laws as more of a reason to question the latter than the former. I say this for two reasons. First, with the possible exception of fairness theories of punishment (which have particular problems with *mala in se* crimes), I suspect that all but the crudest consequentialist approaches will have comparable difficulty with *mala prohibita*. In particular, any theory that includes deontological elements will insist that no one may permissibly be punished unless they do something wrong, and thus virtually all approaches will face similar difficulties capturing why those who commit *mala prohibita* crimes necessarily act wrongly. And second, my hunch is that theorists in philosophy of law tend to be too slow to question *mala prohibita* only because they are unreflective statists; they uncritically assume that if something is standardly practised by all states (including liberal democracies), then it must be morally unimpeachable. So while I have principally analysed this topic in terms of what rights forfeiture theorists can and should say on this issue, I think the enduring lesson of this chapter is that we should be much more suspicious of how freely and generously existing states help themselves to *mala prohibita* legislation.

6

Criminals in Uniform

*John Gardner**

I. Dicey's Doctrine

In England the idea of legal equality, or of the universal subjection of all classes to one law administered by the ordinary courts, has been pushed to its utmost limit. With us every official, from the Prime Minister down to a constable or a collector of taxes, is under the same responsibility for every act done without legal justification as any other citizen. The Reports abound with cases in which officials have been brought before the courts, and made, in their personal capacity, liable to punishment, or to the payment of damages, for acts done in their official character but in excess of their lawful authority.[1]

It is often suggested that this account of the legal position in England, even if true at the start of the twentieth century, was falsified during the course of that century by the rise of modern administrative law. But the rise of administrative law is totally irrelevant to Dicey's point. Administrative law adds new ways to hold public servants and public authorities responsible in law, but it does not take away any of the old ones. Police officers and tax inspectors may still be sued in the civil courts for trespass, defamation, and breach of confidence, just like the rest of us. Prison guards and traffic wardens may still be prosecuted in the criminal courts for theft, perverting the course

* University of Oxford. I was lucky to have detailed written comments on earlier drafts of this chapter from Matt Clayton and Antony Duff. Both advised me to drop what was my focal example of official breach of duty from section II, and doing so has, I think, much improved the chapter. Many thanks to both (without landing either of them with any liability for the new section II). For other helpful criticisms and comments I would like to thank Niki Lacey, Jeff McMahan, Victor Tadros, François Tanguay-Renaud, Friederich Toepel, and numerous other participants in the Stirling criminalization conference (September 2010) and its Warwick follow-up (March 2011).
[1] A V Dicey, *An Introduction to the Study of the Law of the Constitution*, 6th edn (London: Macmillan and Co, 1902) 189–90. I understood our project title *The Constitution of Criminal Law* to be inviting reflections on the relationship between criminal law and constitutional law. Hence my broadly Diceyan themes.

of justice, and blackmail, just like you and me. That MI5 officers, immigration officials, and local authority librarians are banned from murder, torture, and kidnapping comes of the fact that everyone is banned from murder, torture, and kidnapping. That at the time these people were or purported to be occupying their official roles, or fulfilling their official functions, does not in itself give them any legal protection against any criminal charge or cause of action to which they would otherwise be vulnerable.[2]

Of course it is true that many public officials have extra legal permissions that are incidents or constituents of their role. Police officers, for example, have extra permissions to enter onto land, seize goods, and detain persons, all of which give them extra scope to defend their actions in a criminal or civil court beyond what would be possible for an ordinary member of the public in the same circumstances. Dicey never denied this. His point was only that any such extra permissions need to be pleaded as a defence in the ordinary way in an ordinary court in the face of an ordinary charge or claim for an ordinary crime or tort. Both police officers and employees of private utility companies have special permissions to enter onto land. Both customs officers and private bailiffs enforcing judgment debts have special permissions to seize goods. The legal question, when any of these people is sued for trespass or conversion, or charged with burglary or theft, is simply whether he or she had the special permission that he or she claims to have had, not whether the office in virtue of which he or she had it was in the public or the private sector.

This is the 'citizens in uniform' doctrine. There is some poetic licence in the name, because the literal presence of a uniform is neither here nor there,[3] and nor, strictly speaking, is anyone's citizenship. Yet the name conveys the core of the doctrine. It can be expressed as an admonition: 'Don't think that when you step into your official role (your "uniform") you stop being yourself and can abdicate responsibility in your capacity as an ordinary member of the public (a "citizen") for the things that you do. You still answer to the law as yourself, and you can't hide behind your public role when you do it.'

Dicey famously idealized this doctrine, which he rightly took to be a settled doctrine, not only of English law, but also of the British Constitution.

---

[2] Although it certainly adds some, notably misconduct in a public office, which is both a crime and a tort at common law. At common law, bribery (in its 'receiving bribes' form) was also an offence that could be committed only by holders of a public office, but this restriction has recently been removed in England and Wales by statute. For some interesting and pertinent reflections on the reform, see Peter Alldridge, 'Reforming the Criminal Law of Corruption' (2002) 11 *Criminal Law Forum* 287.

[3] On uniforms more literally, see Christopher Kutz, 'The Difference that Uniforms Make' (2005) 33 *Philosophy and Public Affairs* 148.

He cast correspondingly infamous aspersions on the Napoleonic alternative,[4] in which (he claimed) the existence of a special *droit administratif*[5] with special courts of its own was coupled with extensive immunities for public officials from the ordinary processes and liabilities of criminal and private law. As is well known, he thought that English law here conforms to the ideal of the rule of law in a way in which French law does not. In this he was both right and wrong. It depends on how one understands the words 'in a way in which'.

Let me explain. The rule of law, like all credible political ideals, has universal[6] and parochial aspects. Any legal system that does not include an effective way of holding public officials to account in its courts has on any credible view a very serious rule-of-law deficit. It might even be reasonable to claim, on the strength of this deficit alone, that the rule of law does not prevail in that legal system, or in the civilization of which it is the legal system. But the French legal system is clearly not like that. It has an alternative way of holding public officials to account in the courts, namely by providing special courts in which to do so. Given other features of the French legal system, or of French civilization, this may well be the best way of conforming to the ideal of the rule of law in France. By the same token, given other features of English law, or of English civilization, the English way may be the best way of conforming to the ideal of the rule of law in England. We would have to know a lot of other things about each country and its law before we could judge whether things would be better than they are now, from the point of view of the rule of law, if the English adopted the French model, or if the French adopted the English model. It is absurd to think that the rule of law gives its universal blessing to one model over the other. Clearly it allows that different legal systems may find their own ways of conforming, possibly with equal success, to the desideratum of judicial accountability for public officials.

---

[4] Dicey, *Introduction*, n 1 above, eg at p 190.

[5] As Dicey says (Dicey, *Introduction*, n 1 above, at p 486), what French lawyers call '*droit administratif* does not correspond to what English lawyers call 'administrative law'. So I follow Dicey in leaving the expression untranslated.

[6] By speaking of the universal aspects of the ideal, I do not mean to suggest that the rule of law should prevail everywhere. It should prevail, in my view, only where there is or should be a legal system (or something very close to one), which is not everywhere. The rule of law has universal aspects in the less ambitious sense that I am after here so long as there are common desiderata that make it the same ideal, despite variations in its parochial interpretation or implementation, wherever it prevails or should prevail. For analysis of familiar doubts about whether the rule of law has universal aspects even in this sense, see Jeremy Waldron 'Is the Rule of Law an Essentially Contested Concept (in Florida)?' (2002) 21 *Law and Philosophy* 137.

So Dicey is right that the English constitution conforms to the ideal of the rule of law in a way in which the French does not, if that is taken to allow for the possibility that the French model also conforms to the ideal, but does so in a different way. But the statement is wrong if it is taken to mean (as Dicey might have read and approved it) that the English constitution conforms to the rule of law in a *respect* in which the French does not. In one and the same respect—namely in respect of holding public officials accountable before the courts—French law and English law conform to the ideal, but each system has its own way of doing so. That allows us to say, if we like, that there is a French ideal of the rule of law and an English ideal of the rule of law, but that both are parochial renditions of the same ideal, viz the universal ideal of the rule of law. (I bracket the vexed question of whether Dicey got the French position entirely right.[7])

Malcolm Thorburn and I have argued about the Diceyean interpretation of English constitutional law before.[8] He denies that English law includes the 'citizens in uniform' doctrine. He also denies that it would be a good thing, from the point of view of the rule of law, if it did. (I argued with him only about the first point, but as he gleaned from my tone, I tend to disagree with him about the second as well.) One very interesting feature of Thorburn's challenge is that he does not follow Dicey in contrasting the 'citizens in uniform' doctrine with the supposedly Napoleonic alternative, the model of liability in *droit administratif* combined with immunity from various criminal and civil processes and liabilities. Instead, Thorburn contrasts the 'citizens in uniform' doctrine with what I will call the 'officials in plain clothes' doctrine. According to this doctrine, there is a body of rules belonging to the general part of the criminal law that are tailored primarily to regulating public officials in the exercise of their official powers. In this respect, criminal law is a type of public law, a sibling of administrative law.[9] To be more exact: using a cluster of 'justification' defences to criminal charges, the law licenses officials to arrest, to detain, to seize, to search, and otherwise to engage in diverse acts of public defence and public necessity, which are incidents of their specifically public roles. It is true, agrees Thorburn, that versions of the same justification defences are sometimes available to non-officials too. The criminal law permits me, as an ordinary member of the public, to defend and protect people, including myself, in ways that would otherwise incur criminal

---

[7] Cf Dicey, *Introduction*, n 1 above, at p 322, n 1.

[8] Thorburn, 'Justifications, Powers, and Authority' *Yale Law Journal* 117 (2008), 1070; Gardner, 'Justification under Authority' *Canadian Journal of Law and Jurisprudence* 23 (2010), 71.

[9] For further elaboration of the family resemblance, which for Thorburn goes beyond the particular feature I foreground here, see Thorburn's 'Criminal Law as Public Law', in Antony Duff and Stuart Green (eds), *Philosophical Foundations of Criminal Law* (Oxford: Oxford University Press, 2011).

liability. In some cases I am even permitted (and empowered[10]) to make an arrest. When such defences are available to me, says Thorburn, their aim and effect is to make me a public official *pro tempore*.[11] By hypothesis, I have no standing role as a public official, but the criminal law is licensing me to act as a public official right now, in the absence of anyone nearby who has that standing role. So whereas Dicey and I think of the arresting police officer as a citizen in uniform, Thorburn thinks of the ordinary self-defender or defender of others as a stand-in plain-clothes police officer.

In recent work, Thorburn has renewed and redoubled his criticisms of the 'citizens in uniform' doctrine. He now writes:

According to the Diceyan ideal, there is nothing particularly special about the work of public servants. What makes a police officer a police officer, on this account, is little more than his pay cheque: he is paid to do certain things that he would be permitted to do anyway. The aspect of this story that proponents of the Diceyan account like to emphasize is that police officers are not privy to any special treatment – they are held accountable in criminal law in precisely the same way as the rest of us. But the obverse of the same story is the recognition that there is nothing special about the public provision of certain services: nothing of principle would be lost if we were to privatize all public functions: policing, prisons, even the military. Of course, advocates of the Diceyan position might suggest that there are pragmatic reasons for keeping some of these services in public hands, but they would not have any objections in principle to our doing so. I have argued elsewhere that there are important reasons of principle to object to what Paul Verkuil calls 'outsourcing sovereignty' – but they are not reasons that the Diceyan account can articulate.[12]

One curiosity of this 'privatization' objection is that, if sound, it would seem to count against the 'officials in plain clothes' doctrine no less than it counts against the 'citizens in uniform' doctrine. On Thorburn's own view, what is a legally approved act of self-defence or defence of others by an ordinary

---

[10] Thorburn emphasizes powers but (I have argued) what the criminal law cares about must be permissions. Either can exist without the other. See Gardner, 'Justification under Authority', n 8 above, at 85–9.

[11] Thorburn, 'Justifications, Powers, and Authority', n 8 above, at p 1076. ('It is only insofar as they are performing a public function that ordinary citizens have the authority to make such judgments, and accordingly, they are bound by similar normative constraints when deciding what conduct is justified as public officials would be in the same situation.')

[12] Thorburn, 'Two Conceptions of Equality Before the (Criminal) Law', in François Tanguay-Renaud and James Stribopoulos (eds), *Rethinking Criminal Law Theory* (Oxford: Hart, 2011) 12. I have omitted the footnotes in which Thorburn refers to Paul Verkuil, *Outsourcing Sovereignty: Why Privatization of Government Functions Threatens Democracy and What We Can Do About It* (New York: Cambridge University Press, 2007), and to his own 'Reinventing the Night-Watchman State?' (2010) 60 *University of Toronto Law Journal* 425.

member of the public if not a temporarily privatized performance of a police duty? And if such selective privatization of policing is warranted, then why is it not mainly a 'pragmatic' question how far it should be extended—for example, what the balance should be between police arrests and citizens' arrests?

I will not pursue this *tu quoque* response to Thorburn here. Instead I want to ask whether he is right about the moral and political implications of the Diceyan view. I ask because I am in an awkward position if he is right about these implications. If he is right, my views about the best way to implement the ideal of the rule of law in the UK, my own country, (viz by retaining the citizens in uniform doctrine), do not square with my other political ideals. These ideals include a very deep-seated opposition to the transfer or contracting-out to non-public-sector bodies of various hitherto public-sector activities, including (but certainly not limited to) policing, tax inspection and collection, border and immigration control and enforcement, planning and licensing, welfare benefit assessment and payment, diplomacy and consular services, the work of the intelligence agencies and the armed forces, criminal prosecution, the prison and probation services, and—perhaps most crucially of all—the administration of justice in the courts. I will not attempt to defend this opposition here. Instead I will set myself the more limited task of showing that a defender of the Diceyan doctrine can consistently believe that public officials, or some of them, are in a special moral position because they are officials. In other words, they can consistently believe that there is something 'special about the work of [at least some] public servants' when they are occupying their official roles.

To that end, my main thesis will be that, if one is killed or injured or robbed or abused (etc), it makes things morally worse that one is killed or injured or robbed or abused (etc) by a police officer on duty. Consequently, the officer has a *ceteris paribus* harder job of defending his or her actions than he or she would have if he or she were an ordinary member of the public who did the same thing. You will notice soon enough, if you have not done so already, that the special moral position I will be sketching is that of a police officer *qua* police officer, not that of a police officer *qua* public servant. In adumbrating this special moral position I will be assuming, not arguing, that the job of a police officer is and should remain in the public sector. That is what I mean when I say that I will stop short of arguing against the privatization of the police. Nevertheless, I believe that once the special moral position of police officers *qua* police officers is appreciated, it is a fairly short step to seeing why that job should be kept out of private hands, and (in more specific opposition to Thorburn) why the rest of us should not be regarded, when intervening with legally recognized justification in matters that also warrant police intervention, as police officers *pro tempore*.

II. The Morality of Policing

When passer-by Ian Tomlinson was deliberately pushed from behind during the London G20 protests in 2009, and died soon afterwards, the action of the man who pushed him was made more morally lamentable, and hence harder to excuse, by the fact that he, the pusher, was a police officer on duty.[13] When commuter Jean Charles de Menezes was mistaken for a would-be suicide bomber at Stockwell tube station in July 2005, and then killed by bullets fired at close range while he was restrained, the already shocking killing was made more shocking, and put in need of more thorough scrutiny and more compelling justification or excuse, by the fact that the killers were police officers on duty.[14] In explaining why, I will be focusing on these and similar fatal actions by police officers on duty. But let me emphasize from the start that the considerations I will be adducing are of far wider import. They apply no less to police collusion in phone hacking by journalists, to conspiracy between police officers and corporations or politicians to thwart lawful protests or other dissent, to sexual exploitation by police officers of those with whom they come into official contact, to arrest and detention on trumped-up charges as a technique of intimidation, and to obstruction by police officers of the investigation of possible crimes committed by police officers.[15] They also apply to various officials who are not strictly speaking police officers, such as immigration staff, tax inspectors, customs officers, prison guards, intelligence operatives, and soldiers engaging with civilians, to the extent that their work is akin to that of the police. For simplicity I will use the label 'police officers' loosely to refer to the whole range of officials with policing duties. For our main interest is in explaining what, morally speaking, those duties (or some of them) are.

---

[13] 'Ian Tomlinson unlawfully killed, inquest finds', *The Guardian*, 3 May 2011. The officer was subsequently acquitted of manslaughter: 'Ian Tomlinson death: Simon Harwood cleared of manslaughter', *The Guardian*, 19 July 2012.

[14] Independent Police Complaints Commission, *Stockwell One: Investigation into the shooting of Jean Charles de Menezes at Stockwell underground station on 22 July 2005* (London: IPCC, 2007). There has been no prosecution of individual officers involved in the shooting but the Metropolitan Police Service was convicted of an offence under the Health and Safety at Work Act 1974. 'Met police guilty over De Menezes shooting', *The Guardian*, 1 November 2007.

[15] Which was also a feature of the de Menezes case: *Stockwell One*, n 14 above, at pp 165–6.

A. The duty to protect

We all have moral duties[16] not to kill people, and police officers are no exception. But police officers have an additional moral duty to protect people against a wide range of misfortunes, and *inter alia* to protect them against killing. As one young woman wrote after escaping from the Norwegian island of Utøya, where many of her peers were killed by a lone gunman: 'Just think of it, he dressed himself in a police uniform, the symbol of safety and support.'[17] The suggestion here is not that an imposter dressing up as a policeman thereby acquires the moral duties of a policeman (although maybe he sometimes does). The suggestion is only that this killer lulled his victims into a false sense of security by creating the expectation that he would protect them from killing (there being news of a killer on the loose nearby). This expectation of protection is not a specifically Norwegian one. In places (unlike Norway) where police officers routinely fail to provide such protection, so that people come to expect and even accommodate the failure, there remains a sense in which the police are still failing to meet people's expectations. They are failing to meet people's expectations of how police officers should behave. These expectations are normative ones. The police force exists to protect people from (*inter alia*) killing and thus the moral duty to do so goes with the job, irrespective of how often it is breached and irrespective of whether holders of the job, or other people, ever recognize that fact.[18]

---

[16] I put the word in the plural because—although nothing turns on the point here—I believe the moral duty not to kill intentionally is distinct from the moral duty not to kill accidentally (ie where the death is a side-effect, even a known one). Breaches of the second duty are in principle amenable to a wider range of justifications and excuses than breaches of the first duty. It does not follow that intentional killing is morally worse, even *ceteris paribus*: see John Finnis, 'Intention and Side-effects' in R G Frey and Christopher W Morris (eds), *Liability and Responsibility* (Cambridge: Cambridge University Press, 1991) 32 at 60–1.

[17] Emma Martinovic, 'Norway Attacks: a survivor's account of the Utøya massacre', *The Guardian*, 27 July 2011.

[18] It is tempting to trace the moral duties under discussion here to the oath of office, or the contract of service, of a police officer. Although such oaths and contracts are indeed morally binding (so long as they do not purport to abrogate moral duties that exist apart from them and are not extracted by immoral means) it is implausible to think that they are the only or even the primary basis for attaching moral duties to roles, or for holding people to be bound by those duties. For the most part such oaths and contracts exist to solemnize, and hence to reinforce morally and psychologically, and sometimes to give legal effect to, moral duties that belong to the role anyway, thanks to the rationale for the role's existence. So the police duty to protect cannot be avoided simply by refusing to undertake it. A police commissioner cannot relieve her officers of the duty by avoiding any mention of it in their oaths or contracts. Nor can a police officer avoid acquiring it by evading the taking of his oath of office, or by deleting the relevant words from his contract of service before accepting the job. For excellent discussion see Michael Davis, 'Thinking Like an Engineer: the Place of a Code of Ethics in the Practice of a Profession' (1991) 20 *Philosophy & Public Affairs*

There may come a point, to be sure, at which failures to protect, or other moral failures by police officers, become so endemic that doubts start to arise about whether they should still be regarded and treated as police officers. ('What a pathetic excuse for a police force!' 'Call yourself a policeman?') Do such doubts take us back to the problem of the moral duties of imposters? Not quite. There is a difference (although there are certainly borderline cases) between gangsters who dress up as police officers and police officers who behave like gangsters. There are non-moral criteria, in other words, for someone to count as a police officer. There must be. Otherwise those who fail badly enough in the moral duties of police officers (individually or collectively, as you like) are not police officers, and so do not have those duties, and so cannot fail in them.

Now, wearing a police uniform is clearly not one of the non-moral criteria for being a police officer, for in that respect police officers and imposters may be indistinguishable. How about working in the public sector? That would be a turn up for the books—privatization of the police is conceptually impossible!—but I doubt whether it could be sustained. What is among the non-moral criteria for being a police officer, it seems to me, is that police officers have special legal powers to do certain police-characteristic things, which remain their legal powers even when they are systematically abused. With such a criterion in place, 'call yourself a policeman?' and similar reproaches can be taken to convey that, in the opinion of the speaker, the addressee is not fit to be a police officer, or is a degenerate example of a police officer, or is a police officer not worthy of the name, all without denying that a police officer is still what he or she is. Likewise, when we doubt whether such degenerates should be 'regarded or treated' as police officers we may simply mean: don't think of them as your protectors or saviours, don't make them cups of tea, don't help them with their inquiries, don't give them the time of day. Don't credit them, in short, with a fitness for their office of which they are not worthy. Compare the line we should take with bad laws: they are still laws, but errant examples that exert no moral hold over us and so should be ignored as guides to action (and perhaps also derided or subverted).[19]

---

150 at 156ff, and John Kleinig, *The Ethics of Policing* (Cambridge: Cambridge University Press, 1996) 238ff.

[19] This is all consistent with the claim, which I endorse, that someone who doesn't understand the moral duties of a police officer doesn't understand what it is to be a police officer ('Call yourself a police officer? You don't know the meaning of the word!'), or that someone who doesn't understand how legal systems ought to be, morally, doesn't understand what a legal system is. It is one thing to claim that understanding what an X is necessitates understanding how an X ought to be. It is quite another thing to claim that nothing is an X unless it already *is* how an X ought to be. In his *Natural Law and Natural Rights* (Oxford: Oxford University Press, 1980) at 11, John Finnis rejects the

We will return in a moment to the special relationship of police officers to the law. For now our interest is in their moral duty to protect, whether this is reflected in the law or not. There are interesting questions about the stringency of this duty, and in particular about how much protection people should expect from the police. To what extent should people be expected, and hence presumably permitted by law, to protect themselves rather than relying on the authorities? Should those facing more specific or more immediate or more serious dangers get enhanced protection? The cases that concern us here do not, however, raise these questions. It is one thing to be a protector whose protective measures are found wanting. The question can then arise of what further protective measures, if any, should have been taken—of how far the duty to protect reaches. As the Utøya survivor's comments bring out, however, it is quite another thing to be a protector who does the very thing from which he or she is supposed to be providing protection. If one has a duty to protect someone from killing, one breaches it in an especially grave way by killing that same someone oneself. For doing so is not a mere failure in, but rather an inversion of, one's duty as protector. Killing A is as far away from protecting A from being killed as one can get. And the further away one gets from doing one's moral duty, all else being equal, the morally worse one's breach of duty is. In that dimension of moral evaluation, killings by police officers are among the worst there can be.

I say 'among' because police officers (even using that title as broadly as we are using it here, to include a range of police-like officials) are clearly not the only people with duties to protect others from being killed. Such duties—albeit owed to much smaller constituencies of people than the duties of the police—are normal incidents of some personal relationships, such as those between parents and their children, and between one spouse or partner and another. Killings of children by their parents or vice versa, and killings of spouses by spouses, share the morally exacerbating feature that I have just associated with killings by police officers. One is not only killed; one is not only not properly protected from being killed; one is killed by the very person, or one of the persons, who had the job of protecting one from being killed. That person did the opposite of their duty. So the class of worst killings, in the dimension of moral evaluation that concerns us here, is not limited to killings by police officers. Nevertheless, killings by police officers do belong to that class. In this dimension, being killed by a police officer is morally akin to being killed by one's mother or one's husband.

second claim about law, and yet he gives repeated succour to those who accept it by the curious way in which he expresses himself thereafter (viz by sometimes but not always reserving the word 'law' for cases of morally successful law).

Surely this claim cannot be extended to the killing in, for instance, the de Menezes case? True enough, the officers who killed Mr de Menezes could hardly have done a worse job of protecting Mr de Menezes. But they killed him—didn't they?—in the course of performing their moral duty to protect the rest of us. Doesn't that neutralize the special moral awfulness supposedly attaching to their actions? Some people think that an action that was one's only way to perform one's moral duty can never be at the same time a breach of one's moral duty (or at any rate a breach of that same moral duty).[20] Some people think (a different proposition) that a morally justified action can never be a breach of a moral duty.[21] Some people think, moreover, that the killing of Mr de Menezes does not count as a breach of duty thanks to one or more of these propositions. But the propositions are both false, and are anyway irrelevant to the de Menezes case.

That the propositions are both mistaken is the galling lesson of *Sophie's Choice*. 'You choose just one of your children to send to his or her death', says the Auschwitz *Kommandant* sorting those who will live from those who will die, 'or I will send both of them to their deaths'.[22] As a parent, Sophie has a duty to protect her children—both of her children—from being killed. Neither the fact that she was justified in handing over one of her children in order to save the other, nor the fact that handing over her daughter was the only way she had to do her duty to protect her son, entails by itself that she did not thereby breach that same duty as owed to her daughter. That thanks to his proposal Sophie could not but breach her duty to at least one of her children was the main point of the *Kommandant*'s sadistic plan. Indeed the plan, we can now see, was even more sadistic than that. The *Kommandant* did not simply make sure that Sophie violated her parental duty; he ensured that she violated it in a particularly egregious way. He ensured that she condemned one of her children to the very killing from which she, as a mother, was duty-bound to provide protection. He was out to destroy Sophie as a parent by actively involving her in the killing of her own daughter. That she was morally justified in being, and morally bound to be, so involved did not reduce the special moral awfulness of what the *Kommandant* got her to do.

You may say that not every killing by a police officer fits the tragic *Sophie's Choice* model. Surely there are some cases in which a police officer no longer

[20] See eg Barbara Herman, 'Obligation and Performance' in Owen Flanagan and Amélie Rorty (eds), *Identity, Character, and Morality* (Cambridge, Mass: MIT Press, 1990) 311 at 324.

[21] See eg John Skorupski, *Ethical Explorations* (Oxford: Oxford University Press, 1999) 170–1; Stephen Darwall, 'Morality and Practical Reason: a Kantian Approach' in David Copp (ed), *The Oxford Handbook of Ethical Theory* (Oxford: Oxford University Press, 2006) 282 at 286.

[22] The scenario is from William Styron's *Sophie's Choice* (New York: Random House Inc, 1979).

has his or her usual moral duty to protect a particular person whom he or she has in his or her sights? We will come back to that question shortly. For now, my point is only that the special moral awfulness of a breach of duty, when one does the very opposite of one's duty, is not neutralized by the mere fact that one had a conflicting duty to do as one did, nor by the mere fact that the breach was justified.

Still less, we should now add, is it neutralized by the mere fact that one was *trying* to do one's duty, or by the mere fact that one's breach *would have been* justified *if the facts had been as one thought them to be.* These are excusatory considerations, and they are the best that the luckless police officers who mistakenly killed Mr de Menezes can hope to draw upon. Looking more closely it would be seriously misleading for them to claim, as I put it before, that 'they killed him in the course of performing their moral duty to protect the rest of us'. They can only say that they killed him in the course of trying (as assiduously as any police officer could?) to perform what they (on reasonable grounds?) took to be their moral duty to protect the rest of us. And this excuse, even with the parenthetical words included and the question marks deleted, clearly does not in any way diminish the gravity of the breach of duty which it is supposed to excuse. On the contrary, the gravity of the breach is one of the main factors that determines how hard it is going to be to make the excuse, for it is one of the main factors that determines what would count as acceptable steps to ascertain the facts, how much self-restraint or caution would be reasonable, etc.

We could sum up: that doing the opposite of one's moral duty is a particularly grave breach of that duty does not entail, or even suggest, that it is a particularly blameworthy one. It may be wholly justified or excused, and thus entirely blameless. No doubt police officers occasionally have powerful justifications or excuses for killing someone whom they have a duty to protect, and are thus morally exonerated. Their powerful duties to others may be what give them these powerful justifications and excuses. My point, however, is that powerful justifications or excuses are exactly what they need if they are to be exculpated, because the breach of moral duty involved in killing someone whom one has a moral duty to protect is a particularly egregious one, one that calls for (as I put it before) more thorough scrutiny and more compelling justification or excuse than other killings, all else being equal. And even with such compelling justification or excuse, at least some police officers must, like Sophie, carry on their consciences these deadly breaches of duty. Exculpation, as surely they would tell you, is not the same as absolution; a faultless or blameless failure is not the same as no failure at all.

B. The duty to uphold the rule of law

As well as being protectors, police officers are officers of the law, and have a moral duty to uphold the law, as well as to protect people, in their work. The two duties overlap, but each extends beyond the other. The role of the police as protectors is not limited to protecting people against breaches of the law. The role of the police as upholders of the law, meanwhile, is not limited to providing protection, but also includes upholding laws (often very stupid laws) which do not protect anyone. This reflects the fact that the duty of police officers to uphold the law is really but one aspect of their duty to uphold the *rule* of law, the moral ideal according to which everyone is ruled by, and hence answers to, the law. Not all of us have this moral duty. Indeed those of us who are not bound to the law by our occupations (or by other special relationships with it[23]) do not even have a general moral duty to *obey* the law, never mind to uphold it. The police are therefore in the awkward position of being morally bound to uphold the law, and to make it the case that people answer to it, even when (as the police themselves often well know) the law is an ass and has no legitimate hold over those same people. That is another harsh burden of office. It is one that police officers share with prosecutors, judges, and other officers of the law. They have a moral obligation to subject people to the law even when those same people have no moral obligation to submit to it.

The most obvious way in which a police officer can fail in his or her duty to uphold the (rule of) law, already hinted at in these remarks, is by acting illegally himself or herself. Breaking the law is not quite the opposite of upholding the law. The opposite of upholding the law is undermining it, whether or not by breaking it. But breaking the law is nevertheless a long way from upholding it, and is thus a serious breach of moral duty on the part of a police officer, even when the law she breaks is a stupid one. I should emphasize, as I did in connection with the duty to protect, that the fact that the breach is a particularly serious one does not entail that it is a particularly blameworthy one. It need not be blameworthy at all. There may be morally acceptable justifications or excuses for police law-breaking. Sometimes, in a country with laws that are not merely stupid but immoral, civil disobedience or conscientious objection by officers of the law, sometimes by judges as well as by police officers, is called for. My point is only that, since they are then

---

[23] For example, naturalization as a citizen. For discussion, see J Gardner, 'Relations of Responsibility' in Rowan Cruft, Matthew Kramer and Mark Reiff (eds), *Crime, Punishment, and Responsibility: The Jurisprudence of Antony Duff* (Oxford: Oxford University Press, 2011) 87 at 95.

doing something of special moral gravity, their justification or excuse for breaking even such a terrible law needs to be an especially powerful one.

A twist in the tale is that sometimes the law itself will recognize the justification or excuse in question. The law is rather unlikely to recognize civil disobedience or conscientious objection as a justification or excuse, but it might well recognize self-defence or public necessity or duress or mistake of fact. When such defences are recognized by the law, and enable a police officer to be acquitted or not prosecuted according to the proper procedures for determining such things, there is no illegality in the relevant sense. To that extent, the moral duty to uphold the rule of law has not been breached, and no further justification or excuse for breaching it is called for.

There is a strong moral case, however, for the courts to insist that officers of the law produce particularly compelling justifications and excuses before being acquitted in such a situation.[24] Such officers need to show themselves fit for their role as upholders of the rule of law. An officer who pleads provocation to a charge of murdering a suspect, for example, had better not be held to the ordinary standard of self-control applicable to the rest of us. To uphold the rule of law often requires tremendous reserves of self-control and someone who is only ordinarily self-controlled is not fit for police work.[25] Equally, to uphold the rule of law often requires high epistemic competence. A police officer must be particularly free from bias, superstition, gullibility, and prejudice. She needs to be the sort of person who does not maintain easy assumptions or jump to conclusions. In the de Menezes case, the English law of mistake in self-defence and defence of others gave the police officers (just as it would have given you and me) very great latitude in respect of errors of perception and deduction in the lead-up to the decision to kill. Indeed, the reasonableness of the officers having mistaken Mr de Menezes for a would-be bomber is neither here nor there to English law, so long as they really did so mistake him.[26] That degree of excusatory latitude for any of us, but especially for police officers, is in my view indefensible. The effect is that the police officers who were party to the killing of Mr de Menezes could not have been

---

[24] Here I am building on my earlier discussion of the point in J Gardner, *Offences and Defences* (Oxford: Oxford University Press, 2007) 124–6.

[25] In 2000, a UK-wide police recruitment campaign ('Could you?') stressed that not everybody is fit to be a police officer, and in particular that extremely high levels of courage, patience, scrupulousness, and self-control are called for. For a report of the campaign, see http://news.bbc. co.uk/1/hi/902853.stm. Numerous recent cases of unprofessional police behaviour towards public protesters suggest that not all recruits, and maybe not all recruiters, took the point. See eg *Moos and McClure v Metropolitan Police Commissioner* [2011] EWHC 957 (Admin); *R v Barkshire* [2011] EWCA Crim 1885, to mention only examples where the unprofessional behaviour was also illegal.

[26] Settled by *R v Williams* (1984) 78 Cr App R 276 and *Beckford v R* [1988] AC 130, and put on a statutory footing by the Criminal Justice and Immigration Act 2008, s 76.

convicted of murder in England. So the killing did not represent, under the heading of police illegality, a breach of the police duty to uphold the rule of law. But the fact that the law did not allow for their epistemic competence to be tested to make sure that they were fit to be police officers is a bad reflection on the state of the law.[27]

I say 'under the heading of police illegality' because, to repeat, the moral duty of police officers to uphold the rule of law is not only a duty to avoid their own illegality. It also includes, for example, a duty to apprehend law-breakers and to take them through the first stages of accountability to the criminal law: arrest, search, questioning, and charge. This duty to apprehend offenders can make it tempting for police officers, often abetted by politicians and journalists, to regard themselves as existing to protect 'law-abiding citizens' against the 'criminal classes'. But this self-understanding on the part of police officers is already antithetical to the rule of law. Under the rule of law, even the most notorious and dangerous offenders are entitled to the law's protection, just like anyone else. Police officers, as officers of the law, are there to protect the bad guys as much as the good guys, except to the extent that specific protections are withdrawn by the legal mechanisms of accountability to the law itself (arrest, search, detention, charge, remand, trial, sentence) or by the legal recognition of extreme exigencies with which the ordinary legal mechanisms (of arrest, etc) cannot be expected to cope. Subject to these strict exceptions, the police are there to protect looters against shopkeepers no less than shopkeepers against looters, anti-capitalist protestors against corporate interests no less than corporate interests against anti-capitalist protestors, burglars against household-ers no less than householders against burglars, paedophiles against neighbours no less than neighbours against paedophiles, and illegal immigrants against security guards sent to deport them no less than security guards against illegal immigrants.[28] Indeed, the rule of law is not consistent with the police dividing the world up into 'good guys' and 'bad guys', or into 'law-abiding people' and 'criminals', or into 'respectable women' and 'common prostitutes', or into any other classes of people supposedly more and less entitled to the protection of the law and hence of the police as officers of the law. So when vigilantes say that they are merely law-abiding people out to protect themselves against criminals,

[27] To say that is not to advocate a departure from the 'citizens in uniform' doctrine because, as I explained, that doctrine only says that the police are answerable like the rest of us before the ordinary criminal courts on ordinary criminal charges, and cannot hide behind their uniforms as a way of defending their actions. It does not say that the standards of reasonableness used by the courts in assessing their guilt cannot be adjusted to reflect the higher expectations we have of police officers (or of others occupying professional roles, public or not). See *Offences and Defences*, n 24 above, at pp 128–9.

[28] I explored this point, or some applications of it, in my *Offences and Defences*, n 24 above, at ch 11.

the police should reply that one is only ever as law-abiding as the last law one abided by, so that it is always an open question, in any situation of potential conflict, who, if anyone, is (going to turn out to be) a criminal, and hence subject to arrest and other legal consequences.[29]

These are but further aspects of the principle that Dicey calls 'legal equality'. Unlike the more parochial 'citizens in uniform' doctrine, they are aspects that remain even where that principle is not pushed to its 'utmost limit'. The duty to uphold the rule of law is breached when—and hence the rule of law does not prevail to the extent that—police officers hold themselves not to owe the same protection to some person or people (B or the Bs) on the basis that the police exist mainly to protect some other person or people (A or the As) against B or the Bs. So even though the officers who killed Mr de Menezes did not break the law, it is still possible that they breached their moral duty to uphold the rule of law in another way, say by regarding 'terrorist suspects' in general, or Mr de Menezes in particular, as a 'target', less entitled to the protection of the law than other people because of the ongoing threat that they or he supposedly posed to 'ordinary Londoners' or 'decent people'. In the fevered days after the tube and bus bombings of 7 July 2005, and in the morally corrosive climate of the so-called 'war on terror', it would not be surprising (although it would not follow that it would be morally excusable) if at least some police officers fell into this trap, mistaking policing (which has nobody as its enemy) for war (which is waged only against an enemy).[30]

These remarks bring us back to the question, postponed a few pages back, of whether there are cases in which a police officer no longer has his or her usual moral duty to protect a particular person whom he or she has in his or her sights. Our discussion may seem to suggest a negative conclusion. But in fact the answer is more complex and invokes some distinctions which can be hard to draw sharply. Under the rule of law, nobody is an outlaw and nobody should be treated by the police as either above or below the law, or as being either more or less entitled to its protection. Nor can the law itself, consistently with the rule of law, make an outlaw of anyone, so as to license the police to treat him that way. But it does not follow that the police officer's moral duty to protect (the one discussed in A above) is the same duty in all circumstances. It seems to me that, in respect of many circumstantial

---

[29] I have benefited greatly from reading James Edwards' largely unpublished work on this topic (and on several others nearby).

[30] Here I am implicitly rejecting Bruce Ackerman's attempt, in 'This is not a War' (2004) 113 *Yale Law Journal* 1871, to establish a *tertium quid* between policing and military action. To my mind, a fatal muddying of the waters, and a gift to enemies of the rule of law everywhere.

variations, this duty probably resembles the ordinary moral duties not to kill and injure that all of us have. Probably there is a relevant moral difference, for example, between incapacitating wrongdoers in the course of their wrong-doing, and incapacitating others. Killing or injuring bystanders, hostages, passengers, and other innocents in the elimination or mitigation of a threat can sometimes be justified, but it usually remains a serious breach of duty even when it is.[31] Those who are morally implicated in the same threat, on the other hand, may thereby lose some of their rights not to be killed or injured in its elimination or mitigation.[32] This distinction, or something like it, applies to you and me in connection with our ordinary moral duties not to kill and injure people. Probably it, or something like it, applies also to police officers in connection with their special moral duty to protect people from killing or being injured. Thus, police officers who kill or injure for public protection are often, but not always, in *Sophie's Choice* situations. If Mr de Menezes really had been a suicide bomber ready to detonate his explosives, then it seems to me that any attending officer's moral duty to protect Mr de Menezes from being killed would have been abrogated to the extent urgently necessary and proportionate to the cause of eliminating the threat he posed to other people on the tube. Always bearing in mind, of course, that each officer would still have the distinct moral duty to uphold the rule of law in doing so.

III. The Last Line of Protection

I said that being killed by a police officer is morally akin to being killed by one's mother or one's husband. Each of these people is duty-bound to protect one from being killed, and each strays as far as it is possible to stray from performing that duty by becoming one's killer himself or herself. In this

---

[31] Cf Michael Bohlander's reaction to the famous hypothetical discussed by the German Federal Constitutional Court at 1 BvR 357/05 (2006) in which an air force pilot, now on policing duties, is ordered to shoot down a hijacked airliner in order to prevent its being used as a missile by the hijackers against a civilian target. Bohlander writes: 'there is no balancing exercise; [the passengers] are, to put it bluntly, already dead'. See his 'In extremis—hijacked airplanes, "collateral damage" and the limits of criminal law' [2006] *Criminal Law Review* 579. Even Bohlander describes this view as 'harsh'. It is hard to see why he would find it harsh if he really believed it. Not surprisingly, and rightly, the Federal Constitutional Court rejected it, although they bent over too far backwards in doing so, and concluded that the shooting down must be unjustified if the duty to the passengers still holds. Not so. This reasoning reflects the pernicious effects of the propositions about conflicts of duty and justified breach of duty that I rejected earlier (at n 20 and n 21 above).

[32] There is a very large literature on the scope and basis of this loss of right. François Tanguay-Renaud and I have published some reflections on the topic in 'Desert and Avoidability in Self-Defense' (2011) 122 *Ethics* 111, where citations to other recent treatments can also be found.

dimension, I claimed, killings by the police are among the morally worst there can be. But can things get worse still? Yes. There is a further aggravating feature in at least some domestic cases which also extends to many if not all killings by police officers.

Sometimes people have nobody else to turn to for protection beyond the supposed protector who turns on them. Think of children who are sexually abused by their parents, where one parent is the abuser as principal and the other is complicit, usually by turning a blind eye to the abuse, but sometimes in even more degenerate ways. Or think of teenagers hoodwinked into thinking they are going on a family holiday but in fact being kidnapped for forced marriage by their parents. Or think of spouses facing systematic domestic violence from which, gradually deprived by their spouse of any social infrastructure attuned to their urgent needs, they have (or reasonably believe that they have) no realistic means of escape. In such cases it is often not only that the supposed protector does the very things that he or she is supposed to be protecting against; often it is also that there is nobody else to protect against the protector-turned-abuser. It is no good to say: 'Call the police!' 'Tell your teacher!' 'Get a court order!' The victims may reasonably fear that outside interventions will only make things worse, and so do not think of them as providing a further line of protection. Often that judgement is encouraged and then exploited by the abuser. But it need not be encouraged or exploited in order to add yet more to the enormity of his or her wrong. That the abuser is *de facto* the last line of protection against abuse makes his or her protective duty all the more stringent, and his or her violations of it all the worse.

The victims' fears of outside involvement are not always misplaced. Because of ways in which the rule of law ties their hands, or for other institutional reasons, police officers (and other officers of the law) may be unable to provide very effective protection against errant protectors such as these. Sometimes that may itself be a failure of duty on the part of the police, calling for strong justification or excuse (justification or excuse in which the fact that the rule of law ties their hands surely plays a large role). But note that the call for justification or excuse here is made more pressing by the fact that the 'last line of protection' consideration applies *a fortiori* to the police themselves. Under the rule of law, the police are there, *inter alia*, to give everyone somewhere else to turn, a final line of protection when other lines of protection, such as those that are supposed to be built into family relationships, break down. That applies equally to wrongdoers seeking protection from rough 'community' justice. They too are supposed to have the police at their disposal as a last line of protection against the 'community'. So when police officers do the very thing that they are supposed to have protected one against, say by leaving one to the mercies of the baying mob, there is a further aggravation that we have not yet detailed. They not only fail in their protective duty (bad enough); they not only turn that duty on its head (worse); if the rule of law prevails, they also leave those whom they are there to protect, with nowhere else to turn (the worst so far).

You may say that this is an exaggeration. One paltry police officer is rarely one's last line of protection in the relevant sense, for one paltry police officer is not the police. True, if a police officer kills one in an isolated spot then in a sense he or she personally was one's last line of protection; but in that sense any killer who kills one in an isolated spot is one's last line of protection. So that is not the relevant sense. The relevant sense of 'line' here is the 'thin blue line', the police understood as an institution. In the Tomlinson case, for example, the deadly mistake may turn out to have been that of a single officer from whom the police as a force failed, admittedly, to provide protection, but whose actions were not, we may dare to hope, taken on behalf of the police force as a whole. Contrast the de Menezes case, in which—so it appears—the officers present acted in a concerted way and more or less correctly implemented police operational guidelines covering (what they took to be) the situation.[33] Mr de Menezes was not just up against a rogue officer, or even just a rogue team of officers. He was up against a whole system that had, by the time of his death, turned from his protector into his assassin. He had nowhere else to turn because the system that had turned against him was, according to the principles of the rule of law, his last line of protection. That seems to me to make the de Menezes case, in one respect, even more morally troubling.

But here we hit a worry. I said that, if the rule of law prevails, the police are the last line of protection. So, if the rule of law prevails, the fact that it was the police who failed to protect one is a matter of particular moral moment. But if the police fail to protect one, in the systematic way just described, doesn't that entail that the rule of law doesn't prevail? In which case, surely, the failure is promptly rendered less morally momentous, because the condition for its special moral moment ('if the rule of law prevails') is not met? There are several reasons for doubting this argument. Most important, it seems to me, is this: those who have the moral duty to uphold the rule of law (or any other moral ideal) cannot rely on the fact that it is not upheld as any kind of mitigation for their failure to uphold it. The police are duty bound, as upholders of the rule of law, to maintain themselves as the last line of protection, and to prevent rogue forces (vigilante groups, private militias,

---

[33] Possibly they had not been given the order to implement them, itself a very serious breach which I am ignoring here. *Stockwell One*, n 14 above, at p 121.

neighbourhood gangs, mafia protection rackets, renegade intelligence units, and such like) from usurping that position by providing a further line of protection operating above the law. When the police do not provide the relevant protection, it is no excuse that they never do provide it because they are no longer what Robert Nozick calls the 'dominant protective agency'.[34] It is their duty to be that agency. That fact forges a close connection, one of several, between the moral duty to protect that we discussed in section II A and the moral duty to uphold the rule of law that we discussed in section II B.

IV. Dicey's Doctrine Revisited

It may seem that, in all this reflection on the moral position of police officers and police forces, we have lost sight of our original plan. I promised to explain how a defender of the Diceyan 'citizens in uniform' doctrine could consistently believe that police officers are in a special moral position because they are police officers. I have given extended attention to that special moral position, at times analogizing it to the moral position of parents, spouses, friends, and so on, without ever explaining how any of this was meant to relate to the Diceyan doctrine. All I established was (a) that I believe in the Diceyan doctrine as a way of implementing the rule of law in England, and (b) that I believe that the police are in a special moral position. I did nothing, you may say, to show that these two beliefs are consistent, never mind mutually conducive.

But is that true? My discussion was meant to show the appeal of the view that the differences between the duties of police officers and of other people, in other roles, are ordinary moral differences. Although police officers as such are indeed in special moral positions, there is no distinct 'political' morality applicable to them that displaces ordinary moral judgement. Morality is just morality, and it applies to people. It applies to public officials (judges, soldiers, parliamentarians, police officers, local authority librarians, etc) because they are people. They do not stop being people and hence do not stop being bound by morality when they put on their uniforms, or otherwise go on duty.

Of course when they go on duty there are some adjustments in their moral positions, some new moral duties and some new moral permissions, but that is simply because everyone's moral position is affected by the activities they engage in and the roles and relationships they are in when they engage in

---

[34] Nozick, *Anarchy, State, and Utopia* (New York: Basic Books Inc, 1974) eg at 54.

them. *In this respect,* becoming a police officer or a soldier is just like becoming a lover, an architect, a pen-friend, a journalist, a plumber, a member of cabin crew, a polar explorer, a TV chef, a hillwalker, or a foster-parent. It is a morally relevant change in circumstances; there are new tasks to perform and hence new moral duties to fulfil and, sometimes, new permissions to enable them to be fulfilled well. I italicized 'in this respect' to remind you that the various roles on this list are wildly diverse in other respects. It is very important not to think, for example, that police officers owe protection to the public on the same relational basis on which Sophie owes protection to her own (more than she does to other people's) children. A police officer who stops to ask whether the people that need to be rescued from that derailed train or hijacked aircraft are 'our' people has lost his or her way, and should not be working for the police.[35] But that is a problem distinct from the one we have been discussing. I did not suggest here that there is a single basis or rationale for moral duties, or that they all have a standard structure (eg second-personal, relational). I only suggested that they are all part of morality, and that morality binds police officers on duty just as it binds anyone else. Nobody can evade it by saying: 'I work for the government now'. For morality goes with one wherever life takes one, and is never displaced by the supposed demands of one's work, which always, on the contrary, answer to morality and give one, in themselves, no excuse when one violates it.

This view about the unity of morality seems to be what Thorburn has trouble accepting. For him it is 'not at all obvious why ordinary citizens should ever have decision-making authority over their fellow citizens'.[36] What he finds 'particularly troubling about the exercise of such decision-making powers is that they seem to be wielded by individuals with no special status that could explain their authority to make such decisions'.[37] And the main reason why he finds this troubling is that 'if literally *anyone* can make decisions about others' most basic interests in life, liberty, security, and property, then the law's claim that each person is sovereign over herself and her basic interests is hollow indeed'.[38] In other words, he thinks, there is one morality for the rest of us, and there is another for the authorities (even if we sometimes cross the line and stand in for them *pro tempore*). The two moralities have different subject matters. One is the morality of authority and coercion. The other is the morality of, I suppose, everything else. But this underestimates the role of both authority and coercion, their justified role, in

---

[35] For further reflections on this topic, see Gardner, 'Relations of Responsibility', n 23 above.
[36] Thorburn, 'Justifications, Powers, and Authority', n 8 above, at p 1118.
[37] Thorburn, 'Justifications, Powers, and Authority', n 8 above, at p 1125.
[38] Thorburn, 'Justifications, Powers, and Authority', n 8 above, at pp 1125–6, emphasis in original.

ordinary life (and not only with children). Meanwhile it overestimates the role of authority and coercion in the work of public officials. We deliberately did not focus attention, here, on the use of coercion or authority by police officers. We focused attention instead on killings by police officers. That they kill (or injure, exploit, lie, intimidate, conspire, discriminate, steal, etc) in their role as police officers makes a number of moral differences, some of which I sketched. But note that the moral differences as I sketched them are always ordinary moral differences, of a type that we all encounter in our daily lives as we move among our various roles and relationships and try to adapt to their circumstances. As Thorburn anticipates that I will say,[39] being a police officer—and, I would add, a public official of any kind—is just another of those circumstances to adapt to.

Thorburn's resistance to the Diceyan 'citizens in uniform' doctrine comes mainly, I think, from his denial of the unity of morality. My relative ease with the Diceyan doctrine is consonant, in turn, with my acceptance of the unity of morality. In the unity view, to repeat, we are still people, and still answer to morality, even when we put on our uniforms. Likewise, according to the Diceyan doctrine, we always answer to the law as ourselves, and we can't hide behind our public roles when we do it. That doctrine about responsibility before the law parallels closely the moral picture that I have tried to sketch out. Of course, to repeat a point I made in section I, I don't believe that the Diceyan doctrine is the only way to go about regulating public officials that is compatible with that moral picture. The Diceyan doctrine is a particularly radical solution that emphasizes the fundamental similarities between the moral position of public officials and the rest of us, and plays down some of the local differences. In particular, it doesn't attach importance to the mere fact that one is a public official in the way morality in the raw (sometimes) does. Dicey did not disguise the fact that his doctrine was a particularly radical solution. On the contrary, he relished it and trumpeted it. Recall his perhaps excessively proud words: 'In England the idea of legal equality, or of the universal subjection of all classes to one law administered by the ordinary courts, has been pushed to its utmost limit.'

---

[39] Thorburn, 'Two Conceptions of Equality', n 12 above, at p 6.

7

Puzzling About State Excuses as an Instance of Group Excuses

*François Tanguay-Renaud**

I. Why and How to Reflect upon State Excuses

Can the state, as opposed to its individual human members in their personal capacity, intelligibly seek to avoid blame for unjustified wrongdoing by invoking duress, provocation, a reasonable mistake in justification, or other types of excuses? Insofar as it can, should such claims ever be given moral and legal recognition? It is certainly not uncommon to encounter offhand statements to the effect that at least some state excuses are both conceivable and legitimate.[1] However, the issue has yet to receive the sustained philosophical attention it deserves. Few theorists speak to it specifically, and those who do typically discard rather rashly the possibility of genuine state excuses. This theoretical neglect is symptomatic of a more general lack of analytical attention to the conditions that must obtain for the state to be legitimately held responsible for wrongdoing in law and morality. In this chapter, my aim is to start filling this gap by mapping out the topic of state excuses in a way that will, hopefully, spur a more systematic discussion of

* Associate Professor at Osgoode Hall Law School, and Member of the Graduate Faculty of the Department of Philosophy at York University, Toronto. Special thanks are owed to Antony Duff, John Gardner, Stuart P Green, Philip Pettit, Andrew P Simester, Walter Sinnott-Armstrong, Victor Tadros, and Ekow Yankah for constructive discussions, comments, and criticisms. I also thank all participants in the two workshops that led to this edited collection.
  [1] For example, in his recent book on *The Constitutional State* (Oxford: Oxford University Press, 2010) 131, N W Barber remarks in passing that 'A state which enters into an unjust war in a climate of moral panic is, all other things being equal, less reprehensible than a state which enters into that same war whilst fully aware of its injustice'. For an argument assuming the availability of at least some excuses for domestic state wrongdoing, see T Sorell, 'Morality and Emergency' (2003) 103 Proceedings of the Aristotelian Society 21, 33–4.

its various facets, including its relationship with the wider question of when the state may legitimately be singled out to bear adverse normative consequences for wrongdoing. I say that my aim is limited to 'mapping out' the topic because an important first step in understanding state excuses is to identify properly the many complex and controversial theoretical puzzles they raise.

In a bid to remain ecumenical, I adopt a wide understanding of excuses that comprises the core pleas which, for right or for wrong, have sometimes been treated as excuses in recent theoretical debates about individual responsibility in morality and law. By that, I mean claims that although a given course of conduct was, all things considered, wrong, it was not blameworthy—or was less blameworthy, in the case of a partial excuse— because it was (1) 'justified' or 'warranted' from the epistemic perspective of the actor, (2) reasonably motivated by reasonable emotions or other understandable cognitive or affective attitudes, (3) non-responsible, or (4) a hybrid of two or more of these claims. Of course, there are important differences between these four types of claims. In fact, some think of these differences as being so salient that they exclude the first type of claim from the category of excuses altogether and reclassify it as justificatory. Others, who argue that excuses are primarily reasons-based and responsibility-affirming, would differentiate the third type of claim, and perhaps some instances of the fourth, as claims of exemption from, or denial of, responsibility *simpliciter*. While these reclassifications often track deep and important dissimilarities,[2] they remain contentious. Given the exploratory nature of my project, I avoid pre-empting meaningful discussion of any possible state excuses by assuming that restrictive views such as these can simply be transposed onto the domain of state responsibility.

Claims of state justification tend not to elicit the same amount of suspicion as claims of state excuses. For example, arguments about the justification of state coercion, state punishment, and state-led warfare pervade moral, political, and legal philosophy. Yet, it is not unusual to find moral and criminal law theorists who, like Andrew Simester, maintain that excuses 'are simply inapplicable to artificial actors such as the state'.[3] This assumption is also deeply entrenched in other legal fields concerned with the regulation of state wrongdoing. For example, Alan Brudner writes that, while they may be

---

[2] I emphasize some of them in relation to individual excuses in F Tanguay-Renaud, 'Individual Emergencies and the Rule of Criminal Law' in F Tanguay-Renaud and J Stribopoulos (eds), *Rethinking Criminal Law Theory* (Oxford: Hart Publishing, 2012) 21.

[3] A P Simester, 'Necessity, Torture and the Rule of Law' in V V Ramraj (ed), *Emergencies and the Limits of Legality* (Cambridge: Cambridge University Press, 2008) 289, 300.

justified in infringing rights, 'States cannot be constitutionally *excused* for violating rights'.[4]

Such brisk rejections of state excuses are intriguing, especially given the fact that the law of several oft-theorized jurisdictions provides for blame and even punishment of the state and state organs for wrongdoing. For example, the Criminal Code of Canada makes clear that 'municipalities' and other 'public bodies' may, like private organizations, be held responsible and punished for criminal wrongdoing.[5] In the context of some civil actions, public authorities may also be subjected to punitive damages.[6] The constitutional context is no exception. Admittedly, constitutional law continues to be primarily understood in terms of the regulation of the legal validity of exercises of state powers, rather than in terms of the regulation of state wrongdoing, as evidenced by the remedies usually granted for rights violations—that is, legal invalidity and procedural remedies such as exclusion of evidence or stay of proceedings. That being said, state constitutional wrongdoing is regularly condemned and may even be punished. For example, punitive damages are sometimes deemed an 'appropriate and just remedy' for egregiously unjustified violations of rights under s 24(1) of the Canadian Charter of Rights and Freedoms.[7] In international law, the possibility of criminally censuring and punishing states for wrongdoing has often been contemplated and defended over the years, even if the legal status of 'international crimes of state' remains uncertain.[8] Be that as it may, condemnation of state behaviour in United Nations resolutions, as well as through diplomatic channels, is

[4] A Brudner, 'Excusing Necessity and Terror: What Criminal Law Can Teach Constitutional Law' (2009) 3 *Crim L and Philosophy* 147, 148.

[5] Criminal Code RSC 1985 c C-46, ss 2, 22.1, 22.2. Here, Canada is not alone. See eg SP Green, 'The Criminal Prosecution of Local Governments' (1994) 72 *North Carolina L Rev* 1197. Some jurisdictions are more hostile to the idea, like France (Code pénal, ss 121–2) and the Netherlands (R de Lange, 'Political and Criminal Responsibility' (2002) 6(4) *Electronic J of Comparative L* 305, 318–20 <http://www.ejcl.org/64/art64-18.pdf>).

[6] See eg Crown Liability and Proceedings Act RSC 1985 c C-50, ss 17–18 (Canada).

[7] See eg *Crossman v The Queen* (1984) 9 DLR (4th) 588 (Federal Court, Trial Division); *Patenaude v Roy* (1988) 46 CCLT 173 (Superior Court of Quebec); *Freeman v West Vancouver (District)* (1991) 24 ACWS (3d) 936 (Supreme Court of British Columbia). More generally, see *Doucet-Boudreau v Nova Scotia (Minister of Education)*, 2003 SCC 62, par 87, where the Supreme Court of Canada establishes that '[a] superior court may craft any remedy that it considers appropriate and just in the circumstances', for violations of constitutional rights.

[8] For an argument that some international crimes of state are on the threshold between *lex ferenda* and *lex lata*, see N H B Jørgensen, *The Responsibility of States for International Crimes* (Oxford: Oxford University Press, 2000). For a forceful defence of the intelligibility and legitimacy of state criminalization in international law, see D Luban, 'State Criminality and the Ambition of International Criminal Law' in T Isaacs and R Vernon (eds), *Accountability for Collective Wrongdoing* (Cambridge: Cambridge University Press, 2011) 61.

a commonplace. Last but not least, popular and political indictments of states and state bodies as 'wrongdoers' or 'criminal' abound, as do philosophers' characterizations of such entities as moral agents susceptible of moral censure for wrongful deeds.[9]

Of course, the questions of whether and how the state may legitimately be blamed or punished for wrongdoing, as well as what understandings of 'the state' render such enquiries intelligible, require further investigation in their own right.[10] In this chapter, though, I start with the assumption that at least some of the practices of blame and punishment listed above are legitimate and target entities which detractors of state excuses would, or should, themselves readily incorporate in their understanding of the state.

The question then becomes what reasons there may be for thinking that exculpatory claims of excuses—as opposed to, say, claims of justification—are unavailable to the state and, thus, should not be recognized. Some do not share my working assumption, and believe that whatever the state does is necessarily justified. Therefore, they argue, the question of state excuses never arises. This position finds both moral and legal instantiations. At the moral level, some equate the state with the justified pursuit of the public interest and characterize as private, or non-state, any actions that depart from it. At the legal level, the argument is usually that the state is no more and no less than a (domestic) legal system, such that no deed can be attributed to it at the domestic level unless that deed is legally authorized or permitted in some way—for example, through the recognition of a legal justification. Such challenges to the intelligibility of unjustified state wrongdoing and, thus, to the possibility of state excuses are myopic. As I argue elsewhere, they fail to give sufficient consideration to the complexity of what many modern states' socio-legal constitutions enable them to do, sometimes in defiance of morality or extralegally. They also fail to give adequate attention to existing practices of moral and legal censure for behaviour that can be said, to a meaningful extent, to be organizationally programmed by the state.[11] What is more, they tend to ride roughshod over many important puzzles related to

---

[9] Recall, for example, Hannah Arendt's writings on the acts of Adolf Eichmann: 'crimes of this kind were and could only be, committed under a criminal law and by a criminal state'. H Arendt, *Eichmann in Jerusalem: A Report on the Banality of Evil* (New York: Viking Press, 1963) 240. See also J Gardner, 'Prohibiting Immoralities' (2006) 28 *Cardozo L Rev* 2613, 2628.

[10] I make some progress in addressing these underexplored questions in F Tanguay-Renaud, 'Criminalizing the State' (2013) *Crim L and Philosophy* (forthcoming), DOI: 10.1007/s11572-012-9181-x, <http://www.springerlink.com/content/j586831r55125x1/>.

[11] See 'Criminalizing the State', n 10 above, as well as F Tanguay-Renaud, 'The Intelligibility of Extralegal State Action: A General Lesson for Debates on Public Emergencies and Legality' (2010) 16 *Legal Theory* 161.

what specific justifications should be afforded (or not) to the state for prima facie wrongdoing. Thus, I mostly disregard such contentions here.

I say 'mostly' because there may still be a methodological lesson to be drawn from such challenges. Even if we accept that unjustified state wrong-doing is intelligible, there remains an important debate to be had about how it can best be explained. Should we think of states, and state bodies or institutions, as real and irreducible moral agents who, like individual human agents, can perpetrate wrongs and, possibly, also claim excuses for themselves? Or should we instead concede that wrongdoing states are no more than fictions to which the conduct, wrongs, blameworthiness and, perhaps, excuses of certain human agents may legitimately be attributed? This controversy about the nature of the state and state responsibility is not new in moral and legal theory circles, and parallels in many ways debates about the responsibility of organizations more generally.[12] As I indicated earlier, I cannot get to the bottom of it here. Yet, I cannot ignore it completely, given its undeniable relevance to the question of whether and how we should think about state excuses. Therefore, in sections II and III below, I appraise the plausibility of state claims of excuses in terms of both of these leading paradigms, and suggest that some such claims are indeed consistent with both. Note, however, that since excuses are primarily rebut-tals of blameworthiness, since the core case of blame is blame that has a blameworthy moral agent as its direct object, and since the attribution of blameworthiness to, and blaming of, a posited fiction is at best a non-standard case, I will consider the realist paradigm first, and the fiction paradigm second. Note further that, in both cases, I will primarily focus on the possibility of state excuses in morality. While, often, my arguments will also bear directly on the possibility of state excuses in law, and while I will sometimes even explicitly discuss legal excuses, I wish to leave open the further question of whether moral excuses should always be given legal effect.

With such caveats in mind, let me ask again: assuming that unjustified wrongdoing can be attributed to the state, and that the state can be blamed and, perhaps even, punished for it, why should excuses be unavailable to it? Objections are typically of two kinds. Some are metaphysical. They rest on the assumption that excuses reflect profoundly human characteristics and are, therefore, unavailable to organizations such as states and institutional state bodies. Other objections are moral and hold that, even if the state and its institutional organs are entities that can invoke excuses, such claims should

---

[12] For a useful survey of such general debates, see P Cane, *Responsibility in Law and Morality* (Oxford: Hart Publishing, 2002) 143–71.

not be recognized given the moral position of the state. In what follows, I discuss objections of both kinds.

It is worth noting, at this stage, that many objections of the first kind, and perhaps also some of the second, may be aimed at organizations more generally, and not only at the state and its corporate organs. Accordingly, my inquiry will also be of relevance to the question of whether organizations, considered as a class, can intelligibly and legitimately make excuses.[13] I choose to focus on the state, however, out of concern that organizations such as private companies with more restricted constitutional aims and purposes and more constrained means of action may not as persuasively or generally be subject to blame qua irreducible agents—the first paradigm to be investigated.[14] I am also of the view that state excuses call for a discussion of further interesting moral objections that do not apply, or do not apply with the same force, to other organizations. That said, it is my hope that, insofar as my analysis is applicable to other organizations, the reader will be inclined to employ it, *mutatis mutandis*, to elucidate the intelligibility and legitimacy of their excuses.

II. Excusing the State Qua Irreducible Moral Agent?

A. Philip Pettit's model of corporate/state agency

An increasing number of contemporary theorists conceive of the state as a kind of corporate (group, collective—I use these terms as synonyms) organization that can itself be a moral agent. How can this be if, according to the time-honoured objection, corporate organizations have no discernible bodies or minds of their own? The argument tends to rest on the assumption that some groups of interacting human beings can be relatively autonomous agents—that is, that they can form action-directing attitudes such as intentions, develop plans, and perform concerted actions, that cannot be fully reduced to those of their members—thanks at least in part to the operation of

---

[13] The question of the availability of excuses to non-state organizations, such as private corporations, is also notoriously under-theorized. Some theorists assume that corporations can simply 'mak[e] use of any available general excuses'. See J Horder, *Excusing Crime* (Oxford: Oxford University Press, 2004) 262. However, most leading theorists of corporate responsibility just ignore the topic altogether. See eg C Wells, *Corporations and Criminal Responsibility* (Oxford: Oxford University Press, 2001).

[14] About this concern, see further T M Scanlon, *Moral Dimensions: Permissibility, Meaning, Blame* (Cambridge, Mass: Belknap Press, 2008) 165.

a normative framework. Modern states, which are made up of various institutional organs themselves reliant on the agency of countless individuals whose identity changes over time, are often thought to fall into this category, alongside other similarly integrated corporate bodies. These states all have a constitution that constitutes and divides labour between their various organs, lays out principles of governance, and institutes authoritative decision-making, control, and review mechanisms. By jointly committing and adhering to this constitution to a reasonable extent, individual members allow their state qua corporate entity to form judgements and exhibit attitudes as a coherent whole, and to make reasonably consistent decisions over time on the evaluative propositions (including moral and legal reasons) that they present to it for consideration. Individual members also enable their state to execute its decisions by complying with constitutionally-adopted action plans—in the form of rules, practices, directives, and commands—devised to implement them.

The thought, then, is that modern states often have what it takes to be moral agents proper. Like other moral agents, they are regularly confronted with normatively significant choices, involving the possibility of doing right or wrong. Through the intercession of their individual members, they may also have the understanding and access to evidence necessary for making normative judgements about these choices, as well as the capacity to implement them in the world. Crucially, though, as I imply above, if they are to count as moral agents in their own right, states qua corporate organizations must also have the required control over the said judgements. That is, they must be able to judge and plan for action in ways that are irreducible to the judgements and plans of other agents, including those of their members. To see how this is possible, Philip Pettit's recent account of group agency is most helpful. Pettit's account remains one of, if not the, most careful and sophisticated account of irreducible group agency to date, and it is also one of the only such accounts to be quite transparently applicable to complex groups like states.[15] As a result, I use it as the main backdrop for my analysis, with the hope that most of the general insights I derive from its scrutiny will hold even if specific aspects of the account end up being refuted in future arguments.

Pettit argues that groups whose judgements depend on the judgements of more than one individual can be agents insofar as they respond rationally to

---

[15] See especially P Pettit, 'Responsibility Incorporated' (2007) 117 *Ethics* 171. Many of Pettit's insights were developed in collaboration with Christian List, as noted in their recent comprehensive restatement of the argument in C List and P Pettit, *Group Agency: The Possibility, Design, and Status of Corporate Agents* (Oxford: Oxford University Press, 2011). Since the separate articles on which I rely most were authored by Pettit himself, I keep referring to him alone, as a shorthand.

their environment on a reasonably consistent basis. Constitutions facilitate group agency by assigning decisional roles to the group's members and setting limits on what they can and cannot do. To the extent that the group's constitution provides sufficient constraints against internal inconsistencies, the group operating under it may then be a relatively autonomous agent over time (despite deriving all its matter and energy from its individual human members). Pettit argues that constitutional constraints are sufficient for a group to be autonomous in this sense when they ensure that, under normal conditions, reason is 'collectivized,' such that majority views do not always prevail and the group's attitudes cannot be described as a simple majoritarian function of the members' attitudes. In Pettit's own words: 'Autonomy is intuitively guaranteed by the fact that on one or more issues the judgement of the group will have to be functionally independent of the corresponding member judgements, so that its intentional attitudes as a whole are more saliently unified by being, precisely, the attitudes of the group.'[16] He also insists that decision procedures must be in place to guarantee that the group can change and correct its irreducible attitudes over time, so as to ensure the minimal rational coherence and integrity that we expect of agents proper.

The claim, then, is that state constitutions often ensure such relative state autonomy and minimal diachronic rational coherence and integrity by imposing a variety of balances and checks on state decision-making—for example, separation of powers, federal division of powers, judicial review of administrative and legislative action, *stare decisis*, elections, impeachment procedures, and so forth. Depending on how they are constituted, discrete institutional state organs pertaining to the executive, legislative, or judicial branch—sometimes at both federal and state, or provincial, levels—can also be imbued with such relatively autonomous agency. Commonly-discussed examples include municipalities, public corporations, the army, provincial governments, various administrative agencies, as well as the executive as a whole.[17] When such suitably-constituted group organizations arrange for moral or legal wrongs to be perpetrated, given the decisions they license and the constitution by which they channel those decisions, they are fit to be held responsible and, possibly, blamed for them qua irreducible 'source of the deed'.

Focusing on the state as a whole for the sake of simplicity, one may interject here that, even if this account is sound in respect of developed

---

[16] Pettit, 'Responsibility Incorporated', n 15 above, at p 184.

[17] Even if such state organs obviously do not constitute 'the state' as a whole, they typically form significant parts of it, such that consideration of their agency and possible excuses dovetails with a discussion of state excuses. An explanation of the precise nature of their connection to the state is outside the ambit of this chapter.

liberal democratic states, other states may not be sufficiently well organized to respond rationally to their environment on a consistent basis qua irreducible corporate agents. How should we think of such states? Are they states to which a plea of insanity, mental disorder, or straight-out non-responsibility should be available against allegations of wrongdoing? I am tempted to answer with a qualified yes. Insofar as they do not have a sufficiently well-developed constitutional apparatus, or that their individual members do not commit to and comply with it enough, such states do not qualify as relatively autonomous moral agents capable of acting contrary to reason and answering to it. At best, they may be deficiently-constituted 'quasi-states', whose decisions and actions are, in general, reducible to the decisions and actions of some of their individual members. At worse, they are utterly disorganized 'failed states' that possess almost none of the characteristics of what we normally conceive as states.[18]

Here, one may think, lies the main difference with cases of individual insanity or mental disorder. Even when mentally-disordered individuals are thoroughly incapable of responding to reason, they, unlike quasi-states or failed states, remain embodied, identifiable and, in a sense, irreducible entities. Some may also argue that, as mentally disordered as they may be, human beings are deserving of a kind of respect and dignity that is not necessarily warranted, or warranted in the same way, in the case of degenerate forms of human organization like failed and quasi-states. There is certainly some truth to this line of argument. However, I still think the analogy between individual and state insanity can be preserved to a meaningful extent if we insist that failed and quasi-states can remain identifiable in some respects—say, territorially and in the eyes of certain relevant national and international actors—and that, like the mentally disordered, they might, in some possible world, be 'cured' or re-organized in a way that makes state agency possible. For example, it is conceivable that, through its own resources and international assistance, the failed state of Somalia (as we know it today) could one day develop out of its debilitating predicament. Thus circumscribed, the analogy would also seem to be applicable to identifiable institutional state organs and other sub-state corporate entities that lack irreducible agency, yet are susceptible of reorganization that would make it possible.

Unfortunately, this stretched analogy is only the beginning of our troubles. The next and more difficult question is whether a model of irreducible state

---

[18] I borrow this distinction from T Erskine, 'Assigning Responsibilities to Institutional Moral Agents: The Case of States and "Quasi-States"' (2001) 15 *Ethics and Int'l Affairs* 67, 79.

agency such as Pettit's can be consistent with claims of excuses that extend beyond claims of complete lack of responsibility.

B. The challenge of affect-based excuses with a cognitive twist

It is sometimes objected that many common individual excuses are grounded in conscious phenomenal experiences such as affective experiences and that, since states and corporate state bodies do not have such experiences of their own, they simply cannot claim these excuses. Consider the excuse of duress, which Andrew Simester, who champions this objection, explains in terms of unjustified wrongdoing perpetrated out of fear, when the fear in question may have driven a reasonable person to act thus.[19] This affect-based account of the excuse of duress is generally accepted and, *arguendo*, I shall assume its soundness. Simester's objection is that, since corporate organizations such as the state cannot experience the fear that is necessary to ground this excuse, it is not available to them. No doubt, their individual members can experience the required fear, and may sometimes be excused for their wrongdoing on that basis, but states and state bodies qua irreducible corporate agents cannot.

I could not hope to do justice here to the deep and complex metaphysical question of whether corporate entities like states and state bodies can have affective experiences and other conscious phenomenal states of their own. However, some general remarks seem apposite. If functionalist thinkers like Pettit are right about corporate agency, then given some plausible empirical claims about states—that they have decision-making mechanisms, that their decisions can have reasonable coherence over time, etc—there seems to be no principled difficulty in ascribing genuine and irreducible cognitive states to them. According to such a view, states and other appropriately constituted corporate entities can quite literally make judgements, acquire beliefs about what they judge to be the case, intend actions, and so forth. However, the case for corporate affective states and other phenomenal experiences is more difficult to make.

Admittedly, there may be emotions, like anger, that arise among group members (who, by hypothesis, are otherwise never angry) when they are acting as part of a given group—that is, within the processes and relationships that constitute it. This anger might then be described as group, or group-related, anger. However, more needs to be said if the claim that this anger is irreducible to the anger experienced by individual members is to be made

---

[19] Simester, 'Necessity, Torture, and the Rule of Law', n 3 above, at p 299.

out. One could perhaps seek to extend the functionalist argument and claim that phenomenal states are also best explained functionally. Yet, I find it difficult to imagine how this claim could be persuasively developed. As Pettit himself recognizes, functionalist claims that corporate entities have emotions that are relatively autonomous from those of their individual members are generally suspect. It is one thing for states and corporate state institutions to be able to form distinct judgements, beliefs, intentions, and other action-directing attitudes by following, to a reasonable extent, whatever steps are prescribed in their constitution. It seems to be quite another for irreducible affective states to be generated in a similar way. In other words, there seems to be more to phenomenal states—say, to the experience of fear or anger—than mere questions of organizational structure and function.[20] Accordingly, it is at least plausible that Andrew Simester, who appears to think that such states are distinctively human (or, at least, animal as opposed to artificial), is correct.

To be sure, some theorists do defend the possibility of irreducibly collective emotions. However, their arguments tend to rest on the dubious premise that emotions can exist without affective experience. Thus, Margaret Gilbert, the most prominent advocate of collective emotions, adopts early on in her argument Martha Nussbaum's claim that some emotion-types may have no necessary phenomenal concomitant, citing the non-conscious fear of death as an example.[21] Besides the fact that the existence of non-conscious, non-affective emotional states is questionable, it is important to note the difference between the claim that every emotional state does not necessarily come with a specific and distinctive affective experience, and the claim that affect can altogether be absent from emotional experience. While the former claim is admittedly plausible, the latter is rather more counterintuitive. It may well be true that, unlike moods, which refer to purer forms of affective experience—think of free-floating depression, sadness, elation,

---

[20] P Pettit, 'Akrasia, Collective and Individual' in S Stroud and C Tappolet (eds), *Weakness of Will and Practical Irrationality* (Oxford: Oxford University Press, 2003) 68, 79. One should be careful when assessing the implications of this proposition. Many theorists hold that for an agent to be blameworthy and legitimately blamed this agent must be morally responsible in the sense of being able to respond to reasons. Some claim further that this ability requires the emotional capacity to be moved by moral concerns. It follows, they contend, that affect-less corporate organizations can never be blamed legitimately. See especially S Wolf, 'The Legal and Moral Responsibility of Organizations' in J R Pennock and J W Chapman (eds), *Criminal Justice: Nomos XXVII* (New York: New York University Press, 1985) 267. This position rests on an account of legitimate blame which Pettit, along with many other contemporary moral philosophers, forcefully resists. Besides, as I discuss further below, his account also allows that irreducible corporate organizations can, *derivatively*, be moved by the emotions of their constituent individual members.

[21] M Gilbert, 'Collective Guilt and Collective Guilt Feelings' (2002) 6 *J of Ethics* 115, 119–20, citing M Nussbaum, *Upheavals of Thought* (Cambridge: Cambridge University Press, 2001) 61.

or euphoria—emotions also have cognitive components, such as being directed at objects and involving beliefs about them. My fear of a dog, for example, does seem to involve a cognitive construal of a number of the dog's features (its salivating maw, its ferocious bark, its running towards me) as frightening. However, it does not follow that the relevant cognitive aspects of emotions can altogether be devoid of affective experience. Such a position seems radically out-of-touch with the phenomenology of emotions, and much current research has sought to discredit it.[22]

Then again, to the extent that affect-free 'emotional states' do exist or, following Nussbaum, that some 'emotions' are best explained in purely cognitive terms—say, as evaluative judgements that ascribe great importance to certain things or persons—it seems more accurate to treat them generically alongside other cognitive states, rather than as part of a distinctive emotional genre. Indeed, insofar as an 'emotion' is best explained as a mere configuration of beliefs or as a cognitive attitude, I see no reason not to label it and treat it as such. To repeat, according to an account such as Pettit's, suitably-constituted states and state institutions can have cognitive states (such as beliefs) and action-directing attitudes (such as intentions) of their own. It is phenomenal states, such as affective states, they cannot experience.[23]

Does this view entail that states cannot claim excuses grounded in their own affective experiences? The conclusion seems to follow, and follow as much in the realm of domestic law as in the realms of international law and morality writ large. Note, however, that even if states and corporate state institutions cannot claim affect-based excuses—or, more broadly, excuses grounded in their own phenomenal consciousness—they may still be able to claim excuses that are derivative from the phenomenal experiences of their individual members. Remember that, even if the account of group agency on which I am basing my analysis is an account of relatively autonomous group agency, it is still individual group members who supply all its matter and energy. So, for example, it is a state's individual members who introduce information and option-related evaluative propositions for its consideration. Insofar as the information and propositions thus introduced are distorted by, say, the fear experienced by the individuals introducing them, state judgements and intentions formed on their basis may turn out to be mistaken.

---

[22] See eg M Stocker, *Valuing Emotions* (Cambridge: Cambridge University Press, 1996); J Pankseep, *Affective Neuroscience* (Oxford: Oxford University Press, 1998); P Greenspan, *Emotions and Reason: An Inquiry into Emotional Justification* (New York: Routledge Chapman and Hall, 1988).

[23] Insofar as conative attitudes such as wishing, desiring, longing, or craving have phenomenal components, it may also be that corporate agents cannot have them, or can only have them partially. Pro-attitudes devoid of phenomenal components are more straightforwardly available to corporate agents. In this respect, intentions and other cognitively-defined pro-attitudes are least problematic.

Arguably, the greater and the more widespread the fear experienced by the members—which, in a liberal democracy, may include not only officials, but a large part of the citizenry—the likelier it is that their affective experience will influence state decision-making and cause corporate errors.

Consider, for example, the effect that the deep and widespread fear of sudden murderous attacks—which exists amongst important segments of Israel's general population and state officials—might have on state decisions. All else being equal, could this fear excuse, at least partially, some of Israel's harshest reactions, as well as some of the unjustified reactions of specific governmental and defence institutions, to events that do not constitute threats but are collectively perceived as such? All else being equal, could the dread of terrorist strikes that prevailed in the US after the events of 11 September 2001 at least partially excuse some of the state's legally and morally wrongful and unjustified responses—including indefinite pre-emptive detentions of both adults and children at Guantanamo Bay, official sanction and perpetration of degrading forms of treatment as means of interrogation, as well as unwarranted invasive military campaigns? At one point in his brief discussion of state excuses, Simester seems to open the door to this possibility by qualifying his argument, and recognizing that it might just be possible for states to invoke epistemic mistakes as excuses for wrong-doing. 'Epistemic mistake', he writes, is 'a quite different type of case'.[24]

Although Simester does not explain this statement any further, one important distinction is readily identifiable. Unlike duress, epistemic mistake is a cognition-based, as opposed to an affect-based, ground of exculpation. If, indeed, states and corporate state bodies can have cognitive abilities, they too may sometimes fall prey to epistemic failures and, thus, are vulnerable to making mistakes. Beyond what Simester recognizes, they may also fall prey to more radical distortions grounded in irresistible ignorance, as well as in other non-belief-based cognitive attitudes. Even more importantly for our immediate purposes, though, what Simester fails to acknowledge is that the factors that can cause state cognitive distortions not only include individual epistemic limitations—such as misleading or unavailable evidence—and other purely cognitive failings, but also phenomenological distortions experienced by individual members. In other words, when it comes to states and other irreducible corporate agents, cognitive distortions may not always be entirely cognitive. For example, affective distortions of the practical rationality of individual members may sometimes lie at the root of their corporate organization's cognitive failings. In this sense, it might sometimes be possible to speak of states and corporate state institutions that act while being 'blinded

---

[24] Simester, 'Necessity, Torture, and the Rule of Law', n 3 above, at p 300.

by fear' or 'blinded by anger' and then seek to be excused on that ground, with the proviso that the fear or anger in question is the fear or anger of their individual members. The same could also be said of states and state institutions acting in the grip of the (popular) mood of the moment.

Of course, this argument does not amount to a claim that Israel, the US, or any of their institutions *should* be excused for their unjustified wrongs on the ground of affectively-induced epistemic mistakes. What it does, however, is to elucidate further some key intricacies of cognitive distortion as a conceivable ground of excuse for them.

C. Some *sui generis* state qua corporate excuses?

These last remarks warrant a parenthetical note of methodological caution. The analysis as I have conducted it so far assumes that commonly-encountered individual excuses constitute the standard against which the intelligibility of excusatory claims by group agents should be assessed. In other words, my argumentative strategy has so far been to think of excuses in terms of commonly-encountered individual excuses—such as duress, provocation, and mistake in justification—and ask whether such claims are also available to irreducible group agents. Insofar as these agents have what it takes to claim such excuses—and they may not, as in the case of affective experiences—I see no reason why we should not, at least in principle, recognize their possibility (or so I will continue to assume). Then again, my remarks at the end of the last section highlight the fact that irreducible group agents form a special category of agents. Unlike individual agents, their existence and agency depend on, yet are irreducible to, the existence and agency of other (individual) agents. Doesn't this constitutional difference warrant a distinct, or perhaps more complex, approach to understanding at least some conceivable claims of group excuses? I think it might.

What it means for individuals to act appropriately qua ordinary individuals may differ from what it means for them to act appropriately qua members of a group agent, or so they may think or feel. While full commitment of individual members to the group, its constitutional operation, as well as its rational coherence and integrity over time, may ensure that the group behaves in the fashion of a virtuous agent, various members may sometimes be moved, for good or bad reasons, to act in less than committed ways. They may, for example, temporarily turn their eyes away from the group in order to act fairly, charitably, or humanely qua individuals, or because of affective or cognitive distractions, or simply because of selfish or biased inclinations. When this happens, the group may not act in the minimally rationally consistent way that we would expect of an agent proper.[25] Indeed, such lapses may even put the status of the group as an irreducible agent in jeopardy. At the same time, notice that they may not challenge this status to the same extent, as more fundamental structural deficiencies may, as we saw, generate failed or quasi-states.

Consider the case of the United States' failure to join the League of Nations in the 1920s. Although its president at the time, Woodrow Wilson, led an American charge for the League's creation and ensured that its constitutional covenant—contained in the Treaty of Versailles—would be crafted in a way that assumed US membership and leadership, the US Senate refused to ratify the treaty and, therefore, to join the organization. This senatorial rejection, primarily attributable to the opposition of a number of ideologically uncompromising Republican members, sowed the seeds for the League's collapse, which culminated in its inability to prevent the Axis Powers' aggressions that led to World War II.[26] Could Wilson, acting in the name of the United States, have claimed an excuse for his state's harmful volte-face by invoking the erratic character of the US's dualist system of reception of international treaty law—which involves negotiation and signature of treaties by the Executive, and *ex post facto* ratification by Congress? In other words, if a state (or other irreducible group agent) is imperfectly organized in a way that facilitates rational inconsistency of the sort just exemplified, could such a constitutional disorder ground an excuse?

The question is tantalizing since such organizational deficiencies, coupled with individual members' lapses in commitment to group rational integrity, may indeed explain a state's failure to live up to relevant behavioural standards. This kind of explanation may be especially forceful in cases, such as the one just described, where the deficient mode of organization is inherited from the past and is not easily changed, due to constitutional restrictions. Pettit claims that groups that fall prey to such momentary, yet radical, failures in rational coherence and integrity can retain their overall status as irreducible agents. They can do so, he argues, insofar as the bulk of their members remain generally disposed to play their part in the integration of the group as an agent proper. Such groups must also 'prove capable of acknowledging and denouncing the failure and, ideally, reforming their behaviour in the future—or if not actually achieving reform, at least establishing that the

---

[25] A minimum of rational coherence and integrity also seems necessary for individual human moral agency, even if the required threshold likely falls well short of perfection.

[26] See eg W F Kuelh and L K Dunn, *Keeping the Covenant: American Internationalists and the League of Nations, 1920–1939* (Kent: Kent State University Press, 1997).

failure is untypical'.[27] In circumstances in which a group meets these conditions, Pettit speaks of rational unity of 'a second-best sort: a unity that can exist in spite of the disunity displayed in actual behaviour'.[28] In respect of my League of Nations example, it could be argued that the volte-face at issue was untypical of US behaviour (at the time, at least), and that the US subsequently made significant efforts to impress upon other international actors that it should generally be trusted to live up to its representations and commitments (insofar as it made any). Thus, an exculpatory claim to the effect that, given its entrenched constitutional ordering, the US could understandably fail to act as a rationally unified agent in circumstances like the ones that led to its failure to join the League, is at least imaginable. Claims of this sort could also conceivably be made by more discrete state institutions acting within the national sphere.

When, if at all, these claims should be recognized is a further question. For what are mostly prudential (or strategic) reasons, international law tends to be reluctant to acknowledge states' internal deficiencies as acceptable grounds for exoneration. For example, it is often said that such an acknowledgement would inevitably lead to undue erosion of international regimes of state responsibility. However, there is no absolute moral bar against the invocation of internal deficiencies as exculpatory grounds. To return to the analogy with individual defences for a moment, criminal law sometimes recognizes that people who perpetrate harmful deeds while having momentarily lost touch with reason might legitimately be able to deny responsibility for these deeds, either fully or partially. Consider, for example, the oft-encountered defences of automatism and diminished responsibility.

Interestingly, Pettit would likely resist categorizing group claims of momentary constitutional disorder that make reliable decisions difficult as sheer denials of responsibility. He prefers to think of the group failures in question in terms of conflicts of 'inner voices'—that is, the voices of different members—that are analogous to conflicts between 'voices of the heart' and 'voices of the head' that give rise to more reasons-based (and responsibility-affirming) individual excuses such as normal cases of duress and provocation.[29] Of course, this kind of analogy between the excuses-generating 'inner voices' of individuals and groups is bound to be imperfect. The types of conflicting 'inner voices' at play and their role in promoting or impeding

---

[27] Pettit, 'Akrasia, Collective and Individual', n 20 above, at p 85.

[28] Pettit, 'Akrasia, Collective and Individual', n 20 above, at p 82.

[29] On the distinction between denials of responsibility and more reasons-based excuses, see J Gardner, *Offences and Defences: Selected Essays in the Philosophy of Criminal Law* (Oxford: Oxford University Press, 2007) 131–2, 179–82.

agency undoubtedly differ significantly as between groups and individuals. However, argues Pettit, insofar as we conceive of reason as a certain unified sort of pattern, the analogy can be instructive.[30] Notably, it invites us not to overlook the complex role of reason, broadly understood with all its cognitive and affective components, in group claims such as claims of excuses other than sheer insanity.

Pettit's reluctance to analogize too easily cases of group constitutional disorder and individual denials of responsibility also has the potential to shed contrasting light on the alluring analogy between exculpatory pleas of individual infancy and claims that developing states and state institutions may make in relation to various developmental hiccups. While normal young human infants are only minimally responsive to reason, they progressively acquire a more refined understanding of themselves and their surroundings as they age. The range of actions for which they are basically responsible—in the sense of being able to provide rational explanations for them—tends to increase correspondingly. Thus, many modern juvenile justice systems appropriately strive, with varying degrees of success, to hold children responsible only for wrongdoing for which they are basically responsible in this sense, and to modulate their remedies and sanctions accordingly.[31] I say that this approach is appropriate since pleas of human infancy are not claims of conflicting 'inner voices' in Pettit's sense, which may be amenable to appraisal in light of excusatory standards. They are denials of responsibility for alleged wrongdoing (at least in the form in which such wrongdoing is alleged).

States and state institutions may also make exculpatory claims of developmental infancy, yet it is not as clear that all such claims are best explained as sheer denials of responsibility. Consider, for example, the predicament of post-apartheid South Africa where, within a short period of time, a myriad of people of colour who had previously been excluded joined the civil service, and started implementing the Interim Constitution. Although these new state officials were gradually trained and mentored, and their transitional constitutional framework was progressively fleshed out, individual inconsistencies and mistakes were initially bound to take place, resulting in blunders, slip-ups and, possibly, wrongdoing at the corporate level. While, in such a case, it is also the group's capacity to respond appropriately to reason that is at

---

[30] Pettit, 'Akrasia, Collective and Individual', n 20 above, at pp 89–93.

[31] On the nature and importance of the distinction between 'being basically responsible' and 'being held responsible', see J Gardner, 'Hart and Feinberg on Responsibility' in M Kramer, C Grant, B Colburn and A Hatzistavrou (eds), *The Legacy of H.L.A. Hart* (Oxford: Oxford University Press, 2008) 121.

stake, Pettit teaches us that the developmental deficiencies in question may not obliterate the group's basically responsible agency, and susceptibility to be held responsible and blamed for its wrongful exercise. To repeat, there remains for Pettit a 'second-best' sense of unified, irreducible corporate agency which, in the face of teething problems, rests on the group's members' persistent and general commitment to its integration as an irreducibly constituted agent, as well as on the group's *ex post* reaffirmation and readjustment of this integration. Thus, unlike in cases of individual human infancy, corporate bodies that are initially unable to respond to reason appropriately due to developmental hiccups might still at times appropriately be held responsible and blamed for related wrongdoing.[32] Then again, it is also conceivable that these groups' blameworthiness—like the blameworthiness of older, more established groups struggling with constitutional disorders—may sometimes be mitigated, when relevant excusatory standards of institutional resilience, due diligence, as well as *ex post facto* denunciation, are met.[33]

Here, I am not denying that some states and state institutions with infant, frail, or limited decision-making structures may sometimes be basically responsible for some specific actions, while not being basically responsible for others. Indeed, such teetering reality may be especially frequent in infant states with constitutional deficiencies that exceed the mere inability to train officials adequately. In large part, this is because constitutional structures including agency-enabling balances and checks, such as the separation of powers, the rule of law, parliamentary democracy, and judicial review, take time to develop. As it were, France and the United Kingdom did not emerge from the state of nature overnight, and were likely non-responsible for many harms associated with their evolution. My goal here is simply to point out that there is almost certainly more to the corporate agency story than this, and that the possibility of *sui generis* corporate excuses, differing from common individual excuses, should not be overlooked. At the same time, the complex nature of these *sui generis* claims and the magnitude of the philosophical apparatus that would be needed to elucidate them fully prevent me from saying any more here, for fear of losing sight of my initial goal of mapping

---

[32] Note, however, Pettit's subsidiary and fiction-based 'developmental rationale' for holding both children and 'embryonic group agents' responsible and punishing them in some way for harm to which they are merely causally related: it incentivizes them to pull themselves together so as to avoid such harm in the future. Pettit, 'Responsibility Incorporated', n 15 above, at pp 198–201.

[33] This point finds reflection in discussions of how the existence of effective 'compliance programmes' in private corporations may affect how blameworthy they are, and how much they should be punished, for criminal wrongdoing. See eg C Gómez-Jara Díez, 'Corporate Culpability as a Limit to the Overcriminalization of Corporate Criminal Liability: The Interplay Between Self-Regulation, Corporate Compliance, and Corporate Citizenship' (2011) 14 *New Crim L Rev* 78.

out the many theoretical puzzles related to state excuses. Then again, I think have said enough to build at least a prima facie case for the intelligibility of group claims of excuses on the ground of constitutional disorder (short of sheer non-responsibility).

D. The lack of valuable self-interest objection to state excuses

Another prominent set of objections to the possibility of state qua corporate excuses has both metaphysical and moral aspects, which tend to be run together in argument. According to it, even if we grant that states have much of what it takes to make excuses—for example, that they are normally rational agents that can make errors in cognition and perhaps even undergo some forms of affective experiences—we should still never recognize their excusatory claims. The general thought is that corporate agents like states are purely instrumental creations that have no real interests or subjective values of their own. Insofar as they do—after all, the paradigm of corporate agency explored allows for irreducible group judgements and attitudes about what matters to the group's survival and what is important to the realization of its constitutional goals—then such group self-interest and values should never be given weight in law or morality more generally. Corporate agents exist, or should exist, exclusively to promote the interests and values of others—that is, of non-instrumental agents like human beings. Therefore, the objection holds, no recognition should ever be given to their self-interested excusatory claims. No matter what affective pressures they incur, or what mistakes they commit, states and state institutions should never be excused for wrong-fully privileging themselves. Nor should they be excused for any tendency they may have to do so. For example, they should never be excused under the heading of duress for acting wrongfully due to what were perceived as overbearing threats to *their* interests or subjective values.

In my view, the apparent strength of this line of argument comes primarily from its close affinity with the principle of value individualism, according to which the worth of the state (and, indeed, of anything else) must ultimately be appreciated in terms of its contribution to human life and its quality. If, indeed, it is only human interests and values that matter (here, some allow-ance may also be made for interests of other non-human conscious beings), then there seems to be no residual moral space for the recognition of the so-called interests or subjective values of irreducible corporate agents. One possible rejoinder might be that value individualism does not necessarily commit one to a purely instrumentalist view of corporate agency. If one could demonstrate that corporate agents like states or state institutions are intrinsically valuable as necessary constituents of goods that intrinsically enrich human life, then some limited recognition and protection of 'their interests'—or of their natural tendency to protect their interests—could, perhaps, be warranted (for example, in the form of excusatory concessions). Some have recently mounted spirited arguments in favour of the existence and value of groups' irreducible interests along related lines, and it may be that they are onto something.[34] However, powerful objections—questioning the metaphysical soundness of such arguments and the acceptability of their possible moral implications—continue to dominate current debates, and invite great theoretical caution.[35]

What is perhaps a less metaphysically doubtful and morally hazardous way of challenging the interest objection to corporate excuses is to cast doubt on another assumption that underlies it. I am referring here to the assumption that claims of excuses can be reduced to calls for moral or legal leniency for agents who wrongfully, though understandably, disregard the interests of others in order to protect their own. This assumption is unwarranted. It is simply untrue that valid excuses can only arise in the context of dilemmas between self-interest and the interests of others, where the wrongdoer is deemed to have stricken a balance between the two that is sufficiently virtuous to block or attenuate inferences of blame. Many excuses have nothing to do with self-interest, so that the question of whether or not corporate entities like states and state bodies have interests of their own is often quite irrelevant to their ability to make such claims legitimately.

It is true that *some* claims of excuses, such as those relying on sufficient displays of courage in the face of coercive threats, may be connected to questions of self-interest. As Aristotle once dramatized it, using the example of the citizen who risks being killed on the battlefield for the sake of his homeland, courage is a virtue of character that tends to arise out of a struggle between personal safety and external considerations, such as collective victory.[36] However, not all displays of virtue that may yield legitimate claims of excuses have the same structure. For example, loyalty, which the state may invoke in a bid to excuse wrongfully favouring citizens over non-citizens, is a virtue that, at its core, is other-regarding. A theory of morality that would

---

[34] See eg D G Newman, 'Collective Interests and Collective Rights' (2004) 49 *American J of Jurisprudence* 127; J Waldron, 'The Dignity of Groups' in J Barnard-Naudé, D Cornell & F du Bois (eds), *Acta Juridica 2008* (Cape Town: Juta & Company, 2009) 66.

[35] For potent examples of such scepticism, see M Dan-Cohen, 'Sanctioning Corporations' (2010) 19 *J of L and Policy* 15; D Rodin, *War and Self-Defense* (Oxford: Oxford University Press, 2002) 143–4.

[36] On courage generally and on Aristotle's understanding of it, see D Pears, 'The Anatomy of Courage' (2004) 71 *Social Research* 1.

only account for dilemmas between the pursuit of self-interest and the pursuit of the interests of others, exclusively allowing for excuses in such contexts, would be radically deficient. As the example of loyalty highlights, dilemmas of moral life can also arise between different ways of engaging with pursuits that have others' valuable interests at their heart, and valid claims of excuses might well be made in such contexts as well. Moreover, some claims of excuses have very little, if anything, to do with questions of interests writ large. Think, for example, of claims of epistemic mistake, constitutional disorder, or claims more akin to full or partial denials of responsibility (insofar as they are appropriately categorized as excuses). Thus, even if one concedes that states, like other corporate bodies, have no valuable interests of their own, the possibility of state excuses must not necessarily be ruled out. The range of available grounds of state excuses may then differ from the range of available grounds of individual excuses, as may the range of available grounds of corporate excuses in general, but this should not be taken to mean that states, or other irreducible corporate entities, may never make valid excuses.

E. Questioning the irreducible corporate agency model and related-excusatory claims

A more sweeping moral objection to state excuses, understood as excuses claimed by states or state institutions qua irreducible corporate agents, denies the very necessity for such excuses in the first place. Such excuses are thought to be unnecessary since practices consisting in holding corporate agents responsible for wrongdoing and, say, blaming and punishing them for it, are morally redundant. According to this line of objection, both the moral and legal regulation of human actions, be they individual or collective, and practices of accountability for wrongdoing can and should be articulated in exclusively *individualistic* terms. That is, insofar as we understand grounds and practices of moral and legal accountability for wrongdoing in suitably complex and nuanced ways—allowing for sufficiently broad accounts of complicitous and joint wrongdoing—the possibility of holding irreducible groups responsible, blaming them, and punishing them really becomes superfluous.[37] Thus, the question of whether irreducible group agents can invoke excuses turns out to be moot.

One possible rejoinder is as follows: an account of irreducible group agency like Pettit's has the advantage of providing a distinct ground for holding groups

---

[37] Christopher Kutz's work seems at least partly animated by this idea in his *Complicity: Ethics and Law for a Collective Age* (Cambridge: Cambridge University Press, 2000) and related subsequent essays.

such as states and their corporate institutions responsible and blaming them—say, because their actions made harm likely or inevitable—at times when no similar ground is available for holding individual contributors responsible and blaming them. This kind of shortfall of individual responsibility may arise when, for example, individual contributors to state action avoid being held responsible and blamed for their deeds owing to reasonable mistakes or ignorance, due care, duress, or other relevant excuses. Practices of state qua irreducible group responsibility may guard against such scenarios, as well as diminish the incentive for people to arrange things so as to increase their likelihood.

Here, one may be tempted to retort that, even if this rejoinder is sound, it is nevertheless self-defeating. Indeed, if the state can be excused for its wrongs when its individual members are excused for their own wrongful contributions, aren't shortfalls of responsibility unavoidable? This worry is largely unwarranted. First, excusable individual contributions to state action do not necessarily entail excusable state behaviour, and vice versa. For example, it is not because specific individual state members act mistakenly or under duress that their state or corporate state institution will necessarily act mistakenly. Multiple checks and balances are typically in place to reduce the likelihood of the former automatically translating into the latter. Grounds of responsibility may also be different for the state and its members, such that the excuses of one may have nothing to do with the wrongs of the other.

What is more, in respect of reasons-based excuses such as epistemic mistake or normal cases of duress or provocation, role-based considerations must also be factored in. In law, as in morality, excusatory standards often vary according to the roles played by those who claim excuses.[38] Thus, the standards of excusability applicable to individual state officials, although possibly more stringent than the standards applicable to ordinary people, may be nowhere near as stringent as the standards applicable to given corporate state institutions or, perhaps even more strikingly, to the state in all its grandeur. States are typically designed and built to be outstandingly strong and knowledgeable, in order to solve social problems that individuals and smaller corporate entities acting in unco-ordinated ways are unable to solve—such as the securing of social order, safety, trust, and other conditions of societal co-operation. They tend to have access to multiple and often better sources of information than other social actors (including their members taken individually). They also tend to have greater resources, authority over many more people, and more extensive opportunities for contingency

---

[38] See generally Gardner, *Offences and Defences*, n 30 above, at pp 121–39, 245.

planning and training than other agents. With such attributes come greater responsibilities and greater (arguably, much greater) expectations of virtue, skill, and reasonableness. Insofar as the idea of capacity to do otherwise matters to some excuses, different standards may also be applicable to states and their individual members in this regard. Therefore, even in situations where all individual state members are excused for their contributions to state wrongdoing, the state and its institutions may well not be. Of course, the possibility of a shortfall of responsibility always remains. However, if I am correct, such shortfalls are likely to be rare.

Now, it might also be possible to resist the shortfall of responsibility argument at a more general level by arguing that the exonerating force of epistemic limitations and other types of pressures inherent in organizational settings is less significant than has traditionally been believed. One salient reason for this scepticism is as follows: insofar as individuals know—or, perhaps, ought to know—that they are participating in the operation of a group decisional framework that may, by its very constitutional design, yield bad or harmful outputs, it is questionable whether they should ever be able to escape consequential responsibility by invoking the irreducibility of these outputs. Alternatively, it may be that these individuals should only ever be entitled to partial excuses that mitigate their blameworthiness for wrongful participation in collective harm, as opposed to negating it altogether.[39] Of course, this analysis also leaves open the possibility that there may be scenarios in which the conduct of no individual contributor to harmful state action quite amounts to wrongdoing, or only amounts to relatively insignificant wrongdoing. Yet, if the line of argument just outlined is sound, the shortfall of individual responsibility argument may not provide as forceful a case for holding irreducible group agents responsible as some think it does.

Furthermore, even insofar as the shortfall of responsibility argument provides a compelling case for group responsibility, including the possibility of blame and its cognates, some sceptical minds may still object. They may object that, on any plausible account, conditions for irreducible group responsibility will be so demanding that many states and state institutions, such as courts, legislatures, ministerial cabinets, and administrative agencies, are unlikely to meet them, or to meet them on any consistent basis. It cannot simply be assumed, they might insist, that states and their institutions are agents capable of being held responsible and blamed in an irreducible sense, like Pettit and others sometimes seem inclined to do. More radically, some might also advance objections to the very metaphysical possibility of irreducible

---

[39] Jeff McMahan makes a forceful argument along such lines in relation to individual soldiers' decisions to fight in unjust wars in *Killing in War* (Oxford: Oxford University Press, 2009) 137–54.

group agency and responsibility, and simply reject accounts such as Pettit's as misguided.

Even if, *arguendo*, one accepts these objections, care should still be taken not to throw the baby out with the bath water. If, indeed, the shortfall of individual responsibility argument is a valid one, as I think it at least sometimes is, then there will likely remain considerable pressures—grounded in reasons of deterrence, justice, expressiveness and symbolism, as well as various other pragmatic concerns—for practices of group accountability for collectively facilitated harm that cannot be blamed, in whole or in part, on individual wrongdoers. Thus, there may sometimes be good reasons to treat the state—even if only understood as a socio-legal or functional grouping without irreducible moral agency—*as if* it could intelligibly and legitimately be held responsible, blamed, and perhaps even punished, like a fully-fledged responsible agent. In other words, we may sometimes be justified in erecting fictions (or, more loosely put, figurative accounts) of state responsibility and blameworthiness. This may be the case when, for example, such holdings would have significant expressive value—think of situations in which there is mass popular support for, or acquiescence to, unjustified official wrongdoing. Such fictions may also lead to critical reforms in state members' behaviour and contribute to forestalling future misconduct. Such a consequentialist way of thinking about state responsibility for wrongdoing could conceivably complement, or perhaps even replace, more robust models such as Pettit's. Thus, its implications for the possibility of state excuses must also be examined.

III. From Realism to Pragmatic Fiction

A. The general problem

In both law and morality, groups are sometimes treated as agents even when they are not, and held responsible, blamed, and punished for conduct and outcomes that are only fictionally 'theirs'. A case in point is that of regimes of corporate criminal liability which rely on doctrines of identification or vicarious responsibility to hold corporations accountable and blame them for some of the wrongs and harms perpetrated by their members, either individually, aggregatively, or jointly. Many such regimes are premised on the imputation to the corporation of a package, comprising some designated individuals' conduct (including their acts and mental states), that amounts, or is relevantly related to, wrongdoing. Other such regimes involve the sheer attribution of individuals' blameworthiness to the corporation.[40] The question for us is this: insofar as the imputed conduct or blameworthiness is that of individual human beings who are at least partially excused for their own deeds, can their individual excuses ever limit or affect that for which the corporation can legitimately be blamed and punished?

Indeed, the structure of regimes like the ones just mentioned does not necessarily preclude the concurrent imputation to the group of related individual excuses—with all their components, be they cognitive, affective, etc. Insofar as state institutions such as local governments or other public bodies are targets of moral blame or criminal liability in this imputed way, such a structural observation also seems to apply. So does it to cases in which the state as a whole may, in similar ways, be blamed and threatened with sanctions. That is, the excusatory claims of individuals whose conduct or blameworthiness is at stake may conceivably also be imputed to the state and its institutions by means of fictions.

But *should* individual excuses be imputed to groups in such ways? As I indicated at the end of the last section, theorists who think of collective responsibility, blame, and punishment as fictions often justify associated practices in pragmatic terms. Christopher Kutz, for example, argues that such practices can be justified as a means of changing collective behaviour for the better, or as a means of expressing symbolically more significant criticism for the joint perpetration of harm.[41] Now, insofar as the attribution of individual excuses to a group can at least partially exonerate it and, consequently, pre-empt the realization of such valuable reformative and symbolic ends, it is easy to see why pragmatist theorists are reluctant to admit that such attribution is ever warranted.[42] Attribution of individual excuses to groups, their thinking goes, would threaten to undermine the very rationale for blaming and punishing them for the acts of individuals.

The mistake that should not be made here is to assume that the reasons invoked to justify blaming and punishing groups by means of fictions always trump countervailing reasons. Admittedly, there will at times be strong

[40] For a good survey, see Cane, *Responsibility in Law and Morality*, n 12 above, at pp 148–58. Such fictions are also commonly found in morality, even if some seminal discussions of them are prone to exaggeration. See eg J Feinberg, 'Collective Responsibility' (1968) 65 *J of Philosophy* 674, who treats collective moral responsibility as an inherently and necessarily vicarious form of responsibility.

[41] Kutz, *Complicity: Ethics and Law for a Collective Age*, n 37 above, at pp 191–7. Note that the idea of shortfall of individual responsibility tends to underlie discussions of justifications of the second kind.

[42] Thus, in *Complicity: Ethics and Law for a Collective Age*, n 37 above, at p 3, Kutz speaks about pleas for excuse in primarily individualistic terms.

reasons in favour of group accountability, group blame, and even group punishment for harmful wrongdoing. However, there may also be significant competing reasons that can defeat these strong reasons. For example, blaming and punishing groups may stigmatize innocent individual members and cause them to suffer unfairly. The problem of unfair dispersion of group blame and punishment has plagued theorists of collective responsibility for years, and there does not seem to be any easy cure. To be sure, some think that, in light of the seriousness of the problem, we should simply refrain from blaming and punishing groups—and perhaps especially large and complex groupings like states and state institutions.[43] Then again, justice—and, more broadly, morality—may not demand such a radical conclusion, and attribution to groups of relevant excuses, in tandem with wrongdoing, might form part of a more nuanced position that gives due consideration to reasons for blaming and punishing groups as well as to reasons against it, such as unfair dispersion concerns. Attribution of individual excuses to groups may also serve important expressive ends. For example, it may provide a meaningful acknowledgement that, in certain circumstances, there are duties which individual group members should not be blamed, or should not suffer, for failing to discharge either on their own or together. What is more, imputation of excuses to groups might matter outside the context of straightforward blame and punishment. At times, such imputation may suitably mitigate crippling compensatory obligations that befall group members for the erratic and generally detrimental conduct of a few individuals acting, in the group's name, under, say, duress or epistemic misapprehensions. Or in the case of the declaration of an unjust war, attribution of excuses to the declaring state may modulate its members' overall liability to harmful self-defensive action. Of course, all these claims are controversial and arguments beyond what I can provide here would be needed to vindicate them, insofar as they can be. That said, I offer them as plausible candidates of areas in which fictions of group excuses may play an important role and as provocations for further theoretical scrutiny.

One of the fiercest opponents of (legal) fictions, Jeremy Bentham, used to deride them as 'lies' that 'may be applied to a good purpose, as well as to a bad one: in giving support to a useful rule or institution, as well as to a pernicious one'.[44] For Bentham, the only appropriate response to this ambivalent and

---

[43] See eg D F Thompson, 'Criminal Responsibility in Government' in J R Pennock and J W Chapman (eds), *Criminal Justice: Nomos XXVII* (New York: New York University Press, 1985) 201, 212–13, 224.

[44] J Bentham, *The Works of Jeremy Bentham*, vol VII (J Bowring ed) (Edinburgh: William Tait, 1843) 287.

rather unpredictable character of fictions was to get rid of them altogether. However, since fictions of group responsibility can serve important ends, this remedy seems drastic. A more discerning position may be to insist that such fictions must always be justified, in the sense of being deployed for undefeated reasons. As suggested above, it is at least plausible that imputation of individual excuses to groups might, on occasion, help ensure that practices of group—and, more to the point, state—blame, punishment, and their cognates remain so justified.

The point also applies if groups such as states can be irreducible agents and one asks whether the emotions, moods, valuable interests, etc, of their individual members may ever be imputed to them by means of fiction—in ways that could contribute to grounding claims of group excuses. Here again, the issue is one of justification. Yet, in the case of the state, many are reluctant to concede even the very possibility of such justified fictions given what they perceive as the slipperiness of the concession. The state is a purely instrumental creature, they claim, and given its role and position in society, it should embody the epitome of self-control and knowledgeability. As I claimed earlier, there is certainly some truth to this suggestion. But should states—however we understand them—really always be held to standards of perfection in virtue, skill, and reasonableness, such that any talk of state excuses and related talk of state emotions, moods, and interests are really moot *ab initio*?

B. The state as an inexcusable beacon of virtue?

A challenging group of objections take aim at the suggestion that states may legitimately be excused in situations where their 'special relationship' with their human subjects is at issue. The assumption is that, given the nature of the state as an entity whose every function and action should be instrumentally tailored to the well-being of its subjects, such situations are bound to be very common. They are common, if not the norm, and give rise to expectations of state virtue that are so exacting as to create a virtually insurmountable barrier to the legitimate recognition of state excuses. The objections in question tend to target primarily the possibility of domestic state excuses, understood either according to the irreducibility or fiction paradigm, given the profound and inevitable interplay between a state's domestic actions and its subjects' well-being. Yet, international variants are conceivable.

A first such objection rests on the fact that not only does the modern state typically have great resources and opportunities for action; it also characteristically claims a pre-eminent social role for itself as wielder of supreme and legitimate authority over a territory and its occupants. The objection is that, given such attributes, the state should not only seek to be, but be expected to be, a model of virtue for all those who live under it, work on its behalf, or otherwise relevantly cross its path. Indeed, what standing would it have to guide them, hold them responsible, and sometimes even blame and punish them were it not to live up to what it preaches and more? Besides, wouldn't excusing the state for unjustified wrongdoing risk creating erroneous perceptions amongst individual state officials and ordinary subjects that no more is actually expected of *them*? Such moral concerns, and there are no doubt many related others, deserve serious consideration. For some, though, they are so salient as to require holding the state to a standard of virtuous perfection in its dealings with its subjects. In such contexts, the thought goes, even if states can face exigent circumstances and, say, undergo debilitating affective experiences—real or fictionally attributed—they must always be expected to tower above them, with complete equanimity.[45] Therefore, there ought to be no excusatory concessions to state frailty.

Simester emphasizes a distinct, yet related. objection when he argues that 'it is not open for the State, or its officials, to prefer the interests of one person to another, since the State is not entitled to be closer to one person than another. It is equidistant, impartial to all'.[46] Here, the underlying assumption seems to be that, insofar as states have valuable interests and personal values, they are expected never to act on them in their relationships with their subjects. Insofar as they do not have such interests and values, yet one embraces a conception of morality that admits of primarily other-regarding dilemmas, such as dilemmas of loyalty, states are also expected to refrain from engaging in them. Accordingly, even if valid excuses may sometimes be available to individual wrongdoers in similar circumstances, such excuses should never be recognized when invoked by or in the name of the state.

Part of the apparent strength of this last objection derives, in my view, from the powerful liberal idea that states should administer justice impartially and impersonally. Were states not to behave in this way, liberals argue, the very idea of state justice would be severely undermined. I take this position to be quite uncontroversial. However, the administration of justice does not exhaust the activities of the modern state. States also seek to thwart the spread of diseases and risks of natural disasters, they make administrative decisions in matters of taxation, immigration, healthcare and national security, they wage war and engage in all sorts of other pursuits that are not strictly tied to the administration of justice. In the context of these further pursuits, could it

---

[45] This objection was first suggested to me, in spirit, by John Gardner.
[46] Simester, 'Necessity, Torture, and the Rule of Law', n 3 above, at p 302.

not sometimes be excusable for states, state institutions, as well as officials acting in their name and on their behalf to be partial on account of relevant allegiances? For example, whereas it may be morally wrong, all things considered, to expel illegal immigrants who have resided and integrated in, as well as contributed to, a state for a long time, must it really *always* be inexcusable for such a state to give in to intense expulsion pressures stemming from its citizenry?

Some, like Simester, seem to believe that state partiality is indefensible domestically, and that states should be expected to adopt a perfectly impartial and impersonal standpoint in their dealings with their subjects (or, at least, their citizens). Some strict cosmopolitan moral theorists endorse an even more far-reaching version of this view, arguing for equally stringent duties and standards of justice, respect, and beneficence owed to all human beings regardless of territorial jurisdiction, social ties, and political affiliations. These are theorists for whom the objection to state excuses considered here would likely extend to key international dimensions of states' conduct, such as those impinging on the human rights of people who are outside their jurisdiction and are not their subjects. For example, such theorists would likely resist the grant of any excuses to states declaring unjust wars to protect their citizens. This position stands in stark contrast with that of various particularist and pluralist communitarians who readily reject as unrealistic and unreasonable any such premise of perfect state impartiality.[47]

Who is right? I do not intend to delve at length into this debate, nor into the issue of which precise standards of virtue should apply to states. My intention is rather to emphasize an oft-neglected, yet plausible defence of official public attitudes which, despite being conducive to partiality and lesser equanimity, may be consistent with a proper, instrumental account of the role and value of the state.

Consider the gap that sometimes exists, at both state and non-state levels, between what I will call the morality of motives and the morality of actions. For example, take the case of the army officer whose hot-headedness some-times leads them to be less than impartial, treat many of their subordinates harshly, and deal with enemy combatants mercilessly. All things considered, their hot-headed actions may not always be justified. However, for army officers in many important roles, such hot-headedness is a morally desirable

[47] For a thought-provoking discussion of the tension between these two kinds of outlooks, see R Rao, *Third World Protest: Between Home and the World* (Oxford: Oxford University Press, 2010). On the specific question of excuses and reasonable partiality in the context of war, see S Lazar, 'The Responsibility Dilemma for *Killing in War*: A Review Essay' (2010) 38 *Philosophy and Public Affairs* 180, 197–8.

attitude. We would not want them to be such cold fish that they are unable to motivate their troops. Hot-headedness might also be a condition of their success in battle. In short, hot-headedness may be instrumental to the realization of some of the legitimate state purposes that army officers exist to serve qua officials whose conduct is imputable to the state. I believe that this point also holds with respect to a wide range of individual and, possibly, irreducible corporate attitudes that are crucial to the fulfilment of state functions, yet can sometimes drive a wedge between morally acceptable thinking about actions and morally acceptable actions. Think of risk-averseness, carefulness in planning, dedication to people's welfare and responsiveness to their needs, efficiency-mindedness, and so forth.

If not necessarily admirable, unjustified wrongdoings perpetrated on account of morally desirable attitudes may still be understandable and, when relevant standards of virtue are met, warrant excuses.[48] When such excuses are grounded in attitudes instrumental to legitimate state functions, it may then be appropriate to attribute them to the state. Of course, if states and state institutions do not have personal values, valuable interests, or conscious phenomenal experiences of their own qua irreducible group agents, not all types of motivational attitudes that may lead to valid individual excuses may be available to them under that specific understanding of state responsibility. Yet, states and state institutions so understood may still have reasonable cognitive attitudes that are defensible as instrumental to their proper functions, and claim legitimate excuses based on them.

Again, I am not denying that many excusatory standards to be applied to states and state institutions should, as a matter of course, be demanding. Yet, for reasons like the one just introduced, I am unconvinced that virtuous perfection is the required threshold. What is more, if states are, at bottom, collectives of individuals, it seems that our expectations of them should at least partly depend on our expectations of these individuals acting together. Since individuals may sometimes be excused for wrongs perpetrated with others, it would be surprising if state agency arising from their group action could itself never be.

To be sure, we could plausibly conceive of different excusatory standards of virtue applicable to different realms of state activity, with the most stringent perhaps applicable to activities that impinge most severely on basic human rights. We could also conceive of different excusatory standards for the state's domestic as opposed to international incarnations, for the

---

[48] This insight is discussed in part in C Finkelstein, 'Excuses and Dispositions in Criminal Law' (2002) 6 *Buffalo Crim L Rev* 317. Unfortunately, Finkelstein's unflinchingly consequentialist conception of excuses is excessively crude and narrow.

state as a whole as opposed to discrete state institutions, for different such institutions, for states and state institutions at different stages of development, for state institutions as opposed to private corporations or individuals discharging state functions, and so forth. Likewise, even if the state should be expected to be expertly knowledgeable about certain things, excusatory standards for epistemic mistakes may well vary between domains of activity. Indeed, in some such domains, liberal restrictions on what the state should know, and seek to know, may themselves be quite stringent. As discussed earlier, other kinds of excusatory grounds such as complete or partial lack of basic responsibility, the modulating potential of group excuses for concerns associated with group blame and punishment, and valuable symbolism, may also warrant the recognition of at least some state excuses. None of these excusatory grounds are virtue-driven and, like for epistemic mistake and constitutional disorder, they have nothing to do with the permissibility of state partiality. Therefore, the possibility of legitimate excusatory concessions to the state is plainly not as unthinkable as many seem to believe.

IV. Conclusion

In this chapter, I have sought to highlight central theoretical puzzles related to the question of whether state claims of excuses may ever be intelligible and, if so, legitimately recognized. The arc of my argument has been that even if the range of excuses available to the state does not overlap neatly with excuses available to ordinary individuals, excuses may indeed be morally available to states. For some, my argument may raise the spectre of murderous, torturing, or otherwise wicked states being offered unconscionable paths to absolution. I disagree. What my argument does, or at least attempts to do, is to expose the challenge of state excuses for what it is, so that it must be addressed in all its complexity and not simply wished away. Of course, much work remains to be done to determine the appropriate grounds, precise internal structure, and apposite standards of virtue, skill, and knowledge for specific state excuses, in specific contexts. A more refined understanding of the state, its functions, and its susceptibility to holdings of moral and legal responsibility, blame, and punishment would likely assist with this multifaceted task. So might closer scrutiny of the concepts of blame and punishment—individual and collective—and their relationship with excuses, as well as of my generic categorization as 'excuses' of exculpatory pleas that may in fact be saliently different. Finally, it remains an open question whether all excuses morally available to states should be recognized by the law or whether, in some cases, additional concerns stand in the way.

My aim here was merely to map out issues that appear salient to me. For all I know, when all is said and done, the realm of legitimate state excuses may turn out to be very limited indeed. Still, I hope to have said enough to convince you that, in respect of many facets of this debate—as well as of the broader question of corporate excuses considered as a class—the jury is still out. The theoretical road ahead is rich and challenging, and I certainly hope that, in the near future, many more will be travelling it with me.

8

War Crimes and Immoral Action in War

Jeff McMahan

I. The Traditional Theory of the Just War

War crimes are grave violations of the legal principles of *jus in bello*, the principles governing the conduct of war, for which individual combatants may be punished. In international humanitarian law, these principles are found in the Hague Conventions and the Geneva Conventions. They have subsequently been absorbed, though with some modifications, into international criminal law.

As in domestic criminal law, the ideal in the law of war is that all and only those acts that harm their victims and are seriously morally wrong should be criminal, and thus punishable. The law ought, within certain limits, to deter by threat of punishment all acts that are morally impermissible and inflict wrongful harm. Yet it ought not to punish people for acting in ways that are morally permissible. Ideally, therefore, the category of war crimes should include all forms of morally wrong action in war that inflict serious harms on their victims.

In this chapter I will argue that there are insurmountable obstacles to achieving this ideal. I first offer a brief account of the way that *jus in bello* is conceived both by the traditional theory of the just war and by the law. I next indicate why *jus in bello* so conceived cannot be right as a matter of morality and then sketch a revisionist account of the morality of *jus in bello*. Yet I also argue that the requirements of this revisionist account cannot in general be satisfied by those who fight without a just cause. Because *in bello* law has as one of its purposes the effective constraint of the action of those who fight without a just cause, it cannot simply declare that all their acts of war are impermissible. It seems, therefore, that *in bello* law cannot be modelled directly on *in bello* morality. *In bello* law and *in bello* morality must be substantially divergent. I conclude by considering what the criterion, or criteria, ought to be for determining which forms of morally impermissible action in war should be treated as war crimes.[1]

As a preliminary, it is necessary to define a couple of terms. By 'just combatants' I mean those who fight for a just cause in a just war. By 'unjust combatants' I mean those who fight without a just cause. These categories leave out those who fight for a just aim or just cause within a war that is unjust. A war can be unjust overall even if it pursues a just goal. There are several ways in which this might be the case. The war's only aim might be just and yet the war as a whole might be disproportionate or unnecessary for the achievement of the just cause. Or the war might be unjust because, although it pursues a just cause, it also pursues unjust aims that are unnecessary for the achievement of the just cause. Given that the just cause could be pursued by means of war without the pursuit of the unjust aims, the war as a whole is unjust. Combatants who fight in such a war might be able to fight in a way that would advance only the just cause and not the unjust aims. But it is more likely that their contributions to the war would support both the just and unjust aims. If so, both their own status and the moral permissibility of their acts of war are more difficult to evaluate than the status or acts of just combatants or unjust combatants as I have defined them. I will leave these complications aside here.

Jus in bello as understood in traditional just war theory is closely congruent with *in bello* law as it has developed over more than a century. In both, there are three main principles: the requirement of discrimination, the requirement of necessity, and the requirement of proportionality. Particularly in law, there are various other rules governing the treatment of prisoners of war, combatants attempting to surrender, the wounded, and so on. Also in law there are prohibitions of the use of particular weapons and other rules that seem to be wholly conventional in nature. I will not discuss these latter prohibitions here, but will instead explain and then criticize the traditional interpretations of the *in bello* principles of discrimination, necessity, and proportionality.

The requirement of discrimination in its generic form is simply the requirement not to conduct intentional attacks on individuals who are not legitimate targets. Legitimate targets are generally thought of as persons who can be attacked without infringing a right against attack, either because they have waived that right or because they have forfeited it. While some just war theorists argue that all combatants waive their right against attack by enemy

---

[1] In criticizing the traditional theory of the just war and sketching the alternative revisionist account, I must repeat some material that I have published elsewhere. Since I obviously cannot assume that readers will be familiar with my other work, the overlap, though regrettable, is unavoidable.

combatants, I think consent has little or no role in explaining the permissibility of killing in war.[2] The primary moral justification for killing in war is that those who may permissibly be killed have forfeited their right against military attack or, in other words, made themselves liable to intentional, potentially lethal attack.

In law, and according to the traditional theory of the just war, those who are legitimate targets are combatants. Non-combatants are not legitimate targets. In traditional just war theory, this is because what makes people morally liable to attack is that they are *nocentes*, or injurious—that is, they pose a threat to others, so that to attack them is to engage in defence. Those who are not threatening are *innocent*, or not *nocentes*. Hence the familiar identification of those who are 'innocent' in war with non-combatants. Indeed, this assumption of equivalence is so common that the terms 'requirement of discrimination' and 'principle of non-combatant immunity' are generally taken to be synonymous.

In law and traditional just war theory, the *jus in bello* requirements of necessity and proportionality are constraints on the harms that may be inflicted on non-combatants as an unintended side effect of military action. The *in bello* requirement of necessity, or 'minimal force', condemns as impermissible any act of war that inflicts harm on non-combatants as a side effect when there is an alternative act of war that would have an equal probability of achieving either the same military aim or an alternative aim of comparable military significance, yet would cause less harm to non-combatants. The requirement of proportionality is traditionally understood as the requirement that an act of war not cause expected harm to non-combatants that is excessive in relation to the military importance of the act.

II. Critique of the Traditional Requirements of *Jus in Bello*

While there is no disputing that the legal principles of *jus in bello* are as they are, the *moral* principles of *jus in bello* are not best understood in the way they are in traditional just war theory. I have argued against the traditional interpretations at tedious length elsewhere so will here offer only a brief rehearsal of the objections.[3] I do not dispute that there are moral requirements of discrimination, necessity, and proportionality. The problems are in

---

[2] J McMahan, *Killing in War* (Oxford: Clarendon Press, 2009) 51–60. Also see J McMahan, 'Duty, Obedience, Desert, and Proportionality in War: A Response' (2011) *Ethics* 122, 135–67, at 146–50.

[3] See, for example, *Killing in War*, n 2 above.

the ways in which the requirements are interpreted by the traditional theory. These problems derive from the fact that the traditional theory treats *jus in bello* as wholly independent of *jus ad bellum*; that is, it asserts that what it is permissible or impermissible for combatants to do in war is unaffected by whether their war satisfies the requirements of *jus ad bellum*. In particular, what it is permissible to do is independent of whether the war has a just cause. The traditional principles of *jus in bello* therefore make no distinction between just and unjust combatants. They are supposed to be neutral between just and unjust combatants and to be equally satisfiable by either.

The requirement of discrimination as traditionally understood incorporates both a permission and a prohibition. The permission is that all combatants may kill enemy combatants at any time during a state of war. The prohibition is of intentional attacks against non-combatants. The permission, of course, applies to the killing of just combatants by unjust combatants. Just combatants, it is claimed, have lost their right not to be killed by posing a threat to others. Yet people do not forfeit their right not to be killed merely by engaging in morally justified defence of themselves and others against wrongful attacks by those pursuing unjust ends. It is in general impermissible to pursue ends that are unjust, and it is even more obviously impermissible to pursue such ends by means of attacking and intentionally killing people who have done nothing to make themselves liable to attack. It is therefore not, in general, permissible for unjust combatants to kill just combatants in war, though there are exceptions, such as when just combatants would otherwise impermissibly kill or seriously harm people who are not liable to those harms. Although this is less obvious, it is also in general impermissible for unjust combatants to kill just combatants as a means of achieving ends that, although not positively unjust, cannot permissibly be pursued by means of war (that is, neutral ends or even ends that are good but insufficient either to constitute a just cause for war or to establish a lesser evil justification for the resort to war).

The prohibition in the traditional requirement of discrimination, which might be thought to be the more important of the two constituent elements, is also incorrect as a matter of basic morality. That a person is a non-combatant is sufficient to show that he or she cannot be liable to defensive attack on the ground that he or she poses an *immediate* threat of wrongful harm, but it does not entail that he or she cannot be liable to attack on other grounds. An academic physicist in Nazi Germany who would otherwise have provided the breakthrough to enable Hitler to have an atom bomb would have been liable to be killed to prevent him from achieving that breakthrough. Or a wealthy businessman who stood to profit from victory in an unjust war might also be liable to be killed if that was necessary to prevent him from providing his government with the resources necessary to win the war. These are, of course, anomalous examples and it is seldom morally permissible intentionally to attack non-combatants by military means in war. But the examples provide intuitive support for the claim that mere status as a non-combatant is not by itself sufficient to exempt a person from liability to attack in war.[4]

The traditional *in bello* requirement of necessity asserts that any harms that military action causes to non-combatants must be necessary. But necessary for what? It cannot be that they must be necessary for the achievement of a just cause, for the requirement of necessity applies to unjust combatants, who have no just cause. Nor can it be that these harms must be necessary for personal self-defence by combatants, as that would mean that offensive military action undertaken by combatants who were not otherwise under threat would violate the requirement of necessity if it would cause any harm to non-combatants as a side effect—clearly too demanding a requirement. Rather, the requirement seems to be that combatants must not act in a way that harms non-combatants as a side effect if there is an alternative act that would yield at least an equivalent military advantage, would not be significantly costlier to the combatants, and would cause less harm to non-combatants.

Assuming that this principle sometimes requires combatants to expose themselves to greater risks, or to suffer greater costs, to avoid harming non-combatants, it is a substantial and plausible principle. Without that assumption, the principle would simply prohibit the infliction of wanton or gratuitous harm as a side effect. But with the assumption, it is, in its application to unjust combatants, analogous to a requirement that burglars take certain risks to themselves to avoid physically harming those from whom they steal—a strangely permissive but nonetheless plausible requirement.

Just as the traditional theory cites military advantage as the end for which foreseen harm to non-combatants must be necessary, so it also cites military advantage as the end in relation to which foreseen harm to non-combatants must be proportionate. But the assessment of proportionality by reference to military advantage is far more problematic. For military advantage is by itself morally neutral; whatever moral or evaluative significance it has must be instrumental—that is, must derive from the ends it serves, which are the ends or 'cause' of the war. In the case of an act of war by just combatants, any side-effect harms to non-combatants can coherently be weighed against the military advantage yielded by the act because this advantage has value in

---

[4] For a discussion of the limits of non-combatant liability, see J McMahan, 'Who is Morally Liable to be Killed in War' (2011) *Analysis Reviews* 71, 544–59.

proportion to the contribution it makes to the achievement of the just cause. But suppose that the ends pursued by unjust combatants are bad, impartially considered, because they are unjust. In that case, the unjust combatants' means—military advantage—must be bad as well, which makes it nonsensical to suppose that the unintended harms they might cause to non-combatants could be proportionate in relation to military advantage. For the idea that bad side effects could be proportionate (or, for that matter, disproportionate) in relation to intended bad effects is incoherent. It makes no sense to suppose that bad side effects could be justified by being somehow outweighed by other bad effects of the same act. Bad effects can be proportionate or disproportionate only in relation to good effects.

A defender of the traditional theory might argue that if the theory's *in bello* proportionality requirement implies that an act of war that would yield a certain degree of military advantage would be disproportionate if done by just combatants, it must also imply that the same act would be disproportionate if done by unjust combatants. That shows that the requirement is coherent in its application to the action of unjust combatants. But this is only an illusion of moral coherence. The act would certainly be *wrong* if done by unjust combatants, but that is not because it would be disproportionate. For it has no intended effects in relation to which its bad side effects could be either proportionate or disproportionate.

The defender of the traditional theory might next seek to reinterpret the application of the *in bello* requirement of proportionality so that it does compare bad side effects with good intended effects. This might be accomplished by detaching the evaluation of the ends of unjust war from their being unjust, or wrongly obtained. Those who instigate unjust wars believe, usually correctly, that they would benefit from the achievement of their ends. Those benefits, it might be argued, are the good intended effects against which the side-effect harms to non-combatants can be weighed in the assessment of proportionality. Thus, in the assessment of whether an act of war by unjust combatants would be proportionate, the relevant good effects include the benefits to their side of achieving their aims, the prevention of harms to themselves and other unjust combatants on the battlefield, the protection of their own non-combatant population from harms they might otherwise suffer as a side effect of military action by just combatants, and perhaps any good side effects their action might be expected to have. The corresponding list for just combatants is the same except that their ends comprise the good effects that are constitutive of the achievement of their just cause.

To test the plausibility of this suggestion, consider the rough analogy with a nephew whose aim is to kill his uncle as a means of receiving a large inheritance, knowing that this will cause great grief to his aunt as a side effect.

Using the formula just stated to assess whether the killing would be proportionate, we should weigh the benefit to the nephew from the killing against the unintended harm to the aunt and, presumably, the harm caused to the uncle as a means. This seems coherent. Judged in this way, the killing may or may not be proportionate. But suppose it is. Suppose the benefits to the young nephew outweigh the harms to his elderly uncle and aunt. All that would show is that the killing is not ruled out on grounds of proportionality. Proportionality is a constraint, not a justification. Even if the constraint is satisfied in this case, that is irrelevant because the killing is already impermissible because it violates the uncle's right not to be killed. Parallel claims apply to acts of war by unjust combatants.

Yet so far as I am aware, no one has ever understood proportionality in this way. The benefits that wrongdoers derive from wrongful action have not been thought to weigh equally with the harms they inflict on their victims, whether intentionally or as a side effect. Indeed, it has been thought perverse to suppose that they have any weight at all in the determination of proportionality, which is a moralized notion. Proportionality does not simply weigh and compare good and bad effects independently of how they are produced, how they are distributed, and whether people are entitled to them, deserve them, or are liable to them. In particular, when we seek to determine whether the harms that an act would cause to innocent people as a side effect would be proportionate, we weigh them against the act's intended good aims, and at least some of its good side effects, taking 'good' to mean 'morally good', not merely 'good for someone'. To do otherwise would be to allow the benefits that wrongdoers derive from their wrongdoing to weigh morally against harms to innocent people. For example, in determining whether the nephew's act of murder is proportionate, it would allow the benefits he would derive from it to weigh against and perhaps morally outweigh the harm he would cause to his aunt. This seems inadmissible. If that is right, my original claim still stands: assuming that their war is neither just nor justified, it is incoherent to suppose that the harms that unjust combatants cause to noncombatants as a side effect of their military action can be proportionate in relation to the military advantage that action yields.

III. A Revisionist Account if *Jus in Bello*

Even though the *in bello* principles of discrimination proportionality as traditionally interpreted are mistaken as moral principles, and the principle of necessity is bizarrely permissive, there are alternative interpretations that are morally plausible. I will state and elucidate these principles and then argue that they can only rarely be satisfied by acts of war by unjust combatants.

As a purely formal principle, the requirement of discrimination is as I stated it earlier—that is, a requirement to restrict intentional attacks to legitimate targets. One is a legitimate target in war if one has forfeited one's right not to be attacked—that is, if one has acted in such a way as to have become morally liable to attack. The mistake of the traditional theory is to identify legitimate targets with combatants, on the ground that what makes a person liable to attack in war is posing a threat to others. The fundamental problem with this, as I noted, is that one does not make oneself morally liable to attack by posing a threat if one is morally justified in posing that threat. This is particularly clear when the reason one is justified is that the person one threatens is morally liable to suffer the threatened harm.

I have argued elsewhere that the criterion of liability to intentional attack in war is moral responsibility for a threat of serious, wrongful harm, including though not limited to the wrongful harms whose prevention or correction constitutes a just cause for war.[5] There are several points to note about this claim. First, one need not be the immediate agent of a threatened harm to be liable to be harmed in defence of the potential victim; it may be sufficient that one bears some moral responsibility for that harm even if someone else would inflict it. Second, it is not sufficient for liability to defensive harm that one *is* the immediate agent of a wrongful harm; one must also be morally responsible for the harm one would otherwise inflict. Third, responsibility does not entail culpability. There are ways in which one can be morally responsible for a threat of wrongful harm without being culpable—for example, if one has permissibly chosen to act in a way that foreseeably has a very small risk that, through bad luck, one will cause a great harm to innocent people unless one is harmed in their defence.

Given this understanding of liability to defensive attack, the requirement of discrimination in war states that while there is a stringent moral constraint against intentionally attacking those who are not morally responsible for a threat of serious, wrongful harm, it is in general permissible to attack those who are morally liable to be attacked by virtue of their moral responsibility for a threat of wrongful harm to others. Because whether one becomes liable to defensive action by posing a threat of harm to others depends on whether the threat one poses is morally justified, there is a connection between liability and just cause. Those whose war meets the conditions of a just war have a moral justification for fighting and therefore do not make themselves liable to

---

[5] *Killing in War*, n 2 above.

attack unless they pursue their just cause by impermissible means, or pursue impermissible aims within the context of a war that is just overall. By contrast, those who fight without a just cause, and in particular those who fight for a cause that is positively unjust, are generally liable to attack, provided that they are morally responsible for their action, which combatants usually are. There are, however, exceptions. Unjust combatants may not be liable to attack during those times, if any, when they are acting with moral justification to prevent just combatants from acting impermissibly. It is also possible, though not likely, that a war could be justified on grounds of lesser evil even though it lacked a just cause—that is, even though those whom it was necessary for combatants to attack as a means of achieving their aims were not liable to attack. A just war requires two forms of justification: a liability justification for harms inflicted as a means and a lesser-evil justification for harms inflicted on innocent people as a side effect. I call a war that is justified entirely on grounds of lesser evil a merely 'justified' war. Combatants who fight in a war that is justified though not just are 'unjust combatants' but nevertheless have a moral justification for fighting despite the fact that those they attack are not liable to attack. If having a lesser-evil justification for harming non-liable people exempts a person from liability to defensive harm, unjust combatants whose war has only a lesser-evil justification are not liable to defensive attack.

Like the traditional understanding, this understanding of the requirement of discrimination contains both a permission and a prohibition. The permission is in one respect more expansive, for it allows for the possibility of non-combatant liability. It concedes, for example, that the Nazi physicist cited earlier would be liable to attack. But overall the permission is much narrower, since most just combatants are not liable to attack. The prohibition is correspondingly more expansive, as it applies to most attacks against just combatants, but is in another way narrower in allowing for a doctrine of limited non-combatant liability.

Next consider the revisionist interpretation of the requirement of necessity. In elucidating the traditional interpretation, I conceded that it imposes a plausible constraint if it requires combatants to accept greater risks to avoid harming non-combatants if they can do so without any sacrifice of military advantage in the pursuit of their larger goals. But this is a feeble and highly permissive constraint, since it assesses necessity independently of those goals. It plausibly rules out harms that are unnecessary for the achievement of aims that are unjustified, and plausibly requires that unjust combatants accept some sacrifices to avoid causing such harms *if* they are going to pursue unjustified aims; but it also permits harms to innocent people that are necessary *only* for the achievement of unjustified aims. Yet morality demands more than that the harms one causes to innocent people be unavoidable if one is to achieve one's goals, whatever they may be. It holds instead that it is permissible to harm innocent people only when those harms are necessary or unavoidable in the achievement of goals that are morally just or justified and can thus properly weigh against and potentially outweigh the collateral harms. Harms that are necessary only for the achievement of unjust or unjustified goals are not *morally* necessary. The requirement of necessity in war must rule out such harms as impermissible.

The correct *in bello* requirement of necessity thus asserts that an act of war may permissibly harm innocent people as a side effect only if there is no alternative act of war that would make an equal or greater contribution to the just or justifying aims of the war. That an act of war is necessary for a certain degree of military advantage is insufficient to make it necessary in the relevant sense. The military advantage must itself be instrumental to the achievement of an aim that is morally justified.

Two further points are worth making. First, as with the interpretation I offered of the traditional principle, the revisionist principle implies that an act of war that would harm innocent people as a side effect is impermissible if there is an alternative act that would cause less harm to innocent people and make an equal or greater contribution to the achievement of a just or justifying aim, but would also involve a somewhat greater risk or harm to the combatants who would carry it out—though obviously there are limits to how much additional risk or harm just combatants would be required to bear.

Second, there is a question whether the requirement of necessity rules out not only unnecessary harms to non-combatants but also unnecessary harms to enemy combatants. The traditional theory has tended to ignore this question, as its proponents have assumed that all combatants are liable to attack at any time during a state of war and that all harms to enemy combatants lessen their military effectiveness and thus provide some degree of military advantage. But neither of these assumptions is true. There would be no military advantage, for example, in killing the members of a unit that has completed its tour of duty and, though still in the battle area, is awaiting the arrival of transport vessels to return home. As a matter of morality, the *in bello* requirement of necessity applies to intended and unintended harms to both non-combatants and combatants, but I will not pursue further the issue of unnecessary harms to combatants here.

It is, however, important to recognize a parallel claim about the revisionist understanding of *in bello* proportionality. The traditional theory holds that in the determination of whether an act of war is permissible, the only harms that must be shown to be proportionate are those caused to people who are not liable to suffer them, who are assumed to be co-extensive with non-combat-ants. Combatants are all assumed to be liable to be attacked and killed. Harms caused to them are thus considered to be fully justified on grounds of liability, so that it is unnecessary or superfluous to attempt to justify them yet again by weighing them against the good effects that the act that causes them also achieves. But this is a mistake, for, again, it is not true that all combatants are liable to be attacked and killed. Just combatants who fight by permissible means do nothing to make themselves liable to attack. And even some unjust combatants, such as those whose responsibility for being in the military is mitigated by ignorance or duress and who will not contribute significantly to the achievement of an unjust cause or any other harm, are also not liable to attack. Also, the *number* of unjust combatants harmed or killed can render an act of war disproportionate.[6] Suppose that it had been necessary for British forces to kill 50,000 Argentine combatants to preserve Britain's sovereignty over the Falkland Islands. In that case, the Falklands War would arguably have been disproportionate, as, therefore, would most of the constituent acts of war by the British combatants who would have done the killing.

We can refer to proportionality in harms to those who are potentially liable to be harmed as *narrow proportionality*. If a person is, in the circumstances, liable to be harmed in a certain way, harming him in that way is proportion-ate in the narrow sense. If a person is liable to only a certain amount of harm, harming him in excess of that amount is disproportionate in the narrow sense.

It has almost universally been assumed that any harms to which people are liable are ones that it is permissible to inflict intentionally. But people can be liable to suffer harms that occur as unintended effects. And the threshold for liability to suffer unintended harms is generally lower than that for liability to suffer intended harms. A person may not be liable to the intentional infliction of a certain harm and yet be liable to suffer that same harm as a foreseen but unintended effect. In war, unjust combatants tend to be liable to any harms that they might suffer as a side effect of the military action of just combatants. This can also be true, though only rarely, of non-combatants on the unjust side. There can be instances in which some non-combatants on the unjust side bear sufficient responsibility for a threat of wrongful harm that they may have no legitimate complaint if they are harmed as a side effect of military action necessary to eliminate that threat. In such a case, the unin-tended harms to non-combatants are a matter of narrow proportionality.

---

[6] For discussion, see McMahan, 'Duty, Obedience, Desert, and Proportionality', n 2 above, pp 151–7, and J McMahan, 'What Rights May be Defended by Means of War?', in C Fabre and S Lazar (eds), *National Defence* (Oxford: Oxford University Press, 2013).

Even though, contrary to the traditional theory of the just war, wars and acts of war can be disproportionate in the narrow sense because of the harm they cause to enemy combatants, I will not further discuss narrow propor- tionality here. This is because, in practice, most unjust combatants are potentially liable to suffer significant harms and the great majority are liable to intentional military attack.[7]

I will focus instead on what can be called *wide proportionality*, or proportionality in harms caused to those who are innocent in the sense of not being liable to suffer them, either as a means or as a side effect. Such harms to non-liable people caused as a side effect are the ones that the traditional view of proportionality in war has been concerned with, though the traditional theory has also assumed, in my view incorrectly, that the group of those who are innocent in this sense is co-extensive with the group of non-combatants.

It is necessary to consider wide proportionality independently of narrow proportionality, as these different forms of proportionality are constraints on different forms of justification for harming. While narrow proportionality is a constraint on a liability justification, wide proportionality is a constraint on a lesser-evil justification.

Harms to non-liable people may be either intended or unintended. Intended harms to non-liable people violate the requirement of discrimination and are thus generally ruled out. But as it is implausible to take the requirement of discrimination to be absolute, it is possible for there to be a lesser-evil justification for intentionally harming people in ways to which they are not liable. The conditions in which it can be permissible intentionally to attack innocent people in war are generally understood, following Michael Walzer, to be the conditions that define a 'supreme emergency'.[8] ('Supreme emergency' refers to a condition in which the *in bello* requirement of discrimination is overridden. The term has not been used to refer to conditions in which an unjust war fought entirely against non-liable people might be justified as the lesser evil.)

The usual focus, therefore, in the assessment of whether an act of war is proportionate is on the harms the act is expected to cause as side effects (hence the euphemism 'collateral damage') to people who are not liable to be harmed. These bad effects have to be weighed against good effects that are 'moralized' in the sense that they do not include all effects that are good for someone but only those that are morally good. They obviously include the

---

[7] For discussion, see McMahan, *Killing in War*, n 2 above, pp 182–8, and 'Who is Morally Liable to be Killed in War', n 4 above, pp 547–9.

[8] M Walzer, *Just and Unjust Wars* (New York: Basic Books, 1977) 251–68.

good effects that are constitutive of the achievement of a just cause for war and any further good effects that might be caused by the achievement of the just cause. They may include other good effects as well, such as good side effects of a permissible means of achieving a good end. But they do not include the benefits that wrongdoers gain through wrongdoing.

There are other types of morally good side effect whose role in the assessment of wide proportionality seems unclear because of the way in which they are caused. These include morally good side effects (1) of a wrongful means to a good end, (2) of the achievement of a good end through morally wrongful means, (3) of a means to a wrongful end, and (4) of the achievement of a wrongful end.

There are, it seems, three broad possibilities in the case of side effects of these sorts. The first is that the issue of wide proportionality does not arise in the absence of a morally good end that can be pursued by a means that, in itself, is permissible. If the end is bad or the means impermissible, the act is ruled out and there is simply no question of whether it might be proportionate. The second possibility is substantively equivalent. It parallels a suggestion I made earlier—namely, that while such morally good side effects do weigh against all relevant bad effects in determining whether an act is proportionate in the wide sense, this is irrelevant in the case of acts that are impermissible on other grounds. For wide proportionality is merely a constraint, so that when it is satisfied, that means only that one possible reason why an act might be impermissible does not apply. But descriptions (1) to (4) above are of acts that are wrongful on grounds other than proportionality. They are, according to this view, impermissible either because they constitute a wrongful means to the achievement of an end or because they produce or are intended to achieve a wrongful end. They are ruled out even if they are proportionate in the wide sense.

The third possibility is that these morally good side effects count, and indeed count in a way that might not only satisfy the wide proportionality constraint but also provide a justification for acts that have them. Along with any other morally good effects that acts of types (1) to (4) might have, these morally good side effects weigh against any relevant bad effects (though good and bad side effects have, on one version of this view, less weight than equivalent good and bad effects that are intended, either as a means or as an end). If the combined expected good effects outweigh the expected bad effects by a substantial margin, the act is justified on grounds of lesser evil. This possibility is more plausible in the case of acts of types (1) and (2), which have good intended ends. Such cases exemplify a familiar form of lesser-evil justification, in which morally bad means are justified by sufficiently important ends that are morally good, together with morally good side effects. In cases of types (3) and (4), however, in which the intended end is morally bad, one must accept that neither intention nor the causal relations among the consequences matter to the permissibility of the act if one is to accept that such acts can be morally justified.

IV. Unjust Combatants Cannot in General Satisfy the Requirements of *Jus in Bello*

I will argue in this section that acts of war by unjust combatants can seldom satisfy any of the requirements of *jus in bello*, understood in their plausible revisionist forms. It is only rarely that an act of war by an unjust combatant can satisfy even one of the requirements, and more rarely still that such an act can satisfy all three. This is true even of unjust combatants whose war is morally justified as the lesser evil even though it is unjust because some or all of those who must be attacked as a necessary means of achieving the war's aims are not liable to attack. Although many acts of war in a merely justified war can satisfy the *in bello* requirements of necessity and proportionality, they can only rarely satisfy the requirement of discrimination. This is because they are virtually always directed against people who are not liable to attack. Yet the requirement of discrimination is by hypothesis overridden in an unjust but justified war. In such a war, there would be repeated lesser-evil justifications for intentionally harming and killing innocent or non-liable people.

It should not be surprising that unjust combatants cannot in general satisfy the requirements of *jus in bello*. For if a war that lacks a just cause cannot satisfy the *ad bellum* requirements of necessity and proportionality, it is difficult to see how the individual acts of war that are constitutive of such a war could satisfy the parallel *in bello* requirements of necessity and proportionality. And it is relatively uncontroversial that a war that fails to satisfy the requirement of just cause cannot satisfy most of the other requirements of *jus ad bellum*. Indeed, it is generally accepted, even among traditional just war theorists, that a war that lacks a just cause can satisfy only one of their theory's other *ad bellum* requirements—namely, the requirement of *legitimate authority*, which insists that war may be initiated only by a person or persons who are authorized by a people to lead them into war. That requirement is wholly independent of the requirement of just cause. But the other *ad bellum* requirements are not. I will briefly explain why a war that lacks a just cause cannot satisfy the remaining principles of *jus ad bellum* and then indicate how this is relevant to whether unjust combatants can satisfy the principles of *jus in bello*.

First, the traditional principle of *right intention* requires that war be intended to achieve a just cause—that is, that the just cause not be used merely as a pretext for fighting a war for other reasons.

Second, the traditional principle of *last resort*, which is the requirement of necessity under a misleading label, holds that war can be permissible only if it is necessary for the achievement of the just cause—that is, a war is ruled out if the just cause can be achieved by means that would involve the infliction of fewer or less serious wrongful harms.

Third, the narrow *ad bellum* proportionality principle holds that people who are potentially liable to be harmed must not be harmed in ways that exceed the harms to which they are liable. But in a war that lacks a just cause, there are no opponents who are potentially liable to be attacked as a means of achieving the war's aims. So the issue of narrow proportionality simply does not arise.

Fourth, there is the wide proportionality principle, which holds that the harms that a war can be expected to cause to people who are not liable to be harmed must not be excessive in relation to the morally good effects that the war can be expected to have. Among wars that are unjust because they are fought against people who are not liable to be attacked, I have distinguished between those that are justified and those that are unjustified. Those that are justified are so because their morally good effects substantially outweigh their morally bad effects, including the harms caused to innocent people, both intentionally and unintentionally. These wars necessarily satisfy the wide proportionality constraint, for the extent to which the good effects outweigh the bad must be greater for a lesser-evil justification than for a war to be proportionate in the wide sense. But in those cases, if any, in which an act of war can satisfy the wide proportionality constraint, the fact that the war is proportionate is substantively irrelevant unless the extent to which the good effects outweigh the bad is extensive enough to provide a lesser-evil justification. So the relevant questions are whether there are any merely justified wars and, if so, how common they are.

It is, I have argued, possible that a war could be justified entirely on the ground that it is the lesser evil—though this is not a possibility that is recognized by the doctrine of *jus ad bellum* in the traditional theory of the just war. There might be a lesser-evil justification for war if there were a morally extremely important end that could be achieved only by militarily attacking non-liable people. But although a war of this sort is possible, it is, I will argue, unlikely in practice ever to be an option. This is because a war fought for an end that is morally good but is not such that the people who must be harmed as a means of achieving it are liable to be harmed (that is, a good end whose achievement does not constitute a just cause for war) inevitably causes severe and very extensive harms, many of which are intended, to people who are not liable to suffer them. These bad effects include, but are not limited to, (1) intended harms to soldiers on the opposing side who by hypothesis have done nothing to make themselves liable to attack, (2) harms caused to those same soldiers as a side effect, (3) harms caused as a side effect to non-combatants on the opposing side, (4) unintended harms to neutrals, and (5) harms to the unjust combatants' own non-combatant population caused as a side effect of defensive military action by combatants on the opposing side. These are all harms that wrong or infringe the rights of their victims, and those that are intended arguably infringe stronger rights than those that are merely side effects. It is highly unlikely that all these harms could be proportionate in the wide sense in relation to the good end the war seeks to achieve, together with any morally good side effects it might have. And it is considerably less likely, a fortiori, that the good end and good side effects could *substantially* outweigh the many and various wrongful harms, thereby providing a lesser-evil justification for the war. It of course follows, again a fortiori, that it is virtually impossible that an unjust war that pursues morally bad ends could be either proportionate in the wide sense or justified as the lesser evil. For this kind of war causes, in addition to the five types of wrongful harm listed above, the harms to innocent people that either consist in or are side effects of the achievement of the bad end. Thus, it is virtually impossible that such a war could have side effects that would be so good morally that they could outweigh, much less substantially outweigh, the bad end, the bad means, and the bad side effects. So, while it is possible in principle that there could be a war without a just cause that could be proportionate in the wide sense, it is very unlikely in practice. And it is even less likely in practice that such a war could be justified as the lesser evil.

For the sake of completeness, it is perhaps worth mentioning the trad-itional *ad bellum* principle of *reasonable hope of success*. This principle is either subsumed by the principles of proportionality or is mistaken. If it is sub-sumed by proportionality, the claims I have just made about proportionality apply also to reasonable hope of success. But suppose, as traditional just war theorists have thought, that reasonable hope of success is an independent principle. Then consider a war that has a probability of success below the threshold of whatever is considered reasonable but is nonetheless proportion-ate because the achievement of the just cause is sufficiently important that even a tiny probability of achieving it could outweigh all the bad effects. It would be permissible to fight such a war but reasonable hope of success would prohibit it. Hence, if reasonable hope of success is understood as independent of proportionality, it imposes an unreasonable constraint. One might, of course, claim that what counts as success is the achievement of whatever a belligerent's ends happen to be. In that case, the requirement could be satisfied in the absence of a just cause. And such a requirement would prohibit some obviously unjust wars. But it would not prohibit most unjust wars and is thus too anaemic to be a plausible component of *jus ad bellum*. It is better to regard reasonable hope of success as a defeasible element of proportionality.

As this brief survey shows, a state's ability to satisfy the traditional requirements of *jus ad bellum* other than the requirement of legitimate authority depends on whether its war satisfies the requirement of just cause. Two of these requirements—right intention and necessity—explicitly require a just cause. Before I came to appreciate the importance of distinguishing between narrow and wide proportionality and thus assumed as others had done that there was a single, univocal requirement of proportionality, I thought it was also impossible in principle for a war to be proportionate in the absence of a just cause, for I assumed that the only good effects that could properly weigh against the bad were those involved in or consequent upon the achievement of the just cause. I now think that this was a mistake. While I still think that the only good effects that count in the assessment of narrow *ad bellum* proportionality are those associated with the achievement of the just cause, I now accept that other morally good effects, including morally good side effects, can count towards the satisfaction of the wide *ad bellum* proportionality requirement (which is the only proportionality constraint that the traditional theory recognizes). I therefore accept that it is possible that a war that lacks a just cause can be proportionate in the wide sense, though this is irrelevant in practice unless the good effects outweigh the bad to so great an extent that the requirement of just cause is overridden and the war is justified as the lesser evil. As I have noted, however, this is not accepted by the traditional theory, which treats the satisfaction of the requirement of just cause as a necessary condition of the permissible resort to war.

Yet I also argued that in practice it is highly unlikely that a war that lacks a just cause could be proportionate in the wide sense, and even more unlikely that it could be both proportionate and justified. In practice, virtually all unjust wars are disproportionate in the wide sense. According to the traditional theory, however, it is possible for *all* the individual acts of war by unjust combatants who fight in a war that is unjust and disproportionate to be themselves proportionate. (It is also possible, though less likely, according to this view, that a war as a whole could be proportionate even though all the acts of war it comprises are disproportionate.) But how can a war as a whole be disproportionate when all the acts of war of which it is composed are proportionate?

The answer that traditional just war theorists must give is that in assessing wide *ad bellum* proportionality, one weighs the relevant bad effects of a war primarily against the good of achieving the just cause, whereas in assessing wide *in bello* proportionality, one weighs the relevant bad effects of an act of war against the military advantage the act is expected to provide. According to the traditional theory, therefore, *ad bellum* proportionality and *in bello* proportionality are quite different types of constraint. They are similar in that the *bad* effects that count in the assessment of *in bello* proportionality are the same as those that count in the assessment of *ad bellum* proportionality. The traditional theory accepts, in other words, that the bad effects that count in *each* assessment of whether an individual act of war is proportionate are, taken together, the bad effects that also count in the determination of *ad bellum* proportionality—that is, in the determination of whether the war as a whole is proportionate. But the good effects against which these bad effects are weighed in assessing *ad bellum* proportionality are different from the effects (namely, military advantages) against which the bad effects are weighed in assessing *in bello* proportionality. (Recall here that I argued earlier that it is doubtful that serious harms to innocent people can coherently be weighed against gains in military advantage to unjust combatants to yield a measure of proportionality that has any moral significance.)

This seems arbitrary. The natural assumption is that just as *ad bellum* and *in bello* proportionality are concerned with the same bad effects, so they must also be concerned with the same good effects. Given that assumption, a war can be disproportionate only if enough of the acts of war that together constitute it are themselves disproportionate. And that is what one would expect.

To appreciate how problematic the traditional theory's schizophrenic understanding of proportionality is, consider a war that is unjust because the ends it seeks to achieve are ones that would involve the infliction of wrongful harms that would be serious and extensive. The achievement of those ends would, however, provide great benefits to the aggressors. I earlier endorsed the traditional view that such benefits do not constitute good effects against which harms to innocent people can be weighed in the assessment of proportionality. For they are themselves harms to innocent people. On both the traditional and revisionist views, the achievement of these ends counts as a *bad* effect, and one that is weighted for the fact that it would be intended, for the purpose of assessing proportionality. It therefore counts negatively in the *ad bellum* proportionality calculation. Yet the ends of the unjust war are what military advantage is advantageous *for*. If the *in bello* proportionality calculation requires weighing the harms to innocent people against the military advantages that the act of war would provide, the ends of the unjust war seem to count positively, as that which gives military advantage its significance. So unjust ends count negatively in the traditional *ad bellum* proportionality calculation yet positively in the traditional *in bello* calculations.

The traditional theorist would presumably respond by claiming that the bad ends do not count positively because the value of military advantage is, at least in the assessment of *in bello* proportionality, wholly independent of the ends of the war. But this merely returns us to the original problem, which is that military advantage *has* no value that is independent of the ends it serves; therefore military advantage alone cannot weigh morally against and potentially outweigh harms to innocent people. The traditional theorist might argue further that one good aim that military advantage always serves is the defence of the combatants' lives. But that begs the question of whether unjust combatants have a right of self-defence, so that preserving them from harm is morally good in the context. And even if they do have that right, they could better protect themselves by simply terminating their unjust war, which is what they ought morally to do in any case. If their ceasing to fight would result in unjust vindictive action by their adversaries, they might then have a just cause for continuing to fight. If so, their continued war need not be unjust.

It seems, therefore, that the traditional theory's reason for claiming that it is always possible for unjust combatants to fight without violating the *in bello* proportionality constraint, even in a war that violates *ad bellum* proportionality, is unsustainable. I have also argued that unjust wars are almost invariably disproportionate in the wide sense, and that even among those that might be proportionate, relatively few, if any, could be morally justified as the lesser evil. Hence, given that *in bello* proportionality must take into account the ends that the war is intended to achieve (rather than excluding them via some stratagem such as comparing bad side effects with military advantage), it seems that acts of war by unjust combatants can only rarely satisfy the wide *in bello* requirement of proportionality.

It is also only in unusual cases that an act of war by unjust combatants can satisfy the narrow *in bello* proportionality requirement. Part of what it is for there to be a just cause for war is that there are many people who are liable to be attacked as a means of preventing or correcting a serious wrong, or set of wrongs, for which they are responsible. In the absence of a just cause, there are few if any people on the opposing side who are liable to be attacked. Most of the people who are attacked in an unjust war are therefore people who are not liable to attack. Thus the issue of narrow proportionality seldom arises in an unjust war. Recall that an act of war is proportionate in the narrow sense if the harms it inflicts are ones to which the victims are liable. An act of war is disproportionate in the narrow sense if the harms it inflicts exceed those to which the victims are liable. If, as is generally the case in an unjust war, the victims of an attack are not liable to attack at all, there is no issue of narrow proportionality. For the victims are innocent or non-liable people and any harms inflicted on them are matters of discrimination and wide proportionality.

The reason why the issue of narrow proportionality seldom arises in an unjust war is also the reason why unjust combatants can seldom satisfy the requirement of discrimination. This requirement permits intentionally attacking people who are legitimate targets and prohibits the intentional attack of those who are not legitimate targets. Legitimate targets are those who by their action have made themselves morally liable to attack. But combatants who fight by permissible means in a just war have done nothing to forfeit their rights or make themselves liable to attack. And neither, of course, have their civilian fellow citizens. But this means that unjust combatants hardly have any legitimate targets, so that almost all of their acts of war are indiscriminate. Virtually the only occasions on which unjust combatants have legitimate targets occur when just combatants threaten to inflict wrongful harms through impermissible action—for example, when they pursue their just aims by impermissible means, or when they pursue unjust aims within a war that is otherwise just. For when they act in these ways, they make themselves liable to attack. It is only on these occasions, when just combatants become liable and unjust combatants therefore have legitimate targets, that acts of war by unjust combatants can also satisfy the narrow and wide proportionality requirements. (There is a further question whether just combatants make themselves liable to defensive attack when their military action is morally justified but will inflict proportionate harms on innocent people as a side effect, thereby infringing those people's rights. If this does make them liable to defensive attack, unjust combatants may frequently have legitimate targets and their acts of war may sometimes be proportionate. I will not address this issue here, though I have argued elsewhere that when just combatants act with moral justification, the fact that their action will infringe the rights of innocent people does not make them liable to defensive action even by the potential victims, and certainly not by unjust combatants.[9])

There is, finally, the question whether acts of war by unjust combatants can satisfy the *in bello* necessity requirement. Unjust combatants could, of

---

[9] *Killing in War*, n 2 above, pp 38–51. Also see J McMahan, 'Self-Defense Against Justified Threateners', in H Frowe and G Lang (eds), *How We Fight: Issues in Jus in Bello* (Oxford: Oxford University Press, 2013). For a contrary view, see U Steinhoff, 'Jeff McMahan on the Moral Equality of Combatants' (2008) *Journal of Political Philosophy* 16, 220–6.

course, fight in ways that would satisfy the requirement of necessity if what it said is that an act of war can be permissible only if there is no alternative that would both cause less harm to innocent people and have at least an equal probability of achieving whatever the unjust combatants' aim or aims might be. But, as we saw earlier, while that is a plausible requirement as far as it goes, it is far too weak to be the whole truth about the necessity constraint in war. To be permissible, an act of war must, at a minimum, be necessary for the achievement of a morally good aim. While many or even most unjust combatants believe that the ends they pursue through war are morally good, their belief is seldom true. Wars that are unjust are rarely fought, either wholly or even in part, for aims that are morally good. Even self-defence and the defence of other unjust combatants are not morally good effects in the circumstances. And even if they were, attacking just combatants would seldom be a necessary means, since unjust combatants can generally protect their lives by withdrawing from the fighting (by refusal to fight, surrender, or desertion), which is normally what they ought morally to do in any case. The exception to these claims is again the case in which just combatants act impermissibly, either by using impermissible means or by pursuing unjust aims in the context of a just war. In such cases, acts of war by unjust combatants that seek to prevent these impermissible acts can often satisfy the necessity requirement. (Again, if just combatants make themselves liable to attack when their justified acts of war have side effects that threaten the rights of innocent people, many more acts of war by unjust combatants might satisfy the necessity requirement than can do so if the contrary assumption is true. Certainly the prevention of the infringement of a right seems in itself a morally good effect.)

V Why Mere Participation in an Unjust War Should not be Criminalized

We should conclude, I think, that acts of war by unjust combatants can seldom satisfy the *in bello* principles of discrimination, necessity, and proportionality, when these principles are plausibly interpreted. Unjust combatants may be able to satisfy these principles (1) when just combatants threaten to inflict wrongful harms through impermissible action, (2) if a just aim arises within a war that is unjust overall, or (3) when there is a lesser-evil justification for an act of war or, though this is extremely unlikely, for an unjust war as a whole. Otherwise, military action by those who fight in a war that is unjust because it lacks a just cause is likely to involve the objectively impermissible infliction of serious harms on people who are not liable to be harmed. Much of their military action is intended to harm or kill just combatants as a means of securing military advantage, yet most just combatants have done nothing to make themselves liable to attack. And this same action often has as a side effect the harming or killing of innocent non-combatants on the just side as well. Finally, the achievement of the unjust combatants' unjust ends typically involves great and wrongful harms to many people, non-combatants and combatants alike, who are citizens of the state that is the victim of the unjust war.

This generates a serious problem for any morally informed account of war crimes. As I mentioned earlier, it would be ideal if all acts of war that are seriously wrong because they violate important rights and cause great harm could be criminalized—and if *only* such acts were criminalized. But the conclusion I have reached in this section is that the vast majority of acts of war by unjust combatants are wrong because they violate rights that people have, and have not forfeited, not to be seriously harmed. If all acts of war that satisfy that description were criminalized, most acts of war by unjust combatants would be war crimes. And if making a type of act criminal is roughly equivalent to making it legally punishable, most acts of war in an unjust war would render the unjust combatants who did them liable to punishment. Criminalization of seriously wrongful harming in war would be tantamount to making mere participation in an unjust war punishable.

Yet there are many reasons why it would be both unwise and morally wrong to hold unjust combatants liable to legal punishment for fighting in an unjust war. Some of these reasons seem decisive on their own. Together they overdetermine the case against the criminalization of fighting in an unjust and illegal war. Here are some of the main reasons.

1. Individual soldiers are often neither well enough informed nor otherwise qualified to determine with confidence whether the war in which they have been commanded to fight is just or unjust, legal or illegal. And there is no reliable authority, legal or otherwise, that they may consult for guidance. For most soldiers, their own government is the highest form of authority they have, and it tells them to fight. In many cases, therefore, their restricted epistemic situation is an excusing condition that is sufficient to exempt them from liability to punishment, even if it is not sufficient to exempt them from liability to defensive action.

2. They also act under duress, for they are threatened with punishment by their own government if they refuse to fight. Even if there were a reliable and authoritative source of guidance about which wars are just and which are unjust, it might still be unfair to punish genuine unjust combatants for fighting if they would also face draconian punishment domestically for refusing to fight.

3. Given that soldiers are threatened with punishment by their own govern-ment if they refuse to fight, a threat from an external source to punish them if they do fight is less likely to deter them from fighting but may deter them from surrendering, thereby unnecessarily prolonging unjust wars. Indeed, it might provoke unjust combatants to abandon all restraints in a desperate bid for victory as their best hope for avoiding punishment altogether.

4. As long as international institutions of criminal justice remain seriously defective and inadequate, acceptance of the claim that unjust combatants may be liable to punishment involves a risk of 'victor's justice'—that is, a risk that just combatants will be 'punished' by a victorious but unjust adversary, whose claim to have fought a just war cannot be controverted in a way that could prevent it from exacting *post bellum* vengeance.

5. Until international legal institutions are able to provide authoritative guidance to combatants before or during the course of a war on whether their side's war is or would be legal or illegal, it may be unfair to hold combatants legally liable to punishment for fighting in a war that is illegal.

6. Even if the law had the ability to warn combatants in a timely manner that they were fighting in an unjust war, it would be impossible to provide fair trials for them all. It might, of course, be possible to try a limited number of them, perhaps selected by lottery. But in that case the likely deterrent effect would be insufficient to justify using scarce *post bellum* resources in this way.

7. No state could be expected to surrender a large number of its citizens for trial for doing what it had commanded them to do. It would have to be coerced to do so. Yet assuming that peace had been achieved, it would be absurd to suppose that compelling a recalcitrant state to extradite its former combatants for war crimes trials could be a just cause for a further war.

Some of these objections would have less force if there were an impartial international institution that could provide reliable and authoritative judg-ments, while wars were in progress, about which wars were just and legal and which were unjust and illegal, and if states had liberal provisions for selective conscientious objection. In these conditions, a threat of punishment by an international court might have a desirable deterrent effect without being unfair to those who might be punished. Even in these conditions, however, it might be necessary to offer amnesty to unjust combatants to induce them to surrender; but if unjust combatants could anticipate that there would be a significant probability that they would be offered an amnesty, this would diminish any deterrent effect that the threat of punishment might have. And the problem would remain that trials for a large number of former or demobilized combatants would be prohibitively costly, procedurally inadequate and thus unfair, as well as likely to provoke further conflict. So even in conditions substantially more favourable than those that prevail at present, it would still be unwise to criminalize mere participation in an unjust war.

(It is perhaps worth noting that the objections to *criminalizing* most acts of war by unjust combatants do not apply to making those acts of war merely *illegal*. The law could, therefore, condemn such acts without holding offenders liable to punishment for committing them. An unenforced legal prohibition of fighting in an unjust war would have no *deterrent* effect, but it could have the effect of *inhibiting* at least some participation in unjust wars. For an official repudiation of the idea that the law permits fighting for the sake of unjust ends could have a psychological effect in at least some cases.)

VI. The Grounds for Criminalization in War

Even though it is and will likely remain infeasible to criminalize all morally impermissible acts of war by unjust combatants, there are nevertheless moral limits to what may permissibly be done even in a just and legal war and it is necessary that they be recognized and enforced through the threat of legal punishment. And if just combatants are to be potentially liable to punishment, unjust combatants must be as well. Indeed, it is, if anything, even more important to seek to restrain the action of unjust combatants through the threat of punishment. The problem is that, while it is feasible in the case of just combatants to criminalize only seriously wrongful acts, leaving most militarily advantageous acts legally permissible, it would, as we have seen, be both unfair and counterproductive, at least in current conditions, to criminalize all seriously wrongful acts of war by unjust combatants, as that would effectively criminalize their mere participation in the war. The task is thus to determine for which of their morally impermissible acts of war unjust combatants should be held liable to punishment. (Their morally permissible acts of war, of which there could be a few, should be legal. Among their morally impermissible acts, some might be either legal or illegal though not criminal; others would be criminal.)

If there were an international institution that could distinguish, authoritatively and publicly, between just and unjust wars while they were in progress, it might be possible to have a law of *jus in bello* that would be asymmetrical between just and unjust combatants precisely because they could be reliably identified as such. Even though the existence of such an institution would not make it feasible to punish all morally impermissible acts of war by unjust combatants, it might make it possible for the range of punishable acts by unjust combatants to be wider, perhaps significantly so, than the range of punishable acts by just combatants. Yet at present there is no such institution and, at least in the near future, it is highly unlikely that there will be one. Most unjust combatants will therefore continue to believe, as most have done in the past, that they are in fact just combatants, and will consequently assume that the law that applies to them is that which applies to just combatants, whatever that law might be. In such conditions, it is impracticable, indeed futile, to have a law of *jus in bello* that is asymmetrical between just and unjust combatants. Hence, until there is an institution that can authoritatively distinguish between just and unjust combatants, the law of *jus in bello* must remain neutral, or symmetrical, between the two.

One way in which the law of *jus in bello* might be neutral is for it to prohibit all and only those types of act that would be morally impermissible if done by just combatants. Such an arrangement would be non-comparatively fair to combatants on both sides, since it would not legally prohibit any acts that it would be permissible for them to do. But it would be comparatively unfair to just combatants, for they would be punishable for any impermissible act while many impermissible acts by unjust combatants would be exempt from punishment. This is, however, a form of unfairness that exists to an even greater degree in the present law of armed conflict. The comparative unfairness of this possible arrangement is therefore not an objection to a change from the current *in bello* law to a law that would permit all combatants to do only those types of act that are, under some general description, morally permissible for just combatants.

Yet this suggestion would, I suspect, be excessively permissive in its application to unjust combatants. There are various types of action in war that, though nearly always wrong, may in rare instances be morally permissible for just combatants, such as intentionally attacking civilians who contribute in important ways to the enemy war effort, or torturing an enemy agent as a necessary means of gaining information vital to the protection of one's own civilian population. But any provision in the law, however narrowly circumscribed, that would permit the intentional killing of civilians or the torture of captives would almost certainly be repeatedly exploited by unjust combatants in a cynical effort to justify acts that would be objectively unjustified. The same is true, though probably to a lesser extent, of just combatants, who are sometimes ordered to pursue just ends by impermissible means. (Indeed, because just combatants sometimes pursue just ends by impermissible means, or pursue ends that go beyond their just cause, the permission to use torture could in principle extend even to unjust combatants. Suppose, hypothetically, that in early August of 1945, Japanese intelligence agents had known that the US planned to drop a powerful new bomb on a Japanese city. Suppose these agents had then tortured a captive American, thereby learning from him the identity of the targeted city and the timing of the attack, and had thus been able to evacuate most of the civilians from Hiroshima before the atom bomb destroyed the city, thereby saving tens of thousands of innocent lives. I would judge their action to have been objectively permissible, at least on the plausible assumption that the destruction of Japanese cities was neither necessary for nor proportionate in relation to the achievement of the US's just aims at that point in the war.)

If one surveys the history of such practices as intentionally killing civilians in war, killing prisoners of war, and torturing captured enemy agents, one finds that the morally justified instances, if any, are vastly outnumbered by the unjustified instances. This is true whether one examines the conduct of unjust combatants or that of just combatants. In these conditions, if the law cannot permit the justified instances without compromising whatever ability it has to deter or constrain the unjustified instances, it should prohibit all acts of these types. For it is more important for the law to do what it can to prevent the many acts of these types that would be wrong than it is for it to permit those few that would be morally justified.

One may wonder by what criterion I am judging what is more important here. Historically, the aim that has tended to guide both the interpretation of the morality of *jus in bello* and the formulation of the law of *jus in bello* is the reduction or minimization of the overall violence of war, or the harm caused by war. That this is the proper aim of the regulation of the conduct of war is still the consensus view. In an article rightly critical of the conduct of Israel's invasion of Gaza in 2008, Avishai Margalit and Michael Walzer wrote that 'the point of just war theory is to regulate warfare' because 'violence is evil, and . . . we should limit the scope of violence as much as is realistically possible'.[10] More recently, a professor in the Human Rights Institute at Columbia University wrote in a letter to the *New York Times* that 'if "just war" theory has any objective, it is to minimize the use of violence'.[11] Although these claims may seem almost platitudinous, they are wrong. The primary objective of the regulation of war should not be the minimization of violence but the minimization of *wrongful* violence, or the minimization of the violation of rights, weighted for their comparative importance. It is often permissible to engage in greater violence to prevent lesser violence, or to cause more harm than one prevents, provided that the harm one prevents would

[10] A Margalit and M Walzer, 'Israel: Civilians and Combatants' (14 May 2009) *The New York Review of Books* 56, 21–2, at 21.
[11] *New York Times Book Review*, 13 February 2011.

have been inflicted on people not liable to it, while the harm one causes is inflicted on those who are liable to suffer it.

If there are ways of reducing wrongful violence—violence that is indiscriminate, unnecessary, or disproportionate—that also reduce the harm suffered by wrongdoers, they are of course preferable to equivalent reductions in wrongful harm that require the harming of wrongdoers. Some conventions, such as bans of certain types of weapon, offer a reduction in harm to each side without unduly impeding either side's ability to win the war. Although such conventions function to reduce violence and harm overall, the moral reason that just combatants have to respect them may be only to maintain reciprocity and thereby prevent additional wrongful violence by the unjust combatants. While acts prohibited by such conventions are generally *mala in se* when done by unjust combatants, they may be only *mala prohibita* when done by just combatants.

In summary, rather than prohibiting all combatants from doing those types of act that are morally impermissible when done by just combatants, a neutral or symmetrical law of *jus in bello* should criminalize a form of action in war only when doing so would have the expected effect of reducing the amount of wrongful harm inflicted in war or, equivalently, the sum of weighted rights violations. A law of *jus in bello* designed using this criterion of criminalization would be unfair to just combatants in two ways. It would be non-comparatively unfair to them in that it would legally prohibit them from acting in certain ways in which it would be morally permissible for them to act. And it would be comparatively unfair because it would threaten them with criminal punishment for any seriously wrongful act they might do in war while exempting unjust combatants from punishment for a broad range of seriously wrongful acts.

These forms of unfairness seem tolerable. One might, however, think it would not be tolerable if the law were ever to prohibit the *only* possible means by which a people could achieve a significant just cause. Yet there is no objection to legally prohibiting the sole means of achieving a just cause if that means is independently prohibited by morality. Sometimes people are morally required to endure injustice if the only means of avoiding it is morally impermissible. Yet there remains the possibility that the criterion of criminalization I have suggested could, in a particular case, prohibit the only possible means of achieving a just cause even when that means would be permitted by morality. Although this possibility seems remote, it cannot be ruled out. But this too seems tolerable. Law is always imperfect; it cannot anticipate and take account of every contingency. There are therefore occasions on which it is morally permissible, or even obligatory, to violate the law.

There is no reason to suppose that the law of war crimes should be an exception to this.

VII. Discrimination, Necessity, and Proportionality

Having acknowledged that the law of *jus in bello* must for the present be symmetrical between just and unjust combatants and can probably never be asymmetrical to the same extent as the morality of *jus in bello*, we should next consider what the optimal formulations might be, at least for now, of the familiar legal requirements of discrimination, necessity, and proportionality.

By making significant and continuing contributions to an unjust war, civilians or non-combatants can make themselves morally liable to intentional military attack. Yet this is relatively rare, while the temptation to attack civilians for terrorist purposes is often strong, particularly for those who are already pursuing unjust aims, the achievement of which would also harm those same civilians. It is therefore more important to deny any pretence of legal justification to those who are tempted to kill innocent people opportunistically than it is to permit just combatants to kill non-innocent civilians on those rare occasions when that would be morally permissible.

The central problem for the formulation of a neutral requirement of discrimination is the traditional problem of drawing a precise distinction between combatants, who are legitimate targets, and non-combatants or civilians, who are not legitimate targets. The difficulty is that there are often many people who are clearly civilians, and are also non-combatants in that they do not participate in combat, who nevertheless contribute causally to the fighting of a war, sometimes in ways that are more significant than the contributions that most combatants make. The case most often discussed is that of munitions factory workers. Their work may have only one purpose: to provide the weapons necessary for the prosecution of the war. Their causal contribution seems little different from that of military support personnel who deliver weapons to combatants but do not themselves operate those weapons. If it is permissible to kill the latter to prevent the delivery of the weapons, it seems that it should also be permissible to kill the former to prevent the manufacture of the weapons. One might think that it matters that those who deliver the weapons are members of the military while factory workers are not. But consider a society in which the manufacture of weapons is done under the auspices of the military itself, by workers who are officially members of the military but do not have combat roles. It would be arbitrary to suppose that it should be legal to kill munitions workers in that society but not in societies in which the manufacture of weapons was contracted to civilian industries.

Some just war theorists have argued that munitions factory workers may be killed while they are at work but not when they are away from work. This distinguishes them from combatants, who may be killed at any time or anywhere during a state of war. But the suggestion seems to be that when they are at work, their status is also different from that of an ordinary non-combatant, whose killing even as a side effect would be subject to a more stringent proportionality constraint. It seems, therefore, that munitions factory workers are regarded, at least by some just war theorists, as having a kind of status intermediate between that of combatants and that of non-combatants. No status of this sort is recognized in law, but it is worth considering whether there might be advantages to having gradations of legal status rather than the simple and perhaps Procrustean categories of legitimate and illegitimate targets. This would, however, introduce new complexities into the law of war crimes.

The issue is important because there are often people who are unambiguously civilians and non-combatants who nevertheless make extremely important contributions to a state's ability to fight a war. One might think in this connection of certain civilian contractors, who have become increasingly important in recent years, particularly in the wars that the US has fought in Afghanistan and Iraq. But civilian scientists who work to develop new weapons technologies are arguably more important. The outcome in the European theatre of the Second World War would have been quite different if the scientists who were working to provide an atom bomb for Hitler had succeeded. They would clearly have been morally liable to be killed if that had been necessary to prevent Hitler from getting the bomb. But any legal permission, however restricted, to kill scientists in an enemy state seems too dangerous even to contemplate.

Weapons manufacturers, civilian contractors, and weapons scientists are only a few of the types of people who are not comfortably classifiable as either combatants or non-combatants, legitimate targets or illegitimate targets. Others include medics, military lawyers, civilian strategists and others who do consulting work for the military that is relevant to the conduct of war, and so on. The legal status of these and other such people must be clearly and decisively resolved if the requirement of discrimination, and hence the law of war crimes, is to have determinate scope.

Consider next the *in bello* requirement of necessity, or minimal force. To be neutral between just and unjust combatants, it seems that it must stipulate simply that an act of war is permissible only if there is no alternative act that would cause less harm and yet have at least an equal probability of achieving either the same military goal or another military goal of equal importance. As I noted earlier, morality imposes a necessity constraint both on the harming or killing of civilians or non-combatants as a side effect and on the intentional harming or killing of enemy combatants. But in conditions of war, whether the killing of an enemy combatant will contribute to the achievement of one's aims is almost always a matter of uncertainty. For while it may seem that killing a certain combatant would serve no purpose, it is possible that that combatant would otherwise pose a threat later. Because of this uncertainty, it may be wisest not to hold soldiers liable to legal punishment for causing unnecessary harm to enemy combatants, except in such well-defined situations as when enemy combatants are attempting to surrender.

This legal *in bello* necessity constraint is of course a rather weak constraint in its application to unjust combatants, as all it requires of them is that they take some risks to avoid harming innocent bystanders in the course of pursuing their unjust goals. It is analogous to a rule that prohibits burglars from burning down the house they have just burgled and killing its inhabitants, even though by doing so they could eliminate both fingerprints and witnesses.

Finally, how should the legal requirement of *in bello* proportionality be formulated? For the same reasons that the legal *in bello* necessity requirement should not take account of harms caused to enemy combatants, so the legal *in bello* proportionality requirement should concern itself exclusively with harms caused to civilians or non-combatants. That is, while morality imposes a narrow *in bello* proportionality requirement, only a wide *in bello* requirement should be enforced by law. As I argued earlier, unjust combatants can only rarely satisfy the correct moral version of the wide *in bello* proportionality requirement. Yet it is important to try to restrain their action in any ways possible and proportionality is a familiar restraining principle that many combatants, including unjust combatants (most of whom believe that they are just combatants), are motivated to try to respect. The law should therefore include a neutral, coherent, and workable proportionality constraint that serves to diminish the wrongful harms inflicted in the course of war. And at least the most flagrant or egregious violations of this constraint should be punishable as war crimes.

At present, the proportionality constraint in the law of armed conflict requires that expected harms to civilians caused as a side effect of an act of war not be 'excessive in relation to the concrete and direct military advantage anticipated'.[12] But, as I argued earlier, this is incoherent if understood as a

---

[12] Article 51 of the 1977 Geneva Additional Protocol 1 condemns any 'attack which may be expected to cause incidental loss of civilian life, injury to civilians, damage to civilian objects, or a

moral requirement, and it is difficult to make sense of if it is conceded that military advantage has no value independent of the ends it promotes. For *in bello* proportionality, as generally understood, is a relation between the expected bad side effects of an act of war and the act's intended *good* effects (together, perhaps, with certain foreseen good side effects). Yet military advantage is itself not a good effect.

Earlier I suggested, but rejected, the idea that the good effects that count in the proportionality assessment of acts of war by unjust combatants are the benefits that the unjust side would gain from the achievement of its aims. A related though different suggestion is that the relevant good effects consist solely in the protection of combatants on the battlefield.[13] On this view, an act of war is proportionate only if the expected harm it will foreseeably but unintentionally cause to civilians is not excessive in relation to the expected harm it will prevent the combatants themselves from suffering. Since civilians are thought to have a protected status vis-à-vis combatants, a certain harm to a civilian would have greater weight than an equivalent harm to a combatant. And proportionality assessments would tend to give a certain priority to civilians for another reason as well—namely, that the harms to civilians would be ones that the combatants would *cause*, while those the combatants would suffer would be ones they would merely *allow* to occur. Still, all the relevant effects would be confined to the battlefield. The goals for which the different parties were fighting would have no role in the assessment of proportionality. And because of that, the assessment would be entirely neutral between just and unjust combatants. Finally, the good and bad effects that would have to be weighed against one another would all be of the same kinds: the infliction of harms on some individuals would be weighed against the prevention of comparable harms to others. Hence, the problems of incommensurability that plague comparisons between harm to civilians and military advantage would not arise.

But as promising as this suggestion may seem, it is vulnerable to a decisive objection. This is that it rules out as disproportionate any act of war that

---

combination thereof, which would be excessive in relation to the concrete and direct military advantage anticipated'. In international criminal law, Article 8 of the Rome Statute states that the following is a war crime: 'Intentionally launching an attack in the knowledge that such attack will cause incidental loss of life or injury to civilians or damage to civilian objects or widespread, long-term and severe damage to the natural environment which would be clearly excessive in relation to the concrete and direct overall military advantage anticipated.' For a careful argument that the protections afforded to civilians in international criminal law are weaker than those provided by international humanitarian law, see A Haque, 'Protecting and Respecting Civilians: Correcting the Substantive Defects of the Rome Statute' (2011) *New Criminal Law Review* 14, 519–75.

[13] For an earlier discussion, see *Killing in War*, n 2 above, pp 31–2.

would be purely offensive, in that it would be unnecessary for the protection of one's own forces, but would also harm civilians as a side effect, even if the harms would be comparatively slight. Even if such an act would make a significant contribution to the achievement of a just cause, the fact that it would harm civilians but do nothing to protect combatants means that, on this view of *in bello* proportionality, it would be disproportionate.

One might reply that any act of war that increases the probability of victory thereby hastens the end of the war and thus helps to preserve the lives of combatants on that side. But this is not true. Some acts of war increase the probability of victory simply by preventing defeat. These acts prolong the war, usually ensuring that more combatants will be killed than would have been had their side been defeated. Defeat would, of course, mean that their side would lose what it had hoped to achieve by fighting the war, and this would involve harms to the defeated combatants. But such harms do not count in the assessment of *in bello* proportionality, according to this proposal. For the harms involved in defeat are consequent on the failure to achieve the goals of the war; they are not harms caused directly by combat, which are the only harms that this proposal recognizes as relevant to proportionality.

Consider a war of humanitarian intervention. No matter how important the humanitarian aims are and no matter how likely it is that the war would achieve them, the initial attack by the intervening forces would necessarily be disproportionate on this view of proportionality if it would cause even the slightest harm to civilians. For prior to the initial attack, the intervening combatants face no threat from the forces they will attack; therefore the attack cannot protect those combatants from harms caused by combat. Hence, on this view, there are no good effects to weigh against the harms to civilians in assessing the proportionality of the initial attack. But a formulation of the *in bello* proportionality requirement that necessarily rules out the initiation of a humanitarian intervention as disproportionate cannot be correct.

Another proposal for a workable *in bello* proportionality requirement that is neutral between just and unjust combatants is that the harm that an act of war could be expected to cause to civilians should be weighed against the contribution the act would make to the achievement of the aims of the war, taking the aims to be whatever the combatants could most reasonably take them to be on the assumption that they are just combatants. In the initial phases of the Iraq war, for example, most American combatants could have reasonably believed that their victory would prevent the Baathist regime from being able to use weapons of mass destruction against regional enemies or from supplying those weapons to terrorists for use against other countries, such as the US. Perhaps for legal purposes the right way to assess the proportionality of their acts of war was to ask whether the harm such an act would cause to civilians as a side effect was excessive in relation to the contribution the act would make to the goal of eliminating Iraq's weapons of mass destruction. That there were in fact no weapons of mass destruction is irrelevant, on this view.[14]

This proposal has some plausibility when unjust combatants can believe they are just combatants on the basis of false beliefs that are empirical in character, as in the case of American combatants in the Iraq war. But it breaks down when unjust combatants cannot reasonably believe that they are just combatants on the basis of false empirical beliefs, but can believe that they are just combatants only on the basis of a false *moral* belief. Nazi soldiers, for example, may have believed that it was justifiable for members of a superior race to expel inferior races from their lands or to enslave or exterminate them. But harms caused to innocent bystanders as a side effect cannot coherently be weighed against the supposed good of expanding the homeland of a superior people in this way, or against the supposed good of eliminating an inferior people.

Perhaps the *in bello* proportionality constraint as currently stated in the law of armed conflict is the best we can do. Perhaps, that is, unintended harms to civilians must be weighed against military advantage, which is, after all, something that all combatants seek. There is a coherent way of understanding the proportionality constraint in this way, though so interpreted, the constraint does not state a genuine moral principle. The idea is that the military advantage yielded by an act of war would be interpreted to mean the objective contribution that the act makes to the achievement of victory. The military advantage of an act could be measured on a scale, with complete ineffectiveness or no contribution at all at one end and 100 per cent probability of victory at the other. This scale could then be aligned with another that would measure harm to civilians. At one end of the second scale there would be no harm to civilians and at the other would be the maximum harm to civilians (for example, the number of civilian deaths) that would be considered proportionate in relation to the achievement of victory. An act of war would then be disproportionate if the harm it would cause to civilians measures higher on the second scale than the contribution it would make to victory measures on the first scale. This way of assessing proportionality would be equally applicable to the acts of just and unjust combatants, as there is no presupposition that victory has any kind of value. Thus, if some act of war would be decisive in securing victory for the Nazis, it could cause a great deal of unintended harm to civilians and still be proportionate. Perhaps this,

---

[14] I am indebted to Lara Buchak for suggesting to me a view of this sort.

or something quite similar, is what the authors of the proportionality restriction in the current law of armed conflict had in mind.

There are, however, two strong objections to this proposal. One is that if the scale measuring military advantage does not purport to measure anything of evaluative significance, the upper end of the scale measuring harm to civilians must be wholly arbitrary. For the end of that scale represents the maximum harm to civilians that can be proportionate in relation to the achievement of victory. But if victory is morally neutral, there is no way to determine how much harm to civilians is proportionate in relation to it.

The second objection is related to the first. It is that this measure of proportionality treats all victories equally. Suppose that an act of war by the British would have increased the probability of victory in the Falklands War by 50 per cent but that the harm it would have caused to civilians as a side effect nonetheless made it disproportionate. According to the method for determining proportionality we are now considering, if a different act of war by the British would have caused an equivalent amount of harm to civilians as a side effect but would have increased the probability of victory over the Nazis in the Second World War, it, too, would have been disproportionate.[15]

The three proposals I have canvassed are the best I can do, at least at present, in trying to formulate a workable law of *in bello* proportionality. All are inadequate. I hope that others can succeed where I have failed.[16]

---

[15] Thomas Hurka makes a similar point in arguing that it is impossible wholly to divorce *in bello* proportionality from the ends that a war seeks to achieve. See his 'Proportionality in the Morality of War' (2005) *Philosophy and Public Affairs* 33, 34–66.

[16] I am grateful to Massimo Renzo for very helpful written comments and to Victor Tadros for illuminating discussion.

9

Terrorism and the Criminal Law

C A J Coady

Terrorism represents a challenge to the criminal law in a number of ways, partly because terrorist acts confront the settled assumptions and preconceptions of criminal law, certainly of national criminal law. Advancing discussion of this challenge requires achieving some degree of clarity about what terrorism is and what appropriate responses to it might involve, as well as clarifying what the criminal law is, or should be, about. I will principally address the first two, but sketch some possible implications for the third.

I. Preliminaries

On the face of it, terrorist acts involve the use of violence to inflict severe harming or killing of citizens by foreigners, or, often enough, by fellow citizens. They are therefore primary candidates for restraining and punitive action under the domestic criminal law of the relevant nation. What are immediately in play are laws against murder, aggravated assault and so on. These are not esoteric laws, but form part of any criminal law worthy of the name. Whatever the state exists for, whatever justifies its existence, it appears that its laws must sanction such acts. This raises two interesting questions for our discussion. The first is why any new legislation is needed for the prevention and prosecution of terrorist acts. The second is whether killing and harming should always be illegal, and even if they should, whether they might nonetheless be morally justified.

The first question I will postpone for later consideration, noting only that the law has a tendency to partition and treat differently what can seem to be the one crime, witness the different forms of stealing that some criminal codes recognize or the different 'degrees' of murder that some jurisdictions treat differently. More recently, there has been a strong tendency to distinguish on the basis of motive what are otherwise ('externally') the same crimes. So we have the category of hate crimes, ranging from inflammatory speech and insults to killing, and, in international law, genocide. The relevance of this tendency to the enactment of various anti-terrorist laws should be obvious. I don't say that the tendency is wholly bad, or indeed, bad at all. Obviously, the matter should be looked at on a case-by-case basis, with an eye to efficiency and other values, such as civil liberties. The only general thing I would say is that there is a case for bearing in mind a legal analogue to Occam's Razor—don't multiply crimes (or criminal categories) without necessity.

The second question may seem very strange at first, but if the political nature of terrorism is kept in mind it can remind us that many decent societies arguably owe their present relatively benign circumstances to a successful violent revolution which involved just such harms and killings that were and are against the criminal law. Many citizens at the time regarded their revolution as morally justified and many more current citizens of the relevant nation regard it as such today—the United States being a prime example of this tendency. Had the present rhetoric of terrorism been available to the British governors of their North American colonies at the time, they would certainly have characterized the fighters for 'liberty' as terrorists. And when states go to war they train many of their citizens to kill and maim non-citizens (and, indeed, train some of them to do so long before there is any prospect of war) and then unleash them in what would otherwise be regarded within their own jurisdictions as murderous endeavours. At a less political level, many states retain capital punishment for some crimes and all inflict the various harms of detention and deprivation of liberty upon those who break the law. Then there is the matter of euthanasia and, much more ambiguously, abortion. So, not all killing and harming is universally deemed illegal and some that is illegal may be morally justified. (It is worth noting at this point that not all intentional killing and harming need be violent: we can kill someone by calmly and deliberately neglecting to give them a vital medicine they need and that we have a duty to provide.[1])

Of course, these complexities only highlight the fact that states are certain to view political violence that they do not control as something to be punished and suppressed. As Max Weber once argued, states are partly constituted by their having a monopoly on the use of violence within their

---

[1] Issues related to this are discussed in Chapter 2, 'The Idea of Violence', of C A J Coady, *Morality and Political Violence* (Cambridge and New York: Cambridge University Press, 2008).

boundaries. Challenges to this monopoly are inevitably greeted with strong emotional, rhetorical, policing and legal reactions.

We might pause to consider the definition of criminal law. One way of thinking of it is as that part of the law that is concerned with punishment, but unfortunately this just shifts the problem on to the nature of punishment. Footballers are punished by tribunals and referees when they are believed to violate a code, but their offences are hardly criminal. Perhaps we should say that the criminal law is that by which the state (or an international equivalent) licenses the imposition of severe restrictions on personal liberty, such as jail or heavy fines, as a response to violation of publicly declared norms concerned with regulating those aspects of civic life that involve serious harms to citizens and residents. (International criminal law would require some modification to this formula.) This is only a rough approximation for our purposes and perhaps suits the tradition of English law more neatly than some other jurisdictions (see comments on extradition to Poland below).

These background facts lead naturally to another consideration, which is the fact that states, and particularly modern states, exercise tremendous power over their citizens, a power which is, as Lord Acton famously noted, inevitably prone to corruption. This is true even of those states we tend to view most favourably, namely, those we call democratic. One reason for the favourable assessment and for the title 'democratic' is that these states are constrained in the exercise of great power by some recourse, varying in degree and quality, to the will of the people governed, and in those states that are not only democratic but liberal in orientation, there are forms of constitutional protection and redress to protect against abuses of state power or even the power of majorities. But for those of us who believe that state powers are inherently prone to abuse, the crisis brought about by the events of 11 September 2001 and subsequent attacks by Islamic extremists is cause for concern, not only about terrorist events but about government reactions to them. These reactions have not been restricted to internal police, security and legal measures, of course, since they have also involved a considerable military response by many powers, most notably by the USA, but also a number of its allies. This raises a question about the relative value of legal responses and military responses and of the connections between them.

II. What is Terrorism?

But let us turn now to the question of what terrorism is. Politicians, philosophers, political theorists, and lawyers—not to mention ordinary folk—offer a bewildering variety of definitions of terrorism or terrorist acts. My own view, which I have defended at length elsewhere (see n 3), is that we do best to begin with the notion of a terrorist act rather than with that of terrorism or terrorist since it is likely that we call projects, people or policies 'terrorist' because of something distinctive in what they do and likewise with our talk of 'terrorism'. In addition, if we start in this way we have some chance of avoiding misleading accounts of terrorism as a sort of ideology and of terrorists as distinctive sorts of 'other' people. I do not regard terrorism as an ideology or terrorists as a group defined by an ideology or a political programme; rather, people are terrorists when they plan or resort to terrorist acts, and the pattern of such behaviour may rightly be called terrorism. This is important when considering popular or political or legal talk about how to deal with so-called 'terrorist groups'. At a minimum, it would seem a terrorist act is a certain sort of violent act, and if we are going to talk of terrorists and terrorist groups they should be defined by their orientation to deliver that certain form of violence. In addition, terrorist acts are violent acts that are usually regarded as being of a particularly reprehensible nature, though I don't think that this feature should be part of the definition. It is merely worth noting at this juncture.

This starting point may seem very obvious, and indeed it is intended to be so, but it is indicative of some of the difficulties in reaching agreement on starting points concerning terrorism that some theorists don't want to include *any* reference to violence in their definition of terrorism. Robert Goodin, for instance, defines terrorist acts as any acts that are performed 'with the intention of frightening people for political advantage'.[2] In terms of a definition that seeks to capture key elements in the admittedly messy concept of terrorism, an approach that excludes violence from the definition is, I think, simply perverse. Goodin's approach would group together as equally terrorist both the action of a concerned climate scientist delivering a factual speech rightly hoping that it will frighten the audience sufficiently to moderate their contributions to climate destruction, and the bombing of a busload of schoolchildren by a political activist who wants to bring about a change in military policy. My own definition of terrorism is more restricted and would count only the second as a terrorist act.[3] I define a terrorist act as a violent attack upon non-combatants (or their property) by groups or their

[2] Robert Goodin, *What's Wrong with Terrorism?* (Cambridge: Polity Press, 2006) 156.
[3] For a fuller account and defence of my version of a tactical definition and its moral implications see Coady, 'The Morality of Terrorism' in *Morality and Political Violence*, n 1 above. See also C A J Coady, 'Defining Terrorism' in Igor Primoratz (ed), *Terrorism: The Philosophical Issues* (London: Palgrave, 2004).

representatives who launch the attacks for political purposes. By non-combatants I mean those who are innocent of any purported wrongdoing that might serve to legitimate the resort to political violence against the wrongdoers. With this understanding, I will use non-combatant and innocent as roughly interchangeable, though there are complex philosophical issues lurking in the background bushes.[4] This style of definition I call a tactical definition because it concentrates not upon anti-state violence in general, or even politically motivated anti-state violence in general, but upon the specific tactic of targeting non-combatants (or, if you like, innocents). I think that this targeting of people who don't deserve to be targeted is what people are getting at when they speak of terrorism as 'indiscriminate', but I will avoid the term because it can suggest uncontrolled or mindless resorts to violence whereas there is at least a case to be made that terrorism is governed by a certain rationality, even if its aims often fail.

Other versions of a tactical definition are more expansive than mine by including the motive of creating fear, or other features such as targeting one group in order to influence the policies of another. (See, for instance, work by Steve Nathanson[5] or Igor Primoratz.[6]) One might also include (as do most legal definitions) *the threat* of harming non-combatants as part of the definition. But these variations will not matter greatly for what follows.

There is a range of competing definitions in the philosophical, political and legal literature, but one notable competitor, or competitor type, is what I call a political status definition. Unlike the tactical definition, this insists that only certain categories of agents can commit terrorist acts since these are by definition acts committed against the state by sub-state actors. (The term 'sub-state' is meant to operate indexically to mark a contrast with the actions of officially authorized governmental agents, hence the agents of a foreign state could still be terrorists if they committed attacks upon the 'home' state, at least in certain contexts, such as peacetime.) Some political status definitions narrow the field somewhat by holding that only politically motivated attacks against a *legitimate* state will count as terrorist. Either way, these definitions are, I believe, inadequate, principally because they make it impossible to speak of

---

[4] One could use 'civilian', suitably understood, instead of either 'non-combatant' or 'innocent' though a suitable understanding of the term raises further problems.

[5] Stephen Nathanson, *Terrorism and the Ethics of War* (Cambridge: Cambridge University Press, 2010) 24ff. Nathanson agrees with me in excluding the fear reference from his definition but includes a clause about terrorist acts 'generally' being aimed at influencing a wider group than those targeted directly.

[6] Igor Primoratz, 'What is Terrorism?' in Igor Primoratz (ed), *Terrorism: The Philosophical Issues*, n 3 above, especially pp 21–2 and 24. Primoratz emphasizes both fear and the aim of influencing the wider group in his definition.

state terrorism by one's own state and of other states against their own populations, though perhaps there is room for state-sponsored terrorism by other states against one's own. In addition, given the common view that terrorism is always morally wrong, they tar all violent revolutions with the same brush, making it difficult to speak of a just or morally legitimate revolution. (It is particularly ironic that political status definitions are so common in the United States, a nation founded, as noted earlier, by violent revolution that is an object of veneration in that country.) In what follows, I shall have in mind a tactical understanding of the phenomenon, though some of what I say is relevant to political status definitions.

It is worth noting that most of the legal definitions in anti-terrorist definitions are explicitly or implicitly of the political status type. The UK Terrorism Act (2000), with its subsequent amendments, is typical in this respect, as in its blurring of various important distinctions. Although its vague and far-reaching language makes its scope somewhat unclear, it is plain that violence or the threat of it against governments is central to what it seeks to prohibit with the term terrorism. To summarize its convoluted sections and sub-sections, it counts as terrorist (subject to a proviso noted below) those actions that involve either 'serious violence' against a person or property, or that endanger the lives of persons (other than the actor) or 'create a serious risk to the health or safety of the public or a section of the public' or are 'designed seriously to interfere with or seriously to disrupt an electronic system'. Let us call these actions the primary actions.[7]

Primary actions are terrorist provided only that they are first 'designed to influence the government or an international governmental organization or to intimidate the public or a section of the public', and secondly 'the use or threat is made for the purpose of advancing a political, religious, racial, or ideological cause'. In a curious additional clause, however, the first part of this proviso is withdrawn for certain acts by exempting from its governance any use of firearms or explosives to perform one or other of what I have called the primary actions. Someone who has a political grievance against a ramshackle, disused, governmental building structure that impinges upon his or her land in some significant way and who has been unsuccessful in seeking redress through normal channels may be foolish and reprehensible to vent frustration by blowing up the offending edifice, but it seems contrary to common sense to treat the offender as a terrorist. This curious clause (depending upon what is meant by 'serious' and 'electronic system') might also make a terrorist of someone who is enraged with some aspects of government regulation of

---

[7] I am taking the primary acts listed in 1.2 of Part 1 of the Act as disjunctive since it makes no sense to treat them as conjunctive conditions.

telecommunications services and so shoots his or her or another's phone, television set or computer (with a licensed rifle) thus seriously damaging an electronic system in order to make a political statement.

Leaving aside the doubtful effects of this additional clause, we can see that the definition restricts the idea of a terrorist act to acts of violence or serious coercive behaviour by sub-state agents fundamentally aiming to influence government policy. This pro-state bias extends even to the criminalizing (as terrorist) within the UK of such acts directed against governments anywhere in the world, no matter what their political complexion or their oppressive practices. This would make terrorists of Burmese dissidents defending themselves with arms against brutal attacks by government forces, and would retrospectively count as terrorists Jewish armed resisters to Nazi troops in the Warsaw ghetto (as long as such troops could be viewed as representing a foreign government) or French resisters attacking German military facilities, but rule out as terrorist any violent acts against civilians committed by Russian troops in Chechnya, Serbian troops in Kosovo, or government troops in apartheid South Africa. It would also mean that the American revolution of independence consisted wholly of terrorist acts. In fact, the stress on sub-state agents as exclusive perpetrators of terrorist acts is strongly implicit in the legislation rather than openly declared so it is possible to read its provisions as going beyond sub-state agents and covering one government's violent acts against another, so that the 2011 military interventions by Western governments in support of Libyan rebels would be terrorist. It is unlikely that this is the intent of the legislation, though a consequence of its imprecise wording. The Act's inclusion in the primary actions of serious disruption or interference with an electronic system is highly problematic and will be discussed below.

My neglect of the motive of fear in the definition does not mean that the creation of fear is not in fact an important aspect of a good deal of terrorist activity. Some philosophers have been concerned to elucidate something they regard as a distinctive feature of what we might call the moral phenomenology of terrorism. Jeremy Waldron has made a contribution to this in his paper, 'Terrorism and the Uses of Terrorism' and more recently Samuel Scheffler has made much of a role for extreme fear in posing and seeking to answer the question: 'Is Terrorism Morally Distinctive?' in a paper of the same name.[8] There is some interest in this question, though not, I think, as much as the questioners believe. Scheffler wants to avoid defining terrorism at all, though taking certain examples of politically-orientated violence

---

[8] Jeremy Waldron, 'Terrorism and the Uses of Terror' (2004) *Journal of Ethics* 8; Samuel Scheffler, 'Is Terrorism Morally Distinctive?' (2006) *Journal of Political Philosophy* 14.

that people 'would not hesitate, prior to analysis, to classify as instances of terrorism' (p 2) and then analysing what is distinctively morally repellent about them. The answer he produces is that they are committed 'in order to induce fear or terror in others, with the aim of destabilizing or degrading (or threatening to destabilize or degrade) an existing social order' (p 3). These he calls 'the standard cases', though curiously this nomenclature is not intended (he says) 'to beg the very questions of definition that I said I would not be addressing'. I call this curious because a selection of standard cases to the exclusion of what others would equally readily pre-theoretically classify 'unhesitatingly' as terrorist acts is an obvious definitional move, even if it is definition by paradigm case rather than explication of necessary and sufficient conditions or the like. Significantly, many of these other cases are clear counter-examples to Scheffler's thesis, so he has to treat them as somehow peripheral instances of terrorism, or, for one set of cases, as not terrorism at all, but 'terror'. Consider, for example, the numerous examples of terrorist acts in which the aim of the perpetrators has nothing to do with 'destabilizing or degrading an existing social order' such as terrorist acts (in the sense of the tactical definition) aimed at securing the release of political prisoners, or the removal of an occupying force, or the removal of an oppressive government. None of these need aim at the degrading or destabil- izing of the existing social order to which the victims belong; the attackers need not give a fig about that social order, other than its influence on the specific grievances they hope to remedy. Nor, as Scheffler admits, does a great deal of state terrorism have his favoured aim; indeed much of it aims to bolster the existing social order, and, for this reason, he wants to call it 'terror' rather than 'terrorism'—not that he's interested in definition! Some terrorist attacks do indeed have the purpose that Scheffler identifies, but making this the prime focus of our moral concern with terrorism has dangerous implica- tions. One is that the degrading or destabilizing story shifts attention away from possibly remediable grievances that many terrorist acts are concentrated upon. It seems clear, for instance, that much of the stimulus to terrorist activity directed against the United States and its allies arises not from some wholesale rejection of democracy but from hatred of certain American military and geo-political strategies and activities, especially in the Middle East. The presence of US military bases often supporting or countenancing despotic or unpopular regimes combined with almost wholesale support for regionally-detested Israeli policies are potent causes, often invoked in terrorist literature. If terrorist attacks are part of a campaign to achieve, for instance, decolonization, removal of foreign military bases or forces, or what is seen as a foreign invasion or occupation, then the cosmic destabilization/degradation story obscures this reality in favour of what may well be a fantasy. This has serious consequences for counter-terrorist strategies.

For the purposes of this chapter, I will often, in what follows, refer to terrorism or terrorists with basically sub-state agents in mind, for example, when raising a question about whether terrorists should be considered as criminals or soldiers. That question could indeed be raised about states and their agents in a different way, but its usual locus of discussion is with sub-state agents hostile to the state. This pragmatic narrowing of vision for expository purposes should not be seen as any departure from the main thrust of the tactical definition which allows that states can use terrorism (and use it more dreadfully) either against their own people or against other states or external groups. Some states might even qualify for the title 'terrorist state'. Indeed, legal and other measures to prevent state terrorism should preoccupy us more than they do and the prevention of the use of terrorism by states has claims to be a more urgent task than the prevention of terrorist acts by sub-state groups. Nonetheless, sub-state terrorism raises the question of prevention in an acute form since the threat posed is not one that is indicated by massive increase in conventional military forces or the conspicuous build-up of armaments. But first, we need some further clarifications of the tactical definition.

III. Further Clarifications

My tactical definition does not define terrorist acts as immoral, though it does create a presumption of immorality that would have to be rebutted by supporters of terrorism. This presumption rests on the validity of the principle of discrimination that is central to the *jus in bello* of the just war tradition which requires the immunity of non-combatants from direct attack. I treat this principle as a moral principle rather than a legal one though it is mirrored in the legal regulation of war. (It is of course closely related to the moral prohibition on intentionally killing innocent persons (against their will).) Hence, in my usage, a non-combatant is given a moral meaning as someone who is not an agent in the prosecution of a violent objective moral wrong that would license a just cause response of violent defensive war. This has some paradoxical consequences for the legal regulation (and a common understanding) of war, since soldiers who are prosecuting a just war would count as (morally) non-combatants. To avoid this consequence one could amend the definition of non-combatant to replace the word 'objective' with some phrase that referred to a sufficiently reasonable subjective belief. Combatants would then be those who were agents of lethal violence in some political cause presumed by them to be just and non-combatants would be those who were not such agents. There are clear advantages in doing this, but a disadvantage in terms of morality is that, although it helps us keep some connection between non-combatants and innocence, it removes that idea of innocence from application to just combatants. Yet those who fight in an objectively just cause are certainly innocent of wrongdoing in so acting where the aggressors they defend against are not. Another, possibly supplementary, way of handling the problem is to distinguish between a legal sense of 'combatant/non-combatant' and a moral sense. The legal sense will be close to, but not quite identical with, the distinction between 'soldiers' and 'civilians'. It will abstract from the justice of the cause and count as noncombatants all and only those who are not agents of the prosecution of a cause of hostilities whether (within limits) that cause is just or not. A vacillation between the moral and legal senses of the terms combatant and non-combatant partly explains why many people will view attacks upon military targets by sub-state groups as terrorist. They have a tendency to regard their own troops, mercenaries and security companies as almost noncombatants so that attacks upon 'private contractors' in Iraq and Afghanistan seem almost as outrageous (to them) as attacks upon uninvolved civilians, even where those contractors are often armed to the teeth and defending military assets. This tendency is at work even in so sophisticated a theorist as the American philosopher, Virginia Held, who has produced as counterexamples to the tactical definition the suicide-bombing attack upon the United States marine base in Beirut, Lebanon in 1983 which killed 241 American servicemen, and the attack on the USS *Cole* in Yemen in 2000. She thinks the fact that these cases are 'routinely offered as examples of terrorism' shows the defects of the tactical definition, since these were attacks upon combatants.[9] But the 'routine offering' seems to me simply to betray an absurdly benign view of the vast numbers of US military stationed in foreign lands, especially those in the Middle East where their presence provides strong-arm support for regimes and political agendas that many locals cannot regard as anything but hostile and repressive. Indeed, in the Beirut case, the US 'peace-keeping' troops were widely perceived as favouring the Maronite Catholic faction in the Lebanon civil war and US naval gunfire had supported Lebanese army action.

In fact, a version of the legal or regulatory sense is best suited to the discussion of terrorism in most contexts, since we need to distinguish groups using violence on behalf of a political cause who respect the immunity of those who are not

---

[9] Virginia Held, *How Terrorism is Wrong: Morality and Political Violence* (Oxford and New York: Oxford University Press, 2008) 17.

deploying violence against them or those they represent (or not aiding substantially in its deployment) from groups who resort to violence precisely against that category of persons in order to advance their cause through creating fear or anger or whatever. Even here, we should be careful of the labels 'terrorist' or 'terrorist group' since some insurgent or revolutionary groups use non-terrorist tactics, violent or otherwise, for the most part and resort to terrorist tactics occasionally. Branding such groups terrorist and criminalizing support for them risks ignoring the fact that they may be pursuing a legitimate grievance through mostly legitimate means (both violent and non-violent) and external support may be for these possibly legitimate purposes.

What might further concern us is the interesting question that has many practical consequences: whether terrorists should be treated as soldiers or civilians. This tracks the issue whether terrorists should be dealt with by the criminal law, the laws of war, or by mixtures of both. I have so far proceeded by invoking just war categories such as combatant and non-combatant because one locus of attention to terrorism is in the context either of war or of armed struggle for broadly political objectives. It is not surprising that Irish Republican Army (IRA) prisoners in Northern Ireland sought status as prisoners of war instead of criminals in order that it be recognized that they were fighting for political objectives and not the usual criminal aims. Those of them who were terrorists (and not all were, on my definition) should, of course, be regarded as guilty of what would be war crimes in a normal war, so there was certainly a strong taint of criminality in a broad sense about what they did, even if they were also guilty of breaking normal criminal laws, such as the law against murder. Jeff McMahan has argued that it is better to treat terrorists as criminals, though he thinks their status hovers somewhere between criminal and combatant.[10] He is partly moved by worries about the Bush administration's determination to treat them as combatants, indeed 'illegal combatants' or 'enemy combatants' (in an unusual sense of that phrase), so that they could be killed outright rather than arrested and tried. He much prefers the path of arrest and trial. I have a good deal of sympathy with this, but much depends on context. Where the individuals are working on a terrorist project alone or in a small group with only remote and fragile connections to an organized force, it seems better to view them in a context of criminal efforts and seek arrest and trial. This will be particularly pertinent where the suspected terrorists are citizens/residents of the state attempting to deal with them (state A). Where the suspected terrorists are citizens/residents of another country (state B) but planning an attack on state A, then recourse

[10] Jeff McMahan, 'Terrorism and the "war on terror"' in Chris Miller (ed), *War on Terror (Oxford Amnesty Lectures)* (Manchester: Manchester University Press, 2009).

to the policing capacities of state B is again preferable, but that depends, of course, on the integrity and efficiency of those forces.

Where terrorist tactics are used by organized armed forces engaged in insurrection or the like, the response must have more of a military flavour, even if it falls short of all out war. And even the police may have to use lethal violence where necessary against people who are in the process of perpetrating a terrorist attack. Indeed, modern day police have armed response units that have quasi-military roles in, for instance, hostage situations that need not involve terrorists. Even so, the arrest and trial path, in spite of some of its disadvantages mentioned below, has the obvious merits that it is less prone to error, is likely to cause far less 'collateral damage' and has less potential for fanning more terrorist flames than do military measures.

Treating terrorists as criminals raises the question of the utility of the tactical definition in legal practice. Against its use is the understandable reluctance of the state to make distinctions about violence used against it from within. The state sees itself as having a monopoly on the legitimate use of violence within its domain and so is resistant to admitting that individual citizens or, still worse, sub-state groups could in any sense legitimately resort to violence against it. This resistance encompasses both the legitimacy of cause and of means. As to cause, it is understandable that the state, whether democratic or dictatorial, will dismiss the idea that revolutionary or reformist violence could be legitimately or even excusably used against it, even though outsider states and individuals may think otherwise. My concern here, however, is less with this issue than that of distinguishing means, since that is crucial to the tactical definition.

The first point to make is that differentiating violence against the state into different categories does not in itself create a problem for the state's instinct to treat all such violence as illegitimate. Even if violence of this sort is illegitimate (and those who admit just revolutions will deny that this is necessarily the case), there may be some types of violence that are less wrong than others and merit different legal treatment. Although the topic of mercy killing is controversial, there seems a difference of moral category between mercy killing that is effectively assisted suicide and the murder of a kidnapped child who is no longer valued by the kidnappers when the ransom has been paid. Even when treating both such cases as violations of law, there is no reason why the legal processes should not acknowledge the significance of such differences, at least at the point of sentencing, and perhaps in other ways. Similarly, consider the difference between prison escapees who shoot and kill an armed prison guard who is shooting at them while they are attempting to escape and similar escapees who deliberately shoot and kill innocent bystanders in order to distract their pursuers. There is a case for regarding the latter as a more heinous crime even though both are murders. If so, it should be possible to treat political violence directed at state agents (and agencies) that can intelligibly be viewed as opposing forces by those whose grievance leads them to violence in a quite different way from political violence that is manipulatively directed at people who are in no sense opposing forces. Both may be wrong, but they are different wrongs and could very well receive different treatment in domestic law.

I said that in the example of the prison escapees there was a case for regarding the intentional shooting of innocent bystanders as more heinous than killing a prison guard by returning fire. Against this, it may be argued that the state has a special interest in safeguarding those who enforce its laws and so should treat the killing of state officials as more grievous than the killing of ordinary citizens. Certainly, the state needs to be vigilant in defence of those charged with the sometimes-dangerous duty of enforcing the laws and protecting the public, at least where those laws are just and the relevant public deserves protection. But such vigilance need not involve rejection of the point I made, and that for two reasons. First, the vigilant attitude is consistent with there being a requirement for an even more powerful condemnation of such atrocities as the child killing in my example. Second, it should be remembered that there are a range of cases that can fall under the heading 'killing of state officials' and some will be more grievous than others. In a famous case in Australia known as the Walsh Street murders, two young Victorian police constables were lured to a Melbourne suburban street in October 1988 on the report of an abandoned car, then ambushed and shot to death by a group of criminals. The killings were apparently undertaken as revenge for an earlier fatal police shooting of a gang member that was widely viewed by the underworld as an illegal execution. The case created great community concern and even greater police outrage and several career criminals suspected of involvement in the Walsh Street crime were subsequently shot and killed by police in controversial circumstances. The callous killing of the two constables was indeed a horrible crime, but very different from the example of the escapees mentioned above. Indeed, the two young constables might well be regarded as innocent if they were in no way involved in the earlier police killing. This is certainly how they were portrayed in the media. (In fact, there had been a number of earlier police shootings, and one of the murdered constables had been involved in one of these, but that involvement does not seem to have been a reason for the ambush. The killers could not have known who would respond to the report of the abandoned car.)

A further consideration about legal practicality is that, whatever the problems of implementing the tactical definition into law and policing, they create no more difficulties than the existing legal definitions. Indeed, their relative precision contrasts usefully with the sweeping vagaries of such definitions as the UK Act.

IV. Responses to Terrorism

This brings us to the more general question of how best to deal with terrorist attacks. A striking feature of the response to the Islamic militant terrorist attacks on Western 'homelands' has been the deployment of military metaphors and military realities in counter-terrorist measures. They have not been the only forms of response, of course, but they have had a significant role from the slogan 'war on terror' to the invasions of Iraq and Afghanistan. Moreover, employment of the military to deal with terrorism is not new, as witness the British Army's involvement in Northern Ireland. A full discussion of the merits of this sort of response is beyond the scope of this chapter, but I think that overall the record of such military ventures is not encouraging, either in terms of success or in terms of the licence it has given for governments to deploy military force against spurious terrorist threats, as in Chechnya and most recently in the Middle East. I shall merely mention some of the problems with the military approach in discussing the other approaches below.

There seem to be basically (at least) four such non-military approaches: (1) domestic legal and regulatory measures, especially those introduced specifically to deal with terrorism; (2) international legal and regulatory measures; (3) diplomatic measures, both internal and external; (4) removing the grievance. There is some overlap between the categories but it is still useful to distinguish them. I'll examine the pros and cons of each though I will concentrate heavily upon the first.

A. Non-military measures—advantages and difficulties

All of these have the primary advantage over heavily military measures that they do not involve a commitment to killing and maiming on a large or relatively large scale. If the Iraq war was supposed to stem terrorist killing of Americans at home, as some apologists argued, then it has done so (on a dubiously optimistic concession to its supporters) at the cost of more Americans killed than died in the 9/11 attacks, more than 100,000 Iraqi civilians killed, many more wounded, dispossessed, and self-exiled, an economy and social order badly damaged for many years and a great increase in terrorist activity in Iraq itself, still continuing as I write (in early 2012). Somewhat similar considerations apply to Afghanistan. Measures (1) to (4) involve none of this. At worst, their failure may lead to many deaths in terrorist attacks that are not prevented, but, in contrast to military attacks, such deaths are not inevitable, and no measure can guarantee success, certainly not full-scale military measures, as Afghanistan and Iraq in their different ways show. Nor is it clear (to say the least) that the Iraq and Afghanistan invasions have prevented further attacks upon nations outside Iraq and Afghanistan, indeed, they have clearly played a part in provoking such attacks since 2001. By contrast, legal and policing measures, in spite of their problems discussed below, actually seem to have been successful in preventing terrorist attacks, though the extent of that success is difficult to determine. Diplomatic efforts (including some removal of grievance) have also had some conspicuous successes, as (eventually) in Northern Ireland. This presents a good case in favour of (1) to (4), but they have downsides and we need to assess them and assess each category to measure them against the others. In doing so, we need to bear in mind the background facts that I outlined at the beginning of this discussion concerning the innate tendency of great power to be abused and to corrupt.

Re (1), there are many problems with legal measures, some of which will carry over to (2). Those involving the criminal law, and they are the main ones likely to have an appropriate rationale, can be threatening to significant civil liberties within the state enacting them and are arguably superfluous. There is a further question about their effectiveness. There is also the fact that they are stretching the scope of the criminal law in dramatic and, in certain respects, alarming ways. No less a person than Britain's top prosecutor, the former Director of Public Prosecutions, Sir Ken Macdonald, warned of these risks (and realities) in his final speech before leaving office at the end of 2008.[11] He claimed that centuries of British civil liberties were at risk from the relentless pressure of the 'security state'. He referred to various anti-terrorism measures and proposals as the 'paraphernalia of paranoia'. After the defeat of the British Labour Government in 2010, Macdonald was appointed to provide 'independent oversight' to the review of the country's counter-terrorism and security powers by the Office for Security and Counter Terrorism in the Home Office, and his oversight report was published in early 2011.[12] I have no space to discuss the report in detail, but it is worth noting a few points. One is his comment in the Introduction that 'the promise of total security is an illusion that would destroy everything that makes living worthwhile...some risks are worth running in order to enjoy liberty'.[13] He

[11] Frances Gibb, 'DPP chief Sir Ken Macdonald attacks Big Brother state surveillance', *The Times* (London), 21 October 2008.
[12] Lord Ken Macdonald, 'Review Of Counter-Terrorism And Security Powers—A Report By Lord Macdonald Of River Glaven QC' (London: Office of Security and Counter-Terrorism, Home Office, 2011).
[13] Lord Ken Macdonald, n 12 above, at p 2.

supports the reduction of the maximum period of pre-charge detention to 14 days, the abolition of the stop and search provisions of section 44, and the Report's recommendation that groups that espouse violence or hatred should not be proscribed. In connection with the latter, Macdonald argues that the proscription would be 'strikingly illiberal, extraordinarily difficult to enforce and it would probably run counter to the Review's overriding purpose to roll back State powers'.[14] In addition to this, such proscription runs foul of the point I made earlier about the superfluity of some anti-terrorist legislation. It is a superfluous measure since incitements to violence and racial and religious hatred by individuals are already criminal offences, and nothing seems to be achieved (other than the deleterious effects cited by Macdonald) by making them group offences. This is a classic example of the way over-reaction to terrorism produces legislation that is both unnecessary and damaging. The twenty-eight-day detention period has similar problems since, at the time of writing, no recourse to it has been deemed necessary by police since 2007.

It is worth asking whether many other anti-terrorism legislative measures are also superfluous: agencies like police or security services are seldom willing to advise against giving them more and more powers, powers that will invariably work to restrict the liberty of citizens. Of course, the interpretation of the law by judges is sometimes proof against the pressure for more prosecutorial powers and discretions. This was shown in 2010 during proceedings in Britain by six British residents who claim that the British government was complicit in their having been tortured and secretly transferred to Guantanamo Bay: they sued the government for abuse and wrongful imprisonment. The secret agencies MI5 and MI6 urged the courts to suppress a great deal of evidence from the plaintiffs and the public and to make it available only to a judge and specially appointed and vetted counsel. But the Court of Appeal has rejected this procedure as tantamount to 'undermining one of (the common law's) most fundamental principles'. The judges insisted that it was essential that 'a litigant should be able to see and hear all the evidence which is seen and heard by a court determining his case'. Subsequently, the authorities decided not to appeal further and the plaintiffs were bought off with huge taxpayer-funded compensation settlements.

We must not, however, assume that the judiciary will always be a barrier to bad procedures and malpractice in the context of terrorism. The poor record of even very distinguished judges during the 1970s IRA terror alarms in the Birmingham Six, Guildford Four, and the Maguire Seven trials shows that

---

[14] Lord Ken Macdonald, n 12 above, at p 8.

public outrage, political pressure and panic can reach to the highest levels of the law.

A further problem with anti-terrorism laws is that the widening of police and other state powers that they involve presents a permanent temptation to use them or powers that are associated with them against persons other than terrorists. (This parallels, on the international stage, the way that oppressive governments quickly invoke anti-terrorist rhetoric in order to resort readily to military or police violence against non-terrorist protesters, as in Egypt, Libya, and Syria in 2011.) The UK Terrorist Act 2000, as discussed earlier in connection with definitions, includes in its primary actions a reference to serious disruption or interference with electronic systems (whether or not it involves violence), but this would seem to make terrorists of Rupert Murdoch's crew at the *News of the World*, given only that some of their hacking was designed to have a degree of influence on the government. This outcome might be welcome in some quarters, but surely distorts our understanding of terrorism and unduly extends the scope of severe anti-terrorist penalties and emergency investigative techniques. Even more alarmingly, the clause about electronic systems would criminalize as terrorists those dissidents in tyrannical regimes who hack into the phones or computers of government torturers or secret police to get information that will enable them to expose government malpractice and persecution in order to reform or remove the regime.[15] Other aspects of the Terrorist Act, notably those concerning wide powers of search and arrest in section 44 and related sections, that have been criticized by Sir Ken Macdonald and others, have been used in absurd and disturbing ways, as in the case of the photographic artist Reuben Powell, who was arrested in 2009 for photographing the old HMSO print works located near a police station in London. Powell was handcuffed and spent five hours in a cell after police seized the lock-blade knife he uses to sharpen his pencils. His release only came after the intervention of the local MP, Simon Hughes, but not before his genetic material had been stored permanently on the DNA database.[16]

---

[15] Some anti-terrorist legislation has tried to avoid such a consequence by special provisions. The Victorian Government in Australia has even broader prohibitions on interference with electronic systems but, unlike the UK Act, it exempts 'advocacy, protest, dissent or industrial action' where it 'is not intended to cause serious harm that is physical harm to a person, or to cause a person's death, or to endanger the life of a person, other than the person taking action, or to create a serious risk to the health or safety of the public or a section of the public'. See the Victorian Terrorism (Community Protection) Act 2003, Part 1, s 4, especially 4.3 (as amended, 3 November 2011).

[16] Jonathan Brown, 'Photographers criminalised as police "abuse" anti-terror laws', *The Independent* (London), 6 January 2009.

Another problem about the use of legal measures against terrorism concerns the scope and use of legislation that is not specifically geared to counter terrorism but has been motivated by anxiety about terrorism. The extradition processes in the United Kingdom, for example, have come under criticism in recent years because of their connection with the European Arrest Warrant, a legal instrument that was introduced by a European decision made just one week after the attacks of 11 September 2001. It was promoted to the public as a way of ensuring cross-border cohesion in prosecuting terrorists and other serious criminals across Europe. Since then it has been increasingly used to extradite people for alleged offences that are either trivial or not criminal offences in Britain. The extradition proceedings against Julian Assange have highlighted some of the problems with these processes, but there have been even more startling examples. A notable instance, discussed in *The Guardian's* Op Ed pages in December 2010, concerned a Polish man, Jacek Jaskolski, a disabled fifty-eight-year-old science teacher living in the UK since 2004 who was sought for extradition to Poland over a ten-year-old 'offence' of having overdrawn his bank limit. The bank recovered the money and there is no allegation of dishonesty. In Britain, such a case would at most involve civil proceedings, but the desperate desire for new legislation to deal with terrorism has played a part in bringing about this absurd situation—not to mention other absurdities such as the 2008 extradition to Poland of a man who had stolen a dessert from a Polish restaurant![17]

Democratic politics, partly because of its very responsiveness to public feeling and opinion, has a tendency to react to any new crisis by passing a law. Sometimes the relevant law is a good one, but often it is not, since its primary purpose, or effect, is to assure the public that the political leadership is doing *something*. Often those who exercise power under the new laws—police and security agencies—especially in a climate of heightened suspicion and anxiety, will stretch the interpretation of the law. Moreover, once enacted, such 'gut-reaction' legislation has a strong tendency to stay on the books, whatever its defects.

B. The prevention imperative

Many of the problems that arise with the employment of the criminal law in connection with terrorist acts are created by the fact that the primary aim of this employment is direct prevention of crime rather than punishment, reform, deterrence, or communication. One British account of the

---

[17] Afua Hirsch, 'The Mockery of Extradition: Thousands of people are being flown out to face charges which wouldn't warrant arrest in the UK', *The Guardian*, 14 December 2010.

rationale for anti-terrorist law-making talks of the four 'p's: Pursue, Prevent, Protect, and Prepare.[18] Of these, the protecting and preparing are themselves prevention-oriented where pursuit is more related to capture of those who have performed terrorist acts. It would be wrong to see prevention as an entirely new element in law-making and law enforcement since such things as restraining orders, consorting laws, and laws against attempts and conspiracy have a preventative rationale, at least in part. Nonetheless, the rationale is central to a great deal of anti-terrorism legislation in ways that are sometimes more tenuous than in the cases just mentioned. The criminalizing of attempts is partly aimed at preventing their outcomes, but the attempts themselves involve actions that are directly aimed at producing full-blooded crimes, so that they are, in a sense, those crimes already in process of enactment. Restraining orders and restrictions on associating usually arise from crimes or wrongs already committed (eg, assaults, threats, harassment) and likely to be committed again. Conspiracy is somewhat different but, for that reason, the reach of this crime has often been viewed with some suspicion by liberals (and others) who are anxious about the misuse of state power. The primary drive of anti-terrorism legislation is towards prevention broadly considered.

One of the problems relates to the definition of terrorism and terrorist group. Most definitions in the legal campaign in different countries are broader than the tactical definition, and, even where the concerns of the tactical approach are taken into account to some degree, the various offences related to support for or encouragement of terrorist groups or organizations are dangerously broad. Even on the tactical definition, an organization like, say, Hamas, may be engaged in armed struggle against Israeli troops which would not count as terrorism, in various governmental activities beneficial to the people of Gaza (as well as inefficient and corrupt activities related to governing), and also in terrorist acts, such as suicide bombing in crowded civilian areas or delivering rockets against non-combatants. Someone in the UK or Australia sending money to Hamas officials for the non-terrorist and non-corrupt activities may well be caught in the net of support for terrorism, certainly as defined in Australian and UK legal instruments. Where the definitions encompass all acts of political violence against governments, including governments overseas (and they never reach to acts of political violence *by* governments) then they potentially criminalize intellectual or financial support and encouragement of resistance movements that many people plausibly consider legitimate, such as, in former times, the African

[18] Home Office, *Pursue Prevent Protect Prepare: The United Kingdom's Strategy for Countering International Terrorism* (2009) pp 8–9.

National Congress (ANC) struggle against apartheid, much of which (though by no means all) was non-terrorist in the tactical sense. Another example would be support for Burmese dissidents forcefully defending their homes from rapacious government forces. These are examples where the tactical definition of terrorism, even if not explicitly embodied in the law, could be a beneficial influence in determining the nature of anti-terrorism laws or in restricting their scope. It might, for instance, produce more caution about what groups are to be designated 'terrorist organizations' or what defences are available to those who 'support' such organizations.

Although the various legislations in different jurisdictions have many points of divergence, there is a good deal of overlap and there is a general problem with the wide scope of preventive measures and the language used to codify them. Notions like 'facilitate', 'promote', 'support', 'encourage', or 'possession of information useful to terrorism'[19] show an understandable anxiety to forestall terrorist acts, even to forestall the possibility of them, but they are alarmingly open to abuse. A philosophy article offering a limited case for terrorism, or even examining in an objective way plausible arguments for terrorist acts, could easily come under such headings as 'information useful to terrorism'. The UK Act even proscribes inviting some member of an organization deemed to be a terrorist group to give a talk or assist in the organization of such a talk.[20] Admittedly, it is a defence to show that you had had no reason to believe that the speaker's address would 'support a pro-scribed organization or further its activities'.[21] But if some academic invited a significant member of Hamas, for instance, to give a talk on the organiza-tion's political goals, it is barely possible that an inviter could fail to realize that the speaker in the course of his explanations would very likely seek to defend its activities in ways that nullify this defence. Do we really want to limit debate in this way? Of course, one might hope that common sense would prevail at the level of implementing such laws, but liberal democratic societies should not rely too much on such hopes.

Part of the problem of framing criminal laws to deal with politically-motivated violence is that the framing of new laws or the stretched use of existing laws invariably takes place in an atmosphere of heightened fear or even panic. This atmosphere has the understandable effect on politicians, especially democratically elected politicians, that they do not want to be seen to have been remiss in dealing with future threats. They live in apprehension that if a terrorist event occurs, they will be blamed for not having prevented it. These are reactions that often make for bad laws, bad policy and bad policing of laws.

---

[19] See, for example, the UK Terrorism Act 2000, especially ss 3 and 12.
[20] UK Terrorism Act 2000, ss 12.2.c and 12.3.
[21] UK Terrorism Act 2000, s 12.4.

This was abundantly illustrated in the Mohamed Haneef fiasco in Australia where a terrorist attack on the other side of the world (at Glasgow Airport) produced an arrest, lengthy detention and then aborted prosecution of an innocent man for what always seemed at best a trivial 'offence' and turned out to be no offence at all.[22] Haneef, an Indian doctor working in Brisbane, had a relative in Britain who was supposed to have some connection with one of the suspects in the Glasgow incident. He was believed to have given his phone sim card to his cousin in England whose brother was one of the perpetrators of the Glasgow Airport attempted bombing. British police mistakenly reported that the card had been found at the terrorist scene. In the course of this sad process, the court was profoundly misled on central facts by the prosecution, the public was asked to trust the authorities that secret information would justify the process, the character of the accused was besmirched by government ministers, and bail for the accused was effectively set aside by the intervention of the then conservative coalition government's Minister for Immigration who, apparently acting on more secret information, cancelled Haneef's visa. All this, and much more mischief impacting on Haneef, occurred after the Australian Security Intelligence Organization (ASIO) advised early in a report either ignored or 'not seen' by the Immigration Minister that there was no evidence against him.[23]

The preventive imperative not only can involve the clumsy implementation or outright misuse of old or new laws, but can also support governmental resort to non-military policy measures that violate existing laws. The United States government, for instance, secretly instituted surveillance phone hacking techniques on US citizens without any of the required legal warrants at least as early as 2002 even though these were in clear contradiction of the Foreign Intelligence Surveillance Act (FISA). The National Security Agency used the major telecommunications agencies to tap vast numbers of private communications of US citizens in the name of anti-terrorism. The programme was exposed in 2005 by the *New York Times*, but President Bush

---

[22] For a good account of the Haneef case and a discussion of the ethical dimensions of the legal defence (and prosecution) of Haneef see: Francesca Bartlett, 'The Ethics of "Transgressive" Lawyering: Considering the Defence of Dr Haneef' (2009) *The University of Queensland Law Journal*, 28:2, 309–23.

[23] This sort of legal bungling in reaction to heightened fears of 'terrorist' attacks can be paralleled even in the remote past, as the prosecution of Richard Brothers in 1795 for 'imagining the King's death' illustrates vividly. In an atmosphere of anxiety, suspicion and governmental insecurity focussed on the war against republican France and a rising tide of political radicalism at home, proceedings invoking an archaic law were instituted against the weird religious eccentric Richard Brothers who posed no real threat to the regime. For details, see John Barrell, 'Imagining the King's Death: the Arrest of Richard Brothers' (1994: Spring) *History Workshop Journal*, 37, 1–32. See also Hugh Chisholm (ed), 'Brothers, Richard' in *Encyclopædia Britannica*, 11th edn (Cambridge: Cambridge University Press, 1911).

defended the policy and was openly defiant of charges that it breached the clear letter of the law. He and his associates argued that the Patriot Act virtually placed the President above the law. Civil legal proceedings were brought against the telecommunications companies that had palpably broken the FISA law (and several others) in complying with government requests for access to their clients' phones, so a campaign was mounted to exempt them retrospectively from the provisions of the FISA law, a campaign that was eventually successful. Amending and supplementing legislation regarding FISA has been since enacted that seems to give the government increased powers of surveillance while maintaining a semblance of external supervision, but such is the secrecy surrounding the relevant activities of the National Security Agency that it is hard to know how extensive or how illegal current surveillance of citizens remains.[24]

There are many other examples in different parts of the world of the disadvantages that the law faces in dealing with the real or imagined threat of terrorism. These range from the British police shooting dead an innocent man that they misidentified to the numerous squalid detentions in Guantanamo Bay, the revival of torture techniques in democracies, and the victimizations of 'extraordinary rendition'. Moreover, the consternation caused by the terrorist attacks of 11 September 2001 resulted in the arrest of thousands of 'suspects' in the United States, very few of whom have been found to have terrorist connections even after lengthy periods of detention.

C. Diplomacy and removing the grievance

For reasons of space, and because their connection with our topic is indirect, I shall have to be brief in dealing with responses (3) and (4)—diplomacy and removing the grievance. Although these have obvious advantages at first blush, they can be eliminated or much diminished as possibilities by some ways of regarding terrorism. At the extreme, if terrorism can be seen as deranged, as one reading of the idea of 'indiscriminate' violence may encourage, then there is no room to engage diplomatically with terrorists, with groups using terrorism, or with states that encourage or promote terrorist acts. The mantra 'no negotiation with terrorists' partly encapsulates this outlook, though it also has an instrumental rationale concerned with not encouraging further terrorism, a rationale that I don't find decisive and which is often enough abandoned via secret negotiations.

---

[24] There are many accounts of the complexities surrounding the warrantless surveillance scandal, but a good summary is provided in Glenn Greenwald, *With Liberty and Justice for Some* (New York: Metropolitan Books, Henry Holt and Company, 2011) ch 2. Greenwald is primarily concerned with what he argues is the extraordinary routine immunity from the law that the powerful enjoy in America.

The paths of diplomacy and of removing grievances (which can intersect) are also impeded by concentration on the account of terrorist motivation mentioned earlier in discussing Scheffler's version of the distinctive moral wrong in terrorism. As noted then that emphasis on the intent to destabilize or degrade the existing social order makes the perpetrators of terrorism seem quite removed from the category of enemies with whom one could negotiate. Of course, a good deal turns on what such destabilization or degradation is supposed to mean, and Scheffler is quite unforthcoming on this, but it seems to involve such massive damage that there is nothing that could be yielded to such adversaries. But where the enemy has quite specific objectives, such as removing foreign settlements on what he or she regards as his or her land or forcing an occupying power to leave or getting prisoners released, there is clearly much more room for concessions, even if such concessions remain politically difficult. Much will turn on how legitimate the terrorists' grievances are, or how plausible a case they can make for those grievances even where they remain controversial. All compromise, and most negotiation, involves risk and the prospect of a serious degree of loss for both parties. But that is part of the nature of politics, and terrorism and counter-terrorism exist within the domain of politics as well as that of morality and law.

The two great English political philosophers near the beginnings of the modern political era, Thomas Hobbes and John Locke, were both concerned with the need to control violence, animosity, and power, though their methods differed in ways that exhibit the tension discernible in current governmental responses to the threat of terrorism. Hobbes thought that the awful effects of natural tendencies to violence and domination could be controlled by an all-powerful sovereign endowed with the sole 'right of the sword' and empowered to make laws that the sovereign was effectively above and constrained only by regard for the natural law promulgated by God. By contrast, Locke was aware that such untrammelled sovereign power itself posed dangers (even possibly greater dangers) to human security and natural rights. Consequently, Locke thought that citizens had rights, including the right of revolution, against the sovereign who was also under the law and that protections against the abuse of sovereign power were needed. Plainly commenting on Hobbes's doctrine of sovereignty without explicitly naming him, Locke says: 'This is to think that men are so foolish that they take care to avoid what mischiefs may be done them by polecats or foxes, but are content, nay think it safety, to be devoured by lions.'[25] In the face of serious terrorist attacks, the pressure for greater and greater legal (and often enough illegal) measures in the name of national security poses the very danger that concerned Locke.

---

[25] John Locke, *Second Treatise of Government* (New York: Hafner, 1961) ch 7, para 93, p 167.

APPENDIX

The full text of the definitional section (Part 1, Introductory) of the British Terrorism Act 2000 with later qualifications.

(1) In this Act 'terrorism' means the use or threat of action where—
  (a) the action falls within subsection (2),
  (b) the use or threat is designed to influence the government [F1or an international governmental organisation] or to intimidate the public or a section of the public, and
  (c) the use or threat is made for the purpose of advancing a political, religious [F2, racial] or ideological cause.

(2) Action falls within this subsection if it—
  (a) involves serious violence against a person,
  (b) involves serious damage to property,
  (c) endangers a person's life, other than that of the person committing the action,
  (d) creates a serious risk to the health or safety of the public or a section of the public, or
  (e) is designed seriously to interfere with or seriously to disrupt an electronic system.

(3) The use or threat of action falling within subsection (2) which involves the use of firearms or explosives is terrorism whether or not subsection (1)(b) is satisfied.

(4) In this section—
  (a) 'action' includes action outside the United Kingdom,
  (b) a reference to any person or to property is a reference to any person, or to property, wherever situated,
  (c) a reference to the public includes a reference to the public of a country other than the United Kingdom, and
  (d) 'the government' means the government of the United Kingdom, of a Part of the United Kingdom or of a country other than the United Kingdom.

(5) In this Act a reference to action taken for the purposes of terrorism includes a reference to action taken for the benefit of a proscribed organisation.

10

Responsibility and Answerability in the Criminal Law

*Massimo Renzo**

I. Responsibility as Answerability

The current philosophical debate on moral responsibility has paid increasingly more attention to the distinction between two notions of responsibility.[1] One is the notion of responsibility as *attributability*, which specifies the conditions under which a certain act or attitude can be properly attributed to the agent. This ultimately involves assessing the agent's self, as manifested through her conduct, on the basis of some normative standards that he or she is subject to. The other notion is the notion of responsibility as *accountability* or *answerability*, which specifies the conditions under which the agent can be called to answer for her act by the members of the relevant moral community. Once it is clear that a certain conduct can be attributed to the agent in a way that reflects herself thereby making the agent an appropriate object for moral appraisal, we need to ask whether he or she can be *held responsible* (and therefore blamed or praised) for it by the members of her moral community. This will be the case only if the conduct at hand is governed by a set of normative standards that entitle the members of the moral community to make demands on the

* Previous versions of this chapter were presented at the universities of Warwick, Cambridge and Milan. I am grateful to all these audiences as well as to the members of the *Criminalization Project* for stimulating discussions. Special thanks are owed to Alejandro Chehtman, Antony Duff, Simon Hope, Kasper Lippert-Rasmussen, Jeff McMahan, Matt Matravers, Victor Tadros and Bas Van Der Vossen for helpful written comments.

[1] R J Wallace, *Responsibility and the Moral Sentiments* (Cambridge, MA: Harvard University Press, 1994); G Watson, 'Two Faces of Responsibility' (1996) 24 *Philosophical Topics* 227; T M Scanlon, *Moral Dimensions: Permissibility, Meaning, Blame* (Cambridge, MA: Harvard University Press, 2008); J M Fischer and N A Tognazzini, 'The Physiognomy of Responsibility' (2011) 82 *Philosophy and Phenomenological Research* 381.

agent and legitimately expect her to justify her conduct to them. In other words, whereas responsibility as attributability refers to the connection of the agent with her action, responsibility as answerability refers to the interaction between the agent and the moral community to which she belongs.[2]

It is no surprise that the second notion of responsibility has generated particular interest among philosophers working on criminal responsibility, since the very idea of liability to sanctions seems to rely on the practice of calling wrongdoers to account for their criminal acts.[3] Indeed, two prominent attempts to develop a conception of responsibility as answerability are to be found in the work of two influential philosophers of the criminal law: Antony Duff and John Gardner. Duff and Gardner share the view that criminal responsibility should be understood in terms of the reasons offered by the wrongdoer in order to justify her conduct.[4] However, this view is formulated in very different ways by the two.

Duff's account is ultimately founded on the idea that as members of the political community we are criminally responsible to our fellow citizens in relation to those wrongs that 'properly concern' the political community. This is because responsibility, according to Duff, is to be understood in relational terms: X is answerable to Y for her conduct (and vice versa) only to the extent that X and Y stand in a relationship that makes X's conduct Y's business (and vice versa). It is the fact that X and Y are in such a relationship that gives them the right to call each other to account for their conduct with respect to certain matters.

This view fits nicely with the way in which we normally think about our responsibilities. If I cheat on my wife I am certainly answerable to her for what I did.[5] She can legitimately demand that I offer reasons that justify, excuse, or simply explain my conduct. Perhaps, depending on the circumstances, I am also answerable for my cheating to the rest of our family (at least to close family members) or to some of our friends. All of these people can demand that I explain my conduct to them by offering reasons for it, although this demand will have a different strength depending on their specific relationship with me. But these are reasons that I am not also required to offer to passing strangers. The latter can certainly criticize my conduct if

---

[2] Fischer and Tognazzini, n 1 above, at p 381.

[3] Watson, n 1 above, at p 237.

[4] For the purposes of this chapter I will follow Duff and Gardner in using 'answerability' and 'accountability' interchangeably.

[5] I borrow this example from R A Duff, 'Authority and Responsibility in International Criminal Law' in S Besson and J Tasioulas (eds), *The Philosophy of International Law* (Oxford: Oxford University Press, 2010) 589, 597.

they wish, say that cheating was a lousy thing to do, but they do not have the right to call me to justify or explain my conduct to them. My family life is simply none of their business.

Gardner, on the other hand, adopts an agent-neutralist account according to which 'all reasons are ultimately the same reasons for everyone'.[6] Although in a trivial sense the reasons that I have not to cheat on my wife do apply especially to me (logically, I am the only person who can break my wedding vows), those reasons are at the same time reasons that apply to *everyone*. Everyone has a reason to care about the fact that I don't cheat on my wife, to regret that I do so, to contribute to my non-cheating;[7] which explains why, at least in principle, everyone has the right to call me to answer as to whether I am faithful to her.[8]

There are of course pragmatic reasons which explain why most of the time this will be unwise. To begin with, being called to answer for my infidelity by a stranger will often turn out to be of little use, if not altogether counter-productive. Moreover, given the limited amount of time and 'rational energies'[9] at our disposal, it's normally best to attend only to a subset of the reasons that apply to us. (In other words, strangers will typically have better things to do.) Still, in principle, 'everyone's conformity to every reason is everyone's business'.[10] The fact that I have a reason not to cheat on my wife gives, at least in principle, everyone the right to call me to answer for my conduct toward her.

Once applied to criminal responsibility, this view supports the striking conclusion that we can be called to answer by any court in relation to any criminal wrong. In Gardner's words: 'criminal courts have authority over [us] ..., to the extent that they do, irrespective of whether they are [our] ... courts, irrespective of whether they administer [our] ... law, and irrespective of whether this is [our] ... country.'[11]

My own sympathies are with the relational account. Defending this view would require an extensive discussion of issues of practical reason that are

---

[6] J Gardner, 'Relations of Responsibility' in R Cruft, M H Kramer and M Reiff (eds), *Crime, Punishment and Responsibility. The Jurisprudence of Antony Duff* (Oxford: Oxford University Press, 2011) 87, 89. See also J Gardner, *Offences and Defences: Selected Essays in the Philosophy of Criminal Law* (Oxford: Oxford University Press, 2007) 58–66, 177–200, 276–80.

[7] Here I am paraphrasing Gardner, 'Relations of Responsibility', n 6 above, at p 89.

[8] *Offences and Defences*, n 6 above, at p 278.

[9] 'Relations of Responsibility', n 6 above, at p 89.

[10] 'Relations of Responsibility', n 6 above, at p 89. Michelle Dempsey adopts a similar approach in her 'Public Wrongs and the "Criminal Law's Business": When Victims Won't Share', in Cruft, Kramer and Reiff, n 6 above.

[11] 'Relations of Responsibility', n 6 above, at p 95.

beyond the scope of this chapter, but ultimately the problem with Gardner's view is that it misrepresents cases such as the one discussed above. Saying that my cheating is in principle everyone's business, and that strangers should refrain from calling me to account only because this would be counter-productive all things considered, simply distorts the moral situation at hand. As Duff observes, the point is not that strangers have some reasons to call me to account for my cheating, which are then overridden by other reasons they have not to interfere. The point is that my love life is *ab initio* none of their business.[12]

Gardner himself is sensitive to this thought and strives to show how his position can account for it:

Needless to say, I share Duff's view that a stranger's immorality toward her friend or parents may (correctly) strike me *ab initio* as none of my business. The question is: how are we to interpret that verdict? I interpret it to mean that it is not my place to interfere. I have no standing in the matter. I have no relevant right or duty. The question of whether I have such a right or duty arises, however, only because there is a reason for me to intervene and I need to decide (or it needs to be decided) whether or not I am to act on it. If there were no such reason, there would be nothing for me to attend to in the stranger's immorality, and hence nothing for me to take any attitude to, whether *ab initio* or otherwise.[13]

But this way of formulating the problem conflates the question of whether a stranger's immorality is *ab initio* my business with the question of whether it is immediately clear that I have no right to call her to account. There are certainly cases in which, although I do have some reasons to call someone to account, it is obvious—and obvious from the very beginning—that all things considered I should not act on these reasons. But when we say that certain wrongs are not my business *ab initio,* we intend precisely to mark the difference between this type of situation and one in which there is no reason for me to attend to those wrongs in the first place.

Gardner writes that the question of whether we have a right to call someone to account arises only when there *is* a reason for us to do so and we need to decide whether or not we are to act on it, but this way of thinking about the problem seems misleading. The question of whether we have a right to call someone to account does not presuppose that there is a reason for us to do so. Rather, the question arises when we are assessing whether such reason exists.

---

[12] R A Duff, *Answering for Crime. Responsibility and Liability in the Criminal Law* (Oxford: Hart, 2007) 49.
[13] Gardner, 'Relations of Responsibility', n 6 above, at p 90.

When presented with my infidelity you ask yourself if you have the standing to call me to account for it. If we are related in a way that gives you that standing, you have some reasons to do so, and thus you should check whether those reasons are overridden by other considerations (such as those mentioned by Gardner). If we are not related in the relevant way, you do not have any reason whatsoever to call me to account, in which case there is nothing that needs to be balanced with countervailing reasons. Contra Gardner, the mere fact that you can ask yourself whether you have a right to interfere does not presuppose that there is some reason for you to do so. Similarly, the mere fact that you can ask yourself whether you should watch *The Third Man* does not presuppose that there is some reason for you to do so. Perhaps you hate noirs, in which case you do not have any reason to watch it. The question you ask yourself when you wonder whether you should watch the movie arises precisely as part of your inquiry as to which reasons you have to act.

But while I endorse a relational account of responsibility along the lines developed by Duff, I also believe that there are wrongs for which we are criminally responsible to all human beings. Thus, there is a class of wrongs for which my theory and Gardner's coincide, although this is nothing more than an extensional equivalence. I contend that there are wrongs for which any human being can call us to account, but this is not because 'everyone's conformity to every reason is everyone's business'. Rather, it is because all human beings share some important normative relationship that gives them the standing to do so.

This is a view that, understandably, Duff is very cautious about.[14] Although in fact he adopts it himself in relation to a limited number of wrongs, he is wary of the implications that the view has if formulated in the way I will suggest. Indeed, accepting my formulation requires radically revising the way in which we understand criminal responsibility and, particularly, the way in which the distinction between domestic and international crimes is currently drawn. I argue that these worries should not dissuade us. Many wrongs that are currently considered domestic in nature are in fact wrongs for which we are answerable to all human beings, and we should revise our way of thinking about the distinction between domestic and international crimes accordingly.[15] This revision has important practical implications, but they are not as disruptive as we might think.

---

[14] R A Duff, 'Responsibility, Citizenship and Criminal Law' in R A Duff and S P Green (eds), *Philosophical Foundations of Criminal Law* (Oxford: Oxford University Press, 2011) 125, 133, 137.

[15] By 'international crimes' I mean crimes that trigger international punishment, where the latter can be inflicted either by an international institution (such as the International Criminal Court) or by a domestic court claiming universal jurisdiction.

My argument is in four steps. In the next section I provide an account of the distinction between wrongs for which we are answerable to the domestic political community and wrongs for which we are answerable to the whole of humanity. In section III I employ this account to revise the way in which the distinction between domestic and international crimes is currently drawn. I argue that any violations of basic human rights, including those that are not committed in the context of an armed conflict or as part of a wider attack against a civilian population, constitute wrongs for which we are answerable to the whole of humanity, and therefore trigger international criminal responsibility. In section III and section IV I consider and answer two main objections that can be moved against the view I suggest. In section V I compare my relational account with the one defended by Duff and argue that the former provides a more convincing explanation of a crucial distinction that Duff himself intends to draw.

II. The Relational Account of Responsibility

Let me start by providing a more detailed account of the relational conception of responsibility. The main idea is that being responsible is being answerable for something, to someone, in virtue of our occupying a certain role.[16] We are all members of different groups and in virtue of these memberships we share normatively laden relationships with others. An aspect of this picture that tends to monopolize the attention of philosophers is the fact that these relationships ground special duties towards the members of the relevant group (hence the classic discussions about how we should understand our duties to fellow citizens, family members, friends and so on). But a second, equally important, aspect is the fact that such relationships also provide members of the relevant group with the standing to call each other to account in relation to specific matters.[17]

For example, my being a teacher has normative implications to the extent that it grounds duties that I would not have if I did not occupy this role, but also because in virtue of my occupying this role I am answerable to my colleagues and my students in relation to matters for which I am not answerable to others. In the same way that my colleagues have no right to call me to account for my marital infidelity, my wife and my family members normally have no right to

---

[16] Duff, n 12 above, at p 23.

[17] Indeed the two aspects are connected, in that one of the duties incurred as members of a group is typically the duty to answer to the other members in relation to certain issues.

call me to account for showing up late at departmental meetings, since I am accountable to them only for those responsibilities that I have as a member of my family (and not for those that I have as a member of my department).

As it will become clear soon, this picture is too schematic, and one of the aims of this chapter is to complicate it further. Still, it is a good starting point for unpacking the notion of responsibility as answerability, in that it exemplifies how the standing to call someone to account crucially depends on the fact that both parties are members of the same relevant group. What we need to do now is clarify how we can move from moral to criminal responsibility. This can be done in two steps.

First, Duff suggests that criminal responsibility is grounded in citizenship. As citizens, we are answerable to the other members of the political community in relation to those wrongs that 'violate values on which the civic enterprise depends and display a lack of the respect and concern that citizens owe to each other as fellow citizens'.[18] Whereas civil wrongs are private matters between the offender and the victim, criminal wrongs are 'public' in the sense that they properly concern all the members of the political community.[19] Indeed, the very purpose of the criminal law, according to Duff, is to 'identify and declare the public wrongfulness of certain kinds of moral wrongdoing, and to provide for an appropriate public response to them'.[20]

Second, criminal wrongs are so serious that they are properly censured by punishment. Saying that there are wrongs for which we are answerable to our fellow citizens is not yet saying that we should be *criminally* responsible for them, because there are different ways in which we can be called to account. What is special about criminal responsibility is that it warrants the use of punishment as an appropriate form of censure, and the condemnatory force of punishment is such that only particularly serious wrongs ought to be properly censured in this way.[21] Thus, (domestic) criminal wrongs are a subset of those wrongs for which we are accountable to the polity, ie those wrongs that cross the threshold of seriousness required to justify their inclusion in the criminal law.

---

[18] R A Duff, 'Toward a Theory of Criminal Law' (2010) 84 *Proceedings of the Aristotelian Society (Supp. Vol.)* 1, 21. For a discussion of this aspect of Duff's theory, see A Harel, 'The Triadic Relational Structure of Responsibility: A Defence', in Cruft, Kramer and Reiff, n 6 above, at p 103.

[19] Duff, n 12 above, at p 52. But see R A Duff and S E Marshall, 'Public and Private Wrongs', in J Chalmers, F Leverick and L Farmer (eds), *Essays in Criminal Law in Honour of Sir Gerald Gordon* (Edinburgh: Edinburgh University Press, 2010) 70, for some interesting thoughts about how the sharp distinction between criminal and civil wrongs should be revised.

[20] Duff, n 12 above, at p 47.

[21] See G Lamond, 'What Is a Crime?' (2007) 27 *OJLS* 609.

The idea that as citizens we are answerable to the other members of the political community in relation to those wrongs that violate values on which the civic enterprise depends is obviously supposed to account for *domestic* criminal responsibility; but the relational scheme can also be employed to account for international criminal responsibility.[22] In the same way in which domestic courts have the right to call wrongdoers to account in relation to those wrongs for which they are answerable to the domestic political community, international courts (and domestic courts claiming universal jurisdiction) have the right to call wrongdoers to account in relation to those wrongs for which they are answerable to the international community. For if domestic punishment can be justified as a way of calling wrongdoers to account for those wrongs that they are answerable for in virtue of their being members of the polity, international punishment can be similarly justified as a way of calling wrongdoers to account for those wrongs that they are answerable for in virtue of their being members of the community of humanity.

Duff is aware of how problematic this move is and he is extremely cautious about the possibility of portraying the international community as a political community. While he acknowledges that the creation of international institutions such as the International Criminal Court can certainly be seen as 'one of the ways in which the moral ideal idea of a human community might be given some more determinate and effective institutional form', he also maintains that this process is still in its infancy and is probably best seen as an aspiration for the moment.[23] Still, his account of international criminal responsibility ultimately relies on the idea that in the same way in which there are wrongs that should concern us, and are properly our business, in virtue of our membership in the political community, 'some kinds of wrong should concern us, [and] are properly our business, in virtue of our shared humanity with their victims (and perpetrators): for such wrongs the perpetrators must answer not just to their local communities, but to humanity'.[24]

This is a powerful idea and the aim of this chapter is ultimately to explore how this philosophical move and its implications should be understood. In particular, the chapter aims to offer an account of how we should understand the distinction between wrongs for which we are answerable to the domestic political community and to the international community respectively. This is a problem that Duff does not address directly. He seems to assume that the

---

[22] By 'international criminal responsibility' I mean responsibility for international crimes, ie crimes that trigger international punishment (see n 15 above).
[23] Duff, n 5 above, at p 601.
[24] Duff, n 5 above, at p 601.

wrongs for which we are answerable to humanity, rather than to our domestic political communities, are those currently falling within the scope of international criminal law (he discusses war crimes and crimes against humanity), but he never explains why.[25] What is lacking in the picture presented by Duff is an account of what makes certain conduct the business of political communities and other conduct the business of the international community.

Elsewhere I have suggested that in order to explain this distinction we should start by distinguishing between two types of wrongs.[26] Some types of conduct are wrong only in virtue of the restrictions that members of politically organized groups take, more or less voluntarily, upon themselves in order to make their living together possible. These wrongs are contingent on certain rules and principles being adopted by these members in order to structure their relationships in a way that enables them to peacefully live together. Had these principles and rules been different, there would be nothing wrong with engaging in those types of conduct. And indeed, if the number of those who abide by these restrictions is too small, it is questionable that we would still have reasons to observe them.

Other types of conduct, most notably violations of basic human rights, are wrong independently of any of these considerations. The wrongness of these types of conduct is not contingent upon any rules or principles being adopted within the community in which we find ourselves acting, nor is it contingent upon how those around us behave. I contend that wrongs of the first type are to be considered *merely domestic*: they only concern the domestic political community, and this is why no other political institution can intervene to punish them. Wrongs of the second type, by contrast, properly concern the whole of humanity (although, as it will become clear, they can also have a domestic component, under certain conditions), and this explains why the international community has the right to punish them.

Let me illustrate this distinction by briefly comparing theft and rape. Taking something over which someone else claims control is morally wrong only to the extent that we are part of a politically organized group that has adopted a system of private property, ie a system that allocates to specific individuals exclusive control over certain resources. Absent such a system of rules, we would have no moral reasons to refrain from appropriating things over which others claim control. Indeed, it might be argued that absent a system of private property, taking things which others claim control over would not even count as stealing.

[25] Duff, n 5 above, at pp 589–90, 598, 601.
[26] M Renzo, 'Crimes Against Humanity and the Limits of International Criminal Law' (2012) *Law and Philosophy* 31(4), 443–76.

Some might find this view counterintuitive because of the influence of the Lockean idea of a natural right to property, but Hobbes, Rousseau and Kant all defend some version of it. For Hobbes, property is a creation of the sovereign state. Similarly, Rousseau explicitly rejects the idea of a natural right to property and distinguishes between mere possession, which can be achieved in the state of nature, and genuine property which is only possible within an authoritative legal system that defines and enforces property rights. Kant's view is more complex but it ultimately relies on the idea that we can have non-provisional property rights over something only to the extent that others recognize an obligation to refrain from using it. Indeed, for Kant the main reason why individuals must leave the state of nature and enter into a civil condition is precisely to make (non-provisional) property rights possible.

What all these views have in common is the thought that property rights depend for their existence on individuals having entered into a political relationship with those living next to them. Outside the scope of these relationships there are no property rights, or at least no fully-fledged property rights, and therefore it is not wrong to use any of the resources that we come across, no matter who claims control over them. But if the existence of private property depends on the fact that we are part of a political community that implements specific social rules about how to allocate exclusive control over certain resources, it follows that the moral reasons we have not to steal also depend on our being part of such a community. Again, absent such a system of rules (in a state of nature as imagined by Hobbes, Rousseau or Kant), or simply in a social context with rules different from those of private property, we would have no moral reason not to steal.[27]

Consider now, by contrast, crimes such as torture, murder, or rape. How should we account for the difference between these crimes and crimes like theft? The crucial difference seems to be the following: we have a moral obligation to refrain from committing torture, murder, and rape simply in virtue of the respect that we owe to others qua human beings, independently

---

[27] For a defence of the most radical view that there can be no property rights antecedent to the legal system that creates them, see L Murphy and T Nagel, *The Myth of Ownership: Taxes and Justice* (New York: Oxford University Press, 2002). Some attribute this view to Rousseau too (for example, A Ryan, *Property and Political Theory* (Oxford: Basil Blackwell, 1984) 54–5). As I have mentioned, Kant takes the weaker view that property rights do exist in the state of nature, but have a provisional character. Thus 'no one is bound to refrain from encroaching on what another possess' and it is not wrong to interfere with someone else's possession, unless the possession is physically in their hands; see I Kant, M Gregor (ed), *The Metaphysics of Morals* (Cambridge: Cambridge University Press, 1996) 86. For a stimulating discussion of Kant's view, see A Ripstein, *Force and Freedom: Kant's Legal and Political Philosophy* (Cambridge, MA: Harvard University Press, 2008) 86–106.

of the specific social rules adopted by the polity to which we belong. Our obligation to refrain from committing these crimes is not conditional on the existence of the state or of any system of social rules declaring these types of conduct as wrongful.[28] Even if we lived in a state of nature as imagined by Hobbes, Rousseau or Kant, or in any other social context that did not prohibit torture, murder, or rape, we would still have an obligation to refrain from them.[29]

This suggests that while we can account for crimes like theft exclusively in terms of the fact that these crimes 'violate values on which the civic enterprise depends, and display a lack of the respect and concern that citizens owe to each other as fellow citizens', crimes like torture, murder, and rape cannot be characterized in the same way. Crimes that violate basic human rights do not merely violate values on which the civic enterprise depends, nor do they merely display a lack of respect and concern that citizens owe to each other as fellow citizens. They show a deeper and more serious form of lack of respect: lack of respect and concern that individuals owe to each other *qua human beings*, ie independently of their common membership in any social or political community. And for the same reasons why we are answerable to the members of the political community for failing to treat them with the respect and concern that they are owed as fellow citizens, we should conclude that we are answerable to the members of humanity for failing to treat them with the respect and concern that they are owed as fellow human beings.

Thus, this is how we should account for the difference between wrongs for which we are responsible to our domestic political community and wrongs for which we are responsible to the wider community of humanity. But accounting for the distinction between these two types of responsibilities in

---

[28] Although what counts as an instance of rape will certainly depend to some extent on how certain notions (such as consent or sexual integrity) are understood in different contexts.

[29] In Hobbes' theory this might be obscured by the fact that he justifies pre-emptively attacking others as a way of preserving our own life. However, this is not because Hobbes believes that we are not under a duty not to unjustifiably violate others' basic human rights. As he makes clear, doing so would be going against the laws of nature, which prescribe that every man seeks peace. Moreover, he explicitly rules out the infliction of unjustified harm in his discussion of cruelty and of excessive punishment (T Hobbes, R Tuck (ed), *Leviathan*, (Cambridge: Cambridge University Press, 1991) 43–4, 106). Hobbes' point is rather that pre-emptively attacking others is justified because in the state of nature everyone must ultimately rely on their private judgement to decide what will best guarantee their security, and there will be circumstances in which pre-emptive attack will appear to some as the only way to preserve their life. While we might criticize Hobbes for having an overly permissive account of self-defence, according to which we can do anything we see fit to preserve ourselves, Hobbes cannot be criticized for failing to acknowledge the existence of a duty not to unjustifiably violate others' basic human rights.

this way requires that we revise how the distinction between domestic and international crimes is currently conceived, or so I will argue. Before I explain why, however, let me make clear that I do not intend to claim that the latter distinction perfectly maps onto the former. Gaining an understanding of which wrongs should be considered merely domestic is important in that it enables us to identify those crimes that are the exclusive business of the domestic political community, ie crimes involving wrongs for which we are answerable to nobody else but the members of our polity. But not all domestic crimes are 'merely domestic'. The class of domestic crimes is broader than the class of merely domestic crimes, since it also includes crimes that have both a domestic and international component, ie, crimes involving wrongs for which we are answerable both to our fellow citizens and to the international community. The double-layered structure that characterizes these crimes will be examined in the next two sections.

III. Domestic and International Criminal Responsibility

In the previous section I argued that certain types of conduct are wrong only in virtue of particular social rules that have been adopted by the polity to which we belong. For these types of conduct we are only answerable to the members of the polity, as they are nobody else's business. Other types of conduct are wrong independently of the fact that they have been declared so by the polity and, more generally, independently of any social rules that the polity might decide to adopt. It is in virtue of the respect that we owe each other as human beings that we ought to refrain from these types of conduct and, for this reason, it is not only the members of our political community who can call us to account for failing to do so. This is something for which we are also answerable to all human beings.

This move needs now to be clarified both in its foundations and in its implications. A full defence would obviously require two things: on the one hand, we would need a theory of citizenship and political obligation, ie a theory that explains which duties and responsibilities we owe to each other as members of the political community and why; on the other hand, we would need a theory that explains which duties and responsibilities we owe to each other as fellow human beings and why. Obviously I will not be able to provide either here. I will simply assume that there are duties and responsibilities that we have to each other as members of the polity and as fellow human beings, respectively, and focus on the question of how these different responsibilities ought to be treated by the criminal law (whatever our specific views on each of them are).[30] In particular, I will contend that the class of wrongs for which we are answerable to the whole of humanity includes at least violations of basic human rights, where these are understood as rights to the conditions that are necessary in order to have a minimally decent life.

I appeal here to the traditional conception of human rights as those rights that we have simply in virtue of our humanity. The familiar idea is that all human beings are entitled to have a minimally decent life, and this requires that they are not treated in certain ways. The function of human rights is to provide individuals with protections against being treated in these ways, and this is why these rights are pre-institutional: their existence is not conditional on their being embodied in any political institutions or on their being recognized in any political doctrines. Human rights are possessed in a pre-political condition because they belong to human beings *as such*.[31]

If the distinction that I outlined in the previous section is plausible, we should conclude that we are answerable for crimes that violate basic human rights not only to the other members of our local political community, but also to the international community. For violations of basic human rights are wrong independently of the specific social rules adopted by the polity to which we belong, and in this sense they cannot be considered merely domestic crimes. These crimes have an international dimension because they involve wrongs for which we are answerable to the whole of humanity, rather than merely to the domestic political community to which we belong.

Clearly this is a highly revisionist view, since according to international law violations of basic human rights are to be considered international crimes only when they are committed in the context of an armed conflict (in the case of war crimes), as part of a widespread or systematic attack on a civilian population (in the case of crimes against humanity), or with the intent to destroy a group (in the case of genocide). According to the view I suggest, on the contrary, any violations of human rights, including those lacking any of these 'contextual elements', are to be considered international crimes.

---

[30] For my views on the justification of political obligation, see M Renzo, 'State Legitimacy and Self-defence' (2011) 30 *Law and Philosophy* 575 and 'Associative Responsibilities and Political Obligation' (2012) 62 *Philosophical Quarterly* 106. Duff's views are presented in his *Punishment, Communication and Community* (New York: Oxford University Press, 2001) 35–74. For a relational account of the moral duties that we owe to each other in virtue of our personal dignity, see S Darwall, *The Second-person Standpoint: Morality, Respect, and Accountability* (Cambridge, MA: Harvard University Press, 2006).

[31] See, for example, A Buchanan, *Justice, Legitimacy and Self-Determination* (Oxford: Oxford University Press, 2004); M Nussbaum, *Frontiers of Justice* (Cambridge, MA: Harvard University Press, 2006); J Griffin, *On Human Rights* (Oxford: Oxford University Press, 2008).

In the remainder of the chapter I will argue that the consequences of adopting this view are ultimately not as radical as we might first think, and that to the extent that adopting this view does call for revisions, these revisions are indeed desirable. Let me however begin by stressing that the claim that we are responsible for violations of basic human rights to all human beings is still less radical than Gardner's claim that we are answerable 'to everyone [we] ... come across'[32] in relation to all kinds of wrongs and that 'criminal courts have authority over [us] ..., to the extent that they do, irrespective of whether they are [our] ... courts, irrespective of whether they administer [our] ... law, and irrespective of whether this is [our] ... country'.[33] The class of wrongs for which my view invokes answerability to all human beings is a subset of the class of wrongs for which it is invoked by Gardner's view.

Let me also stress that for the purposes of this chapter I will leave open the question of whether there are other types of wrongs for which we are answerable to the whole of humanity. Some might argue that other wrongs, for example verbal abuse, constitute ways of treating the victim without the respect owed to her as a fellow human being, even when these wrongs do not involve violations of basic human rights. Remember however, that here we are interested in *criminal responsibility* rather than moral responsibility, and as we have seen, we can only be criminally responsible for particularly serious wrongs. Given the great condemnatory force that punishment has as a form of censure, only wrongs that cross a given threshold of seriousness ought to be properly censured in this way. Thus, even if we agree that verbal abuse or other forms of offensive behaviour are wrongs for which we are answerable to the whole of humanity, this is not enough to conclude that they should be covered by criminal responsibility.[34]

---

[32] Gardner, *Offences and Defences*, n 6 above, at p 187.

[33] Gardner, 'Relations of Responsibility', n 6 above, at p 95. Gardner's view, as I understand it, nicely reflects the so-called *Lotus principle.* The principle, articulated by the Permanent International Court of Justice in 1927, states that international law does not include any prohibition against states extending 'the application of their laws and the jurisdiction of their courts to persons, property and acts outside their territory'. Rather, the presumption is that states are permitted to do so unless specific prohibitive rules are in place (*S.S. Lotus (Fr. v Turk.)*, 1927 P.C.I.J. (ser. A) No. 10 (Sept. 7)). Notice however, that despite its popularity, the *Lotus principle* is rarely invoked in international law (in fact, the *Lotus* decision was later overruled by the 1958 High Seas Convention) and has been widely rejected in the literature; see M N Shaw, *International Law*, 5th edn (Cambridge: Cambridge University Press, 2003) 582; R Cryer, *Prosecuting International Crimes: Selectivity and the International Criminal Law Regime* (Cambridge: Cambridge University Press, 2005) 88; H Lauterpacht, *The Function of Law in the International Community* (Oxford: Oxford University Press, 2011) 102–4.

[34] Indeed, the threshold of seriousness that needs to be met for a wrong to be included within international criminal law is normally supposed to be higher than the threshold for inclusion within

In any case, in this chapter I am more interested in testing the plausibility of a philosophical move, ie expanding the scope of international criminal responsibility for a group of wrongs that are currently considered merely domestic, than in fully determining the limits of the move itself. Some will agree with my suggestion that certain wrongs currently considered domestic in nature are in fact wrongs for which we are answerable to the international community, but will disagree as to what these wrongs are exactly. It is not my intention here to address this problem. If my argument has any purchase, it has it at least in relation to wrongs that consist in violating basic human rights, so I will limit myself to considering these wrongs.[35]

The idea that we are answerable to the international community for crimes such as rape or murder, even when committed in isolation from a wider attack against the members of a group or outside the context of war, will raise two main concerns. Firstly, this view will look counterintuitive to the extent that it seems to have the implausible implication that each and every individual case of rape or murder should be prosecuted by an international court. The conclusion that national sovereignty can be justifiably infringed not only in order to punish crimes against humanity, war crimes, or genocide, but every time a single rape or a murder is committed seems to constitute a *reductio ad absurdum* of the view I suggest. Secondly, and independently of the unpalatable implication just described, my position will seem implausible simply because crimes such as murder or rape are normally considered classic examples, indeed, paradigmatic examples, of domestic crimes. Hence, the scepticism about the idea that we should see them as *international* crimes.

However, I believe that both of these worries can be dispelled. I will start with the second, since the answer to it can then be employed to address the first. The key move here is to clarify that, as I have mentioned already, when I say that violations of basic human rights are wrongs for which we are answerable to the international community, I do not mean to suggest that for these wrongs we are *only* answerable to the international community. Remember that domestic crimes are those that 'violate values on which the civic enterprise depends, and display a lack of the respect and concern that citizens owe to each other as fellow citizens'.[36] Now, this is certainly true not only in the case of crimes such as theft, but also in the case of crimes such as

---

domestic criminal law. This is because international criminal law is a delicate tool which involves the right to trump national sovereignty, and thus can justifiably be employed only for grave wrongs.

[35] Elsewhere I suggest that all crimes that violate basic human rights should be considered crimes against humanity (Renzo, n 26 above). Although I still hold this view, I will leave it aside here. The argument presented in this chapter is not conditional on accepting this further claim.

[36] See above, p 217.

murder and rape. Crimes such as murder or rape will violate the fundamental values of any political community that aspires to be minimally decent because any decent political community will declare them as public wrongs and, consequently, will want to call its members to account for them.

It is important here to distinguish the question of what makes a certain conduct wrong from the question of what makes it the business of the political community. Sometimes the two coincide: what makes the pro-hibited conduct wrong is that it breaches the duties we owe to our fellow citizens, and this is also what makes it their business. (This is what happens in the case of merely domestic crimes.) But sometimes they do not: murder and rape are wrong independently of the respect that is owed specifically to fellow citizens; still, these are wrongs that concern the political community to the extent that they violate its fundamental values, and this is why the polity has the right to call wrongdoers to account for them. In this sense, these wrongs are similar to theft: they properly concern the members of the political community to the extent that the political community has declared them as public wrongs. My point however, is that murder and rape differ from theft because they *also* concern all human beings, independently of the fact that they are declared as public wrongs by the polity in which they are committed.

Thus, the distinction between the two kinds of wrongs identified in the previous section is not supposed to account for the distinction between domestic crimes and international crimes, but rather for the distinction between what we might call 'purely domestic crimes', ie crimes for which we are *only* answerable to the members of the political community, and international crimes, ie crimes for which we are *also* answerable to the international community. But saying that we are answerable for a certain crime to the international community does not exclude that we can be also answerable for it to the domestic community. Indeed, this is the case with crimes such as murder or rape.

Philosophers tend to discuss cases in which the duties and responsibilities we have in virtue of the different roles we occupy are in conflict with each other, but in fact most of the time these duties and responsibilities overlap. This means that we are often responsible for the same course of action to different audiences. Domestic abuse is an obvious example. Those who perpetrate the abuse are accountable to the other members of the family for failing to treat the victim with the respect owed to her as a member of the family, but also to the domestic political community for failing to treat her with the respect owed to her as a fellow citizen. My claim is that violations of basic human rights have the same structure. We are answerable for them to our fellow citizens because, to the extent that they are declared as public wrongs by the polity, in perpetrating them we fail to treat the victim with the respect owed to her as a fellow citizen. But we are also answerable for them to the whole of humanity because in committing them we also fail to treat the victim with the respect owed to her as a fellow human being.[37]

Thus, my view should not be confused with the view that the only crimes for which we are answerable to the domestic political community are those crimes that I have called 'purely domestic', ie those crimes whose wrongness depends on the restrictions that members of political communities take upon themselves. Nor should it be confused with the view that violations of basic human rights are wrongs for which we are only answerable to the international political community. My claim is rather that whereas merely domestic crimes only concern the domestic political community, violations of basic human rights do not. Violations of basic human rights certainly do have a domestic dimension in that any minimally decent political community will declare them as public wrongs and, consequently, will take a proper interest in condemning them and responding to them; but they also have an international dimension. They have this double dimension because in addition to failing to treat the victim with the respect and concern owed to her as a fellow citizen (a wrong for which we are answerable to the domestic political community), these crimes also fail to treat the victim with the respect and concern owed to her as a fellow human being (a wrong for which we are answerable to the whole of humanity).

IV. International Crimes and National Courts

The distinction I drew in the previous two sections might look at first as a mere restatement of the classic distinction between *mala prohibita* and *mala in se*, but the two are only partially overlapping. The distinction between *mala prohibita* and *mala in se* accounts for the difference between conduct that is wrongful in virtue of its being criminalized or in virtue of its being legally regulated (depending on which account of the distinction we adopt) and conduct that is wrongful independently of its being criminalized or

---

[37] Of course some forms of domestic abuse involve violations of basic human rights. For these wrongs we are answerable to (at least) three groups: the members of our family, our fellow citizens, and the whole of humanity. Far from being a problem for my view, this confirms the point I am making in the text, namely that typically our responsibilities overlap and that, consequently, we can be answerable to different groups for the same wrong. I further discuss this problem in Renzo, n 26 above, at pp 467–72.

legally regulated.[38] Here, by contrast, I am interested in conduct that is wrongful in virtue of our membership in the political community, whether or not the conduct in question is criminalized or regulated by the law. All *mala prohibita* obviously fall within this group, but not all the wrongs in this group are *mala prohibita*.

For example, it is widely believed that in virtue of our membership in the political community we have a duty to serve in the military when our country is unjustly attacked. If this view is correct, it would be wrong not to do so, even if there were no laws regulating or criminalizing failure to serve in the military. In this case, we would be answerable to the members of the polity for failing to contribute to the defence of our country, even if the conduct in question would not be a *malum prohibitum*.

Of course, typically conduct that is wrongful in virtue of our membership in the political community is in fact criminalized or regulated, which might explain why the distinction I suggest is normally ignored. But even if in fact these wrongs are normally also *mala prohibita*, the distinction is conceptually important. And once we accept the distinction and combine it with the relational account of responsibility presented above, the conclusion that violations of basic rights constitute wrongs for which we are answerable to the international community naturally follows. Some conduct is wrong only in virtue of our membership in the political community, because it shows lack of respect and concern that we owe to our fellow citizens qua fellow citizens; some conduct is wrong independently of our membership in the political community, because it shows lack of respect and concern that we owe to our fellow human beings qua human beings. For the former we are only answerable to our fellow citizens, which is why only the domestic political community can call us to account for it; for the latter we are also answerable to all human beings, which is why the international community can call us to account for it. Violations of basic human rights belong to the second group.

In the previous section I have explained why this view is not subject to the second of the two main objections that could be moved against it, ie, that it fails to account for the idea that crimes such as murder or rape are paradigmatic examples of domestic crimes. I now need to address the first objection, ie, that excluding violations of basic human rights that do not include a 'contextual element'[39] from the scope of international criminal law is necessary in order to avoid continuous interference with domestic jurisdictions.

---

[38] D Husak, *The Philosophy of Criminal Law: Selected Essays* (Oxford: Oxford University Press, 2010) 410–32; Duff, n 12 above, at pp 89–93.
[39] See above, p 221.

This worry can be dispelled by simply noting that saying that all violations of basic human rights fall within the scope of international criminal law is not tantamount to saying that these violations ought to be prosecuted exclusively by international courts.

There are obvious pragmatic, as well as principled, reasons why we should let national courts deal with crimes of this sort, when they are not committed in an armed conflict or as part of a wider attack on a civilian population. Let me just mention two obvious ones:[40] first, national courts are normally in the best position to investigate and prosecute crimes committed in their states' territory. Second, the costs of infringing states' sovereignty are so high that doing so will normally be justified only in the case of crimes that do have a contextual element, and particularly in the case of mass atrocities perpetrated by state officials or by members of politically organized structures.

Still, acknowledging that in principle individual violations of basic human rights properly concern the international community, and thus also have an international dimension, does have important implications. To begin with, this means that when these violations are punished by domestic courts we should see these courts as acting not only on behalf of the polity but also on behalf of humanity. Thus, when a domestic court is prosecuting someone for theft or tax evasion, the court should be seen as acting only in the name of the polity, but when the same court is prosecuting someone for murder or rape, the court should be doing so *also* in the name of the whole of humanity. For in the latter case, the wrongdoer is being called to account at the same time by his fellow citizens and by all human beings.

The idea of a domestic court acting at the same time on behalf of the international community might sound strange, but it is common in international law. It is already the case that the majority of international crimes are prosecuted by domestic courts acting as enforcers of international criminal justice, and it is already acknowledged that in these cases courts act as international judicial bodies playing 'the double role both of guardians of national law and agencies of enforcement (or at least implementation) of international legal standard'.[41] Likewise, the idea that international crimes

---

[40] For further discussion, see Renzo, n 26 above.

[41] A Cassese, 'The Rationale for International Criminal Justice', in A Cassese et al (eds), *The Oxford Companion to International Criminal Justice* (Oxford: Oxford University Press, 2009) 123, 124. Here Cassese parts ways with Georges Scelle, who had originally presented the idea of 'dual role' of domestic courts (see G Scelle, *Précis de Droit des Gens. Principes et Systématique* (Paris: Sirey, 1932–1934)). Whereas for Scelle courts act either as domestic or international organs, depending on whether they are dealing with issues of domestic or international concern, Cassese seems to suggest that the two roles are fulfilled simultaneously (see also his 'Remarks on G. Scelle's Theory of Role-Splitting in International Law' (1990) 1 *Eur J Intl L* 210).

have a double-layered dimension is already familiar in international law: these crimes 'constitute criminal offences in domestic legal systems . . . in that they infringe municipal rules of criminal law. In addition, they have an international dimension, in that they breach values recognized as universal in the world community and enshrined in international customary rules and treaties.'[42]

Secondly, acknowledging that violations of basic human rights properly concern the international community means that, at least in principle, crimes such as rape or murder should be covered by the *complementarity principle*. This means that in case domestic courts are unable or unwilling to prosecute and punish these crimes, another court has in principle the right to do so. This court could be either an international court, like the International Criminal Court, or another domestic court claiming universal jurisdiction.[43] Although, as we have seen, there are normally both pragmatic and principled reasons to let domestic courts deal with crimes such as murder and rape when they do not have a group-based or a policy component, I contend that there are cases in which this right ought to be exercised.

Consider for example the case of an Italian citizen who commits a sex crime in Thailand and then flees to France.[44] Suppose that whilst clear evidence that the crime has been committed is available, both Italy and Thailand fail to prosecute the wrongdoer. (We can imagine that Italy is simply trying to protect one of its citizens, whereas Thailand's main concern is to avoid a prosecution that might discourage sex tourism). According to the current view, the role of France in this case is merely to extradite the wrongdoer if Italy or Thailand requests it, whereas according to my view France would have a right to prosecute and punish the crime—a right that I believe France in this case should act upon.

This is a case in which my view does have clear practical implications which are at odds with what is currently permitted under international criminal law. However, these implications seem to me entirely desirable. No doubt giving France the right to prosecute this crime against the will of Italy and Thailand will create some diplomatic tensions, but arguably these tensions will not be much different from those currently generated when

---

[42] A Cassese, *International Criminal Law*, 2nd edn (Oxford: Oxford University Press, 2008) 54.

[43] The complementarity principle currently only regulates the functioning of the International Criminal Court, but there is no reason to think that it could not also be applied to national courts claiming universal jurisdiction, once suitably adjusted. For a detailed analysis of the principle, see M El Zeidy, 'The Principle of Complementarity: A New Machinery to Implement International Criminal Law' (2002) 23 *Michigan J Intl L* 869.

[44] I originally considered this hypothetical case in Renzo, n 26 above.

states decline extradition. Since the latter case does not seem to undermine international stability, there is no reason to believe that the former should.

In fact, I intend to defend the stronger claim that there are circumstances in which the wrongdoer should not be extradited, even if extradition is requested. This is the case when there is a serious risk that, if extradited, she would be persecuted or exposed to human rights violations. In these circumstances, France should exercise its right to punish the wrongdoer, notwithstanding the fact that Italy or Thailand has requested extradition. Once again, this seems a desirable consequence of my view, as it spares France a choice between two evils: either declining extradition in order to prevent the wrongdoer's persecution, where this comes at the price of letting her go unpunished, or agreeing to extradite the wrongdoer in order to ensure her punishment, where this comes at the price of exposing the wrongdoer to the risk of persecution. A theory that spares states this sort of dilemmas is, I think, one that we should look favourably upon.

It is interesting to notice that a similar approach was adopted in the Austrian case of *Public Prosecutor v Milan T*,[45] which is considered by some as the earliest case of universal jurisdiction internationally reported.[46] Here, Austria tried a Yugoslavian citizen for domestic criminal offences committed in Yugoslavia, after declining extradition because there was a risk that he would be subjected to political persecution. However, this case supports a more expansive use of universal jurisdiction than the one I am arguing for, as the defendant was prosecuted for property crimes (fraud), rather than for crimes involving basic human rights violations. I hope the reasons I have offered in favour of limiting the use of universal jurisdiction to violations of basic human rights will convince the reader that expanding the scope of international criminal responsibility so much would be not only impractical, but unsustainable on principled grounds.

V. Answerability to Humanity: A Relational Account

In the previous sections I have argued that we should develop the relational account of responsibility defended by Duff in a direction that he intends to resist: we are criminally responsible for crimes such as murder and rape to the whole of humanity, even when they do not include a 'contextual element';

---

[45] Oberste Gerichtshof, 29 May 1958, reprinted in Oberste Gerichtshof, Serie Strafsachen, XXIX, No 32; edited version (in English) published in (1963) 28 *Intl LR* 341.
[46] L Reydams, *Universal Jurisdiction: International and Municipal Legal Perspectives* (Oxford: Oxford University Press, 2004) 98.

and this is why (under certain conditions) these crimes can be prosecuted by an international court or a national court other than those of the states involved. The aim of this section is to consider the main objections raised by Duff against this idea and show that these objections do not pose an insurmountable obstacle to it. Indeed, I will argue that my view enables us to better account for an important distinction drawn by Duff himself in his theory.

In rejecting the idea that an Italian wrongdoer could be called to answer in a French court for a crime committed in Thailand, Duff appeals to the relational character of his conception of responsibility.[47] As he puts it, 'there must be some relationship between B who calls and A who is called that gives B the right or the standing thus to call A: some relationship that makes A's alleged wrongdoing B's business, and that entitles B to make this demand'.[48] But as it should be clear by now, none of this is at odds with the view I defend because my view is also relational in the same way.

My disagreement with Duff is not over the question of whether criminal responsibility should be understood in relational terms, but over the question of which relationships are salient in attributing criminal responsibility for crimes such as murder or rape. Duff suggests that the salient relationship is the one we share with our fellow citizens. Answerability to humanity seems to be invoked only when these crimes include a contextual element (ie when they have a group-based or a policy-based component). However, he does not explain why the audience to which we are criminally responsible for collective violations of basic human rights should be different from the audience to which we are answerable for the same violations when they lack a group-based or policy-based component. My claim is that if it makes sense to invoke answerability to humanity for crimes such as murder or rape when they have such a component, the same type of answerability should be also invoked for these crimes when they do not have it.

Nor do I disagree with Duff over the question of how we should understand the relationship between law and morality, for I also believe that the criminal law should not be used to address every kind of moral wrongdoing, but only 'public wrongs', ie wrongs that properly concern the public. The question is rather what should count as the relevant public here. I claim that whilst the public properly concerned with crimes such as theft is only the

---

[47] Of course Duff does grant that the offender might be arrested and extradited to Thailand (or Italy) to face trial, but he rightly observes that to extradite the offender is not a way of calling her to answer. Rather, it is a way of assisting the country to which the offender is extradited in holding her to account under its jurisdiction; see Duff, n 14 above, at pp 134–6.

[48] Duff, n 14 above, at p 132.

domestic political community, violations of basic human rights also concern a wider public, namely the international community. This is because in addition to violating values on which the civic enterprise depends, these crimes also violate more fundamental principles that regulate our relationships with our fellow human beings, independently of the fact that we are part of the same political community.

Notice, finally, that I do not deny that violations of basic human rights might be more serious when they have a group-based or policy-based component than when they do not.[49] My claim here is simply that it is not clear why this component should be the ground on which we decide whether we are answerable for them to the domestic or the international community.[50] On the view I suggest, the distinction between wrongs for which we are only responsible to the political community and wrongs for which we are also responsible to the international community (although not only to it) tracks the distinction between conduct whose wrongness only depends on our membership in the polity and conduct whose wrongness is independent from such membership. We ought to refrain from conduct of the first type in virtue of the respect that we owe each other as fellow citizens, and we are answerable to the political community when we fail to do so. We ought to refrain from conduct of the second type in virtue of the respect that we owe each other as fellow human beings, and we are answerable to the international community when we fail to do so. Since violations of basic human rights clearly fall within this second group, even when they do not have any group-based or policy-based component, there is no reason to limit international criminal responsibility only to violations that have such a component.[51]

---

[49] Although this might also be questioned. See M Renzo, 'A Criticism of the International Harm Principle' (2010) 4 *Criminal Law and Philosophy*, 267, 270 and Renzo, n 26 above, at p 463.

[50] I am not the only one to question this idea; see A A Haque, 'Group Violence and Group Vengeance: Toward a Retributivist Theory of International Criminal Law' (2005) 9 *Buffalo Criminal Law Review* 273. In a similar vein, Kit Wellman has recently argued that in principle, national sovereignty could be violated in order to prevent not only widespread human rights violations, but also individual ones (C H Wellman, 'Taking Human Rights Seriously' (2012) 20 *Journal of Political Philosophy* 119). Wellman's view is admittedly less radical than the one I am suggesting, for it is certainly less controversial to claim that national sovereignty can be trumped in order to prevent a single human rights violation than it is to suggest that sovereignty can be trumped in order to punish such violation once it has been perpetrated. Still, both views are driven by the thought that taking human rights seriously requires revising our current understanding of state sovereignty in a way that makes this notion sensitive to the importance of individual human rights violations.

[51] The only valid reasons to limit international criminal responsibility in this way have to do with the costs of violating sovereignty but, as we have seen, these reasons do not tell against my theory, because my theory does *not* require that individual violations of human rights be punished by an international court when the costs of violating sovereignty are too high.

Interestingly, Duff grants that there is at least one case in which wrong-doers can indeed be called to account by a polity other than the one to which they belong for crimes that do not have a collective or policy element. This is the case of crimes committed by visitors and temporary residents, such as the crimes committed by an Italian citizen in France. But on what grounds is the Italian wrongdoer answerable to the French political community in this case? If domestic criminal responsibility is founded on the idea that we are answerable to our polity for violating the fundamental values of our political community and failing to treat our fellow citizens with the respect and concern that we owe them as fellow citizens, it seems doubtful that domestic criminal responsibility can ever be attributed to non-members of the polity. On this view France cannot have the standing to call an Italian wrongdoer to account for the obvious reason that France is not her political community; nor can the wrong at hand be characterized as one that fails to display the respect and concern that the wrongdoer owes to the victim as a fellow citizen, for the victim is not a fellow citizen of the wrongdoer.

To avoid this problem, Duff must provide a separate argument to justify the right of France to punish the Italian wrongdoer, and his argument is that states can call visitors and temporary residents to account 'as guests'. Since visitors and temporary residents are accorded many of the rights and protec-tions enjoyed by regular citizens, they are also expected to accept some of the responsibilities and duties that citizens normally incur. It is in virtue of these responsibilities incurred as a guest that the Italian wrongdoer can be called to account for the crime perpetrated on French territory.

This argument seems to me plausible in relation to what I have called 'purely domestic crimes': as a guest, the Italian wrongdoer incurs a duty to respect local laws when in France, and this involves refraining from conduct that is declared as a public wrong in France, whether or not the same conduct is also considered wrong in Italy. The same argument, however, is less plausible if applied to crimes such as murder or rape. Duff obviously acknowledges that these types of conduct are wrong wherever they are committed, but suggests that they become the business of 'our polity' and of 'our criminal law' only when they are committed on our territory:

we should not say to a wife-beater . . . that he ought to refrain from beating his wife whilst he is here out of respect for local laws; we should say that wife-beating is a wrong that he ought not to commit anywhere, and for which we will call him to answer if he commits it here. . . . [In this case] the significance of the location is not that it makes wrongful what might not have been wrong elsewhere, but that it makes our business a wrong that would not have been our business had it been committed elsewhere.[52]

---

[52] Duff, n 14 above, at p 143. See also at pp 139–40.

However, it is not clear why the fact that the crime is committed on our territory makes it our business. If we have the standing to tell the wrongdoer that wife-beating is a wrong, that he ought not to commit *anywhere*, why can we do so only when he commits it here?

We should bear in mind that, at least according to Duff, the standing to call someone to account has nothing to do with the place where the relevant wrong has been committed. It has rather to do with the relationship that exists between the wrongdoer and those who call her to account. (There must be 'some relationship that makes A's alleged wrongdoing B's business, and that entitles B to make this demand'.) Unless Duff intends to resort to a territorial criterion of criminalization, as opposed to one based on citizenship, he should explain why this relationship only exists when the wrongdoer is on our territory and not when he or she leaves.[53]

Duff's point seems to be that the Italian wrongdoer becomes answerable to France when she commits her crime on French territory because one of the responsibilities that we incur as guests is to answer to our hosts for our conduct in their home,[54] but this move is unpersuasive. If your diet is none of my business, I do not have the standing to call you to account for eating too much ice cream independently of whether you eat it at my place, in the street or in your house. Vice versa, if your behaviour toward your children is abusive to the point that I have the right to say something, I can do so whether or not the episode takes place in my house, in yours or elsewhere (subject, of course, to the pragmatic constraints that this will not be counter-productive, all things considered).

Of course I do agree that there are cases in which I have the standing to address your wrongful conduct simply in virtue of the fact that you happen to be my guest—for example, I have the right to ask you to leave my party for having insulted another one of my guests, whereas I could not do so if I was not the host. But this is precisely one of those situations where my right depends on the fact that as a guest you have incurred a duty to respect the rules of my house (where one of the rules is not to offend the other guests). I do not have the standing to censure your behaviour because what you did was 'a wrong that you ought not to commit anywhere'. I can only require that you do not keep that behaviour in my house and criticize you for failing to comply with my request.

[53] Alejandro Chehtman presses a similar objection in his 'Citizenship V. Territory: Explaining the Scope of the Criminal Law' 13 (2010) *New Crim L Rev* 427.

[54] Thanks to Antony Duff for pressing this line of argument.

In other words, the host-guest relationship does not seem to be able to do the work that Duff would like it to because, by definition, such relationship only pertains to the responsibilities that wrongdoers incur *as guests*; while the right to call wrongdoers to account for crimes such as murder or rape cannot be accounted for on this basis. Thus, Duff seems to be facing a dilemma. Either he gives up his relational account of criminal responsibility based on citizenship and resorts to a mixed account—one that is partly based on territorial considerations—or he maintains a purely relational account, but identifies a relationship other than the host-guest relationship to explain why France has the right to call an Italian wrongdoer to account for crimes such as murder and rape.

The view I suggest, by contrast, does not have the same problem. This is because its starting point is precisely the claim that anyone can be called to account for crimes such as murder, rape or wife-beating, wherever they are committed and whatever the nationality of the parties involved; for violations of basic human rights are wrongs for which we are accountable to all human beings. The reasons why France should take precedence in prosecuting the crime committed by an Italian wrongdoer on its territory is simply that it is best placed to do so and that sovereignty should be respected whenever possible. Thus, my view does not have the problem of explaining why France does not have the right to call the Italian wrongdoer to answer for murders or rapes committed elsewhere, because according to my view France *does* have this right, although there are normally reasons not to exercise it.

In conclusion, let me stress how my view accounts for the main idea that Duff seems to be after in drawing his distinction. Duff claims that when visitors engage in conduct whose wrongness merely depends on the fact that it is prohibited by the local rules, they can be called to account for 'failing to respect a justified convention', whereas in the case of crimes such as murder, rape, or wife-beating 'our claim should be more robust': visitors can be called to account because their conduct is wrong, wherever it is committed.[55] It seems to me that this distinction ultimately relies precisely on the one I draw between wrongs that depend for their existence on our membership in the polity and wrongs that are independent of such membership.

Since the former type of wrong identifies conduct that is wrongful merely in virtue of how the members of the political community decide to regulate their living together, we cannot expect visitors to endorse this particular understanding of what counts as wrongful conduct. Nonetheless, we should certainly expect them to refrain from it in virtue of the fact that they are

---

[55] Duff, n 14 above, at pp 142–3.

guests, and call them to account for failing to do so. Violations of basic human rights, by contrast, are wrongful independently of what the political community decides. When we punish foreigners for committing this type of wrong we call them to account for conduct which they should refrain from independently of where they are, and our standing to do so does not depend on our being their host. These are crimes that properly concern the international community, and it is on behalf of the international community that we act when we punish the wrongdoer for committing them on our territory.[56]

VI. Conclusion

I began by distinguishing between responsibility as attributability and responsibility as answerability. I then considered two possible ways of understanding responsibility as answerability. One model, defended by John Gardner, is 'non-relational' in that it assumes that all moral reasons ultimately apply to everyone and that 'everyone's conformity to every reason is everyone's business'. This means that, although there are obvious pragmatic reasons to limit the practice of calling each other to account, in principle we are answerable to everyone for everything. The other model, defended by Antony Duff, is relational in that it ties the right to call someone to account to the existence of a normative relationship existing between the members of specific groups. In particular, Duff ties criminal responsibility to membership in the political community: being criminally responsible is being answerable to our fellow citizens for those wrongs that violate the fundamental values of the political community.

While espousing the relational model defended by Duff, I have suggested that there is an important class of wrongs, namely violations of basic human rights, for which we are criminally responsible not only to our fellow citizens,

---

[56] It might perhaps be argued here that these crimes also have a double-layered structure similar to the one I have ascribed to murder and rape when they are perpetrated as domestic cases. For once the host political community has declared murder and rape as public wrongs, visitors can be said to be accountable not only to the international community for failing to treat the victim with the respect owed to her as a fellow human being, but also to the host political community for failing to respect local rules and local understandings of what counts as wrongful conduct. Even so, this second dimension would be at most of secondary importance in explaining why visitors can be called to answer for these crimes. For we should expect foreigners to refrain from murder and rape first and foremost in virtue of the respect that they owe others as human beings, and this is the main justification for our right to call them to account for these crimes wherever they are committed. The problem with Duff's view is that this second dimension is the one supposed to be doing all the work in explaining foreigners' accountability for these crimes.

but also to all human beings. This is because while we can account for the wrongness of crimes such as theft or tax evasion simply by appealing to Duff's thought that these crimes violate the fundamental values of the political community, the wrongness of crimes such as murder or rape cannot be reduced to that. We are certainly answerable for these crimes to our fellow citizens because, to the extent that our polity declares them as public wrongs, in perpetrating them we fail to treat the victim with the respect owed to her as a fellow citizen. But we are also answerable for them to the whole of humanity because in committing them we also fail to treat the victim with the respect owed to her as a fellow human being.

Index